★

THE HOMESICK TEXAN'S FAMILY TABLE

1 Pecan pie

1 cup sugar
½ cup white Karo
3 eggs lightly beaten
½ cup pecans

Mother Hulson

Chet Cook
Jordan J Meat

The
HOMESICK TEXAN'S
FAMILY TABLE

Lone Star Cooking from
My Kitchen to Yours

LISA FAIN

TEN SPEED PRESS
Berkeley

Library of Congress Cataloging-in-Publication Data is on file
with the publisher.

Hardcover ISBN: 978-1-60774-504-4
eBook ISBN: 978-1-60774-505-1

Printed in China

Design by Katy Brown

10 9 8 7 6 5 4 3 2 1

First Edition

For my family

CONTENTS

INTRODUCTION ★ 1

1. BREAKFAST AND BREADS ★ 13

2. STARTERS AND SNACKS ★ 51

3. SALADS AND SIDES ★ 75

4. CHILIS, SOUPS, AND STEWS ★ 115

5. THE MAIN EVENT ★ 137

6. SWEETS ★ 201

7. ACCOMPANIMENTS ★ 239

RESOURCE GUIDE ★ 268

ACKNOWLEDGMENTS ★ 269

MEASUREMENT CONVERSION CHARTS ★ 270

INDEX ★ 271

INTRODUCTION

★

There's this recurring dream that I have. I'm in a field—my great-grandma's Texas cornfield to be exact. A long table loaded with dishes, bowls, and platters full of good food stretches through the green stalks, and surrounding the table is most everyone I've ever known, both family and friends. My great-grandmother is there, and she waves me over. "Mighty fine food and mighty fine people to eat it!" she says as I take a seat. I then begin to eat a most memorable meal.

It's been said that if you ask a Texan about their most memorable meal, they won't tell you about a coveted reservation at a five-star temple of dining, or an exotic feast served after an airplane flight halfway across the world. Nope, most Texans will say that their most memorable meal was home-cooked, shared at the family table.

At least it's that way for me.

But to be honest—despite my recurring dream—I hadn't really pondered the question until some New York friends and I were having dinner at my apartment. Now, before I continue, let me say I'm a seventh-generation Texan who happens to live in New York, and one of my favorite pastimes is to share the joys of my home state with my non-Texan friends.

That particular evening was Tex-Mex night. As we sat around dipping tortilla chips into salsas and quesos, my friends talked about elaborate meals from fine establishments located in places such as Napa Valley or Spain. But when it was my turn to answer the question, even though I've enjoyed eating in a fair share of fancy restaurants, I realized my most memorable meal was the potluck we had for my grandparents' fiftieth anniversary.

"A potluck?" said my friends.

"Yes, a family potluck," I said. Then I told them about the meal.

It was early July, and while Texas is notorious for being hotter than heck during the summer, that day was blessed with a gentle breeze. The party was held at my grandparents' North Texas farm—a beautiful spread of green pastures, rolling hills, and a pond—which has been continuously owned by my family since the 1840s.

Through the course of the party, more than one hundred people came by to pay their respects—a lively gathering of folks young and old. I had recently moved to New

York, so for me, a visit to the peaceful farm was a much-needed tonic from the craziness of city life. But beyond seeing the beautiful land, it was a treat to visit with dear family and friends, many of whom I hadn't seen in years.

The food at the anniversary party was typical mid-summer Texan fare—cold salads, hot rolls, chicken, cake, and pies. The food was good, as it was all made with love. But what made the meal truly special were the connections made with family and friends, old and new.

Whether it was getting to hug cousins I hadn't seen since we were kids, hearing stories about my grandparents' wedding from guests who had been there that day, or eating homemade pies rolled out with a pin that had been a hand-carved wedding gift fifty years earlier—the meal made me smile. It was a most memorable meal.

And that's what *The Homesick Texan's Family Table* is all about—making memories at the table with those whom we love. No matter if they are memories of sitting together for a simple weeknight dinner or jostling for space during a large holiday gathering, some of my fondest moments have occurred at the family table. Perhaps you feel the same way.

Sure, Texans spend time at the table for the major milestones such as births, weddings, anniversaries, and deaths. But we're also inclined to break bread together just because it's a clear evening, and our friend's back porch has a spectacular view of the sunset, or it's a Sunday afternoon in spring, and we want to toast the arrival of our state flower, the bluebonnet. No special occasion is ever really needed: Texans gather at the table simply to reconnect with our family and friends.

This is not to say that food isn't also important. On the contrary, we love to eat and we love to eat well. And what we eat plays such an important role in our lives, if you're a homesick Texan such as myself, you'll find that cooking and eating certain dishes will instantly take you back home.

For instance, on cold winter nights I'll brighten people's spirits with ranch-style beans and jalapeño cheese enchiladas. Or to commemorate Texas Independence Day, I might offer bowls of chili and slices of pecan pie. Fiery wings, peppery ribs, and choriqueso are always welcome before the big game. And when the world begins to awaken in spring, thick slices of balsamic-tarragon glazed ham along with strawberry shortcakes are a fine way to celebrate the world in bloom.

The recipes I'm sharing with you are inspired by old favorites that I culled from recipe cards, dinners, and conversations with family and friends across the state, dishes that are as wide and varied as Texas itself. Whether it's seafood from the Coastal Bend, beef dishes from the arid west, Mexican-influenced dishes from the Rio Grande Valley, or traditionally Southern dishes from the east—Texas's food reflects the diversity of its regions and people.

If you're familiar with my first book and my blog, you might be aware that I have been known to take certain liberties with Texas cuisine. For instance, I tend to eschew

processed and packaged ingredients in favor of their fresh equivalents. I also try to cook with fruits and vegetables that are in season as much as possible.

Simply put, my approach to cooking is to make each dish as flavorful as possible. This can be achieved, for example, by using fresh ingredients, by adding an extra squeeze of lime juice, or by throwing in a jalapeño slice or two. But while I may tweak the classics and create new dishes from old standards, their spirit and soul is always Texan.

But enough about the book—let's get cooking. Please pull up a chair and join me at the table, where's there's plenty of mighty fine food, and mighty fine people to eat it.

ABOUT THE RECIPES

KITCHEN EQUIPMENT

My kitchen is small. If I stand in the middle of it, I can spread my arms and reach the outer boundaries on each side. There is one counter, a stove, and a narrow, shallow sink. There is no dishwasher, there is no walk-in pantry, and while there is a refrigerator, it doesn't fit in the space allotted and instead is halfway in the kitchen and halfway in the living area, straddling the border of both.

I share this with you not to complain, but rather to assure you that if I can cook all of these dishes in my tiny New York City kitchen, then you can, too, wherever you may be. Of course, having a small kitchen means that I need to keep only the essentials on hand, but that's fine as I typically use the same ingredients and tools over and over.

Because my kitchen is so small, I keep my equipment needs to the bare minimum. Here are a few things that are a must for me.

CANDY THERMOMETER: This thermometer can measure temperatures up to 500°F. Now that's hot! It's invaluable when frying foods and—no surprise, given the name—making candy.

CAST-IRON SKILLET: I use my cast-iron skillet for just about everything—from deep-frying to sautéing to even baking. Pretty much the only things I *don't* make in the cast-iron skillet are soups and some baked goods. I prefer cast iron because when it's been well seasoned, it conducts heat well, is naturally nonstick, and lasts a lifetime. Actually, it lasts more than a lifetime: most of my cast-iron cookware has been passed down for generations in my family. They are a wonderful heirloom.

PALOTE: This thin, short rolling pin is ideal for rolling out homemade flour tortillas as it gives you more control. If you can't find a proper *palote*, however, you can use a 1-inch-thick dowel that's been cut to 6 inches in length. Also, many Asian groceries sell rolling pins for dumplings that are almost identical to a *palote*.

JARS FOR CANNING: Most of my pickle and jam recipes could easily be stored in plastic containers, but if you want to process your jams and pickles in a boiling water bath (see page 267), then you'll need proper glass canning jars. While the jars can be reused, you'll need new lids for each batch, because the lids can only be processed once. (Though if you're simply storing the jars and lids without doing a water-bath process, you can use the lids again.)

A NOTE ABOUT SALT

I prefer to cook with flaky kosher salt, so when a precise quantity of salt has been specified in a recipe, I call for kosher salt. Kosher salt has larger crystals than most table salts, so if you decide to use a finer-grained table salt, it's best to halve the amount to start and then add more to taste if you feel it's necessary. For recipes where I ask you to salt to taste, feel free to use any salt that you wish.

TO PEEL OR NOT TO PEEL?

For fruits and vegetables, the recipes will note if they should be peeled or not. The exception to this is for garlic and onions, which should *always* be peeled even though it's not specified.

CHILE PEPPERS

Texan cuisine is big and bold, and chile peppers—both fresh and dried—contribute largely to that flavor profile. Whether it's a jalapeño's piquant heat or a dried ancho chile's bittersweet tones, chile peppers add distinct flavor. Here is some information about the chile peppers used in this book.

Fresh Chiles

I've never met a fresh chile I didn't like. Raw, pickled, or cooked, fresh chiles add heat, flavor, and life to Texan dishes. Fresh chiles have a relatively short season during the summer and early fall when they're at their best, but you can usually find out-of-season fresh chiles in the store year-round. When buying fresh chiles, lightly thump the skins—they should be firm without any soft, mushy spots. They should be fragrant if they're fresh, and some hotter chiles, such as jalapeños, are sometimes so pungent, they might make your eyes water.

Fresh chiles are usually sold when they're green, though most of them will eventually turn red if permitted to stay on the plant long enough. I find that when you do find a red fresh chile, it tends to be hotter (but this is not scientifically proven).

To store fresh chiles, keep them individually wrapped, separate from each other in the crisper drawer of the refrigerator.

When working with fresh chiles, I recommend wearing gloves because their heat can linger on your hands. If you don't wear gloves, running milk over your hands will help get rid of the heat. Either way, be especially careful not to touch any sensitive spots on your body after working with the chiles.

While there are many different varieties of fresh chiles, these are the ones that you'll find used in this book.

FRESNO: This red, short, triangular chile ranges in heat from medium to hot. It's similar to the jalapeño, but has a fruitier flavor.

HATCH: The Hatch chile is mild-to-hot, light green, slender, and long. Its name refers to its origin, the Hatch Valley in New Mexico, and not the type of chile that it is, as it's properly known as a New Mexico chile. Unlike most fresh chiles, Hatch chiles are only sold fresh during their brief season, which is late summer and early fall. They do roast and freeze well; if you can't find them, you can substitute the more common Anaheim instead, which comes from the same family. It has a thick skin, which you need to remove before eating by roasting (see page 9).

JALAPEÑO: While the jalapeño is not a Texas native, no other chile is more closely identified with Texan character and cuisine. We love our jalapeños and their bright and lively flavor. This chubby, short, and pointed chile—usually sold as a green chile but sometimes as a red chile—can range from medium to hot. While it's difficult to know the chile's heat level before taking a bite, I find that the truly hot ones will emit volatile oils that will make my eyes water just to look at them.

POBLANO: This thick, heart-shaped long chile has a mild to medium heat level

and is usually a dark green color. It has a thick skin, which you need to remove before eating by roasting (see page 9), a process that gives this chile a deep, earthy flavor.

SERRANO: This slender, short chile is like a thinner, meaner version of the jalapeño, because it is hot with a crisp bite. It's usually sold as a green chile, though it can also be found as a red chile.

Dried Chiles

Dried chiles are the foundation of many Texan dishes, especially Tex-Mex dishes. As the name implies, a dried chile is simply a fresh chile that has been dried and sometimes, as in the case of the chipotle chile, smoked. Because of the drying process, they have a robust, earthy depth that adds a lot of flavor to dishes.

When buying dried chiles, look for chiles that are soft and pliant like raisins, rather than hard and brittle, as these will be the freshest. The chiles should be whole, without cracks or tears. They should also be fragrant.

To store dried chiles, keep them in an airtight container, such as a jar. While they don't need to be refrigerated, it is important to store each type of chile separate from the others as they have different flavors.

To use dried chiles, you'll need to rehydrate them first (see page 9). If you've never used dried chiles, don't be intimidated! They're fun to cook with and add so much to each dish that I know you'll grow to love them as much as I do. The ones you'll find in this book are listed on the next page.

ANCHO: This chile is the heart and soul of Tex-Mex cuisine. Triangular and dark red, the ancho chile is the dried version of the fresh poblano and has an earthy flavor with hints of raisin and chocolate. The ancho is the base for most commercial chili powders and its flavor will be familiar if you've ever had a bowl of chili or a plate of enchiladas drowning in brown gravy. Their heat level is mild to medium-hot. Sometimes they can be bitter, so I always rinse mine after roasting and rehydrating them before proceeding with a recipe.

CHILE DE ÁRBOL: This short, thin red chile is hot and adds spark wherever it's added.

CHIPOTLE: This is a dried jalapeño chile that's been smoked. As such, it has a smoky flavor and a lot of heat. When buying this chile dried, it will have either a dusty brown color or it will be a deep, rich red, depending on how it was processed. Most of the time this dried chile is sold in cans in a sauce known as adobo, which is made with vinegar, tomatoes, sugar, and spices. When using the canned chiles, you'll want to include some of the sweet and smoky adobo sauce, too. Know that this chile is hot, so proceed with caution—and when a recipe calls for the canned chipotle chile, it will refer to one or two from the can, not the whole can! Since most of the time you won't be using a whole can of chipotle chiles, you can transfer them to an airtight container and store them in the refrigerator for a couple of weeks, or in the freezer for 6 months.

GUAJILLO: This is a bright red, long, and slender chile with a berry-like flavor and medium heat. It doesn't have a strong presence, so it tends to be more of a team player than the dominant star in a dish. It has a tough skin, so you'll need to soak it longer than most dried chiles when rehydrating it. Some cooks also strain it when making a puree, but I find that if you run the blender for a few extra minutes, this is not a necessary step.

PASILLA: The pasilla chile is the dried version of the chilaco chile, which is not often found fresh in many American markets, though it is popular in Mexico. This long, dark-brown, dagger-like chile has an earthy flavor similar to the ancho chile, but it tends to be a little more bitter and has a touch more heat.

Ground Chiles

Using chiles that have already been ground into a powder is a simple way to bring some heat and flavor to a dish.

CAYENNE: This bright red chile powder packs a lot of heat. It adds brightness to dishes and also has the ability to make other flavors sing louder as well.

CHILE POWDER: This is a powder made from a single chile pepper, such as a chipotle chile powder. It is pure and has not been mixed with other ingredients.

CHILI POWDER: This differs from chile powder in that chili powder is a spice blend, made of ground chiles, usually ancho, along with garlic, cumin, clove, and allspice.

SMOKED PAPRIKA (PIMENTÓN): This is a Spanish chile powder that comes from chiles that are slowly smoked over wood. It tends to be mild to medium-hot. While it has a strong, fire-kissed flavor, there is also a bit of sweetness present, too. This is a terrific way to add a smoky dash to a dish when you don't want the heat that comes from a chipotle chile.

Making your own chile powder

You can find pure chile powders in the spice aisle or at specialty grocers, but it's also simple to make your own. To do this, in a dry skillet over high heat, toast 2 ounces of any dried chile for about 10 seconds per side, or just until they start to puff. Remove the seeds and stems, and then place the chiles in a spice or coffee grinder and process until finely ground.

Making your own chili powder

Take a pure chile powder and then combine it with ground cumin, garlic powder, ground allspice, and ground cloves. While I like to play around with the ratios, a good place to start is ½ cup ancho chile powder mixed with 1 teaspoon ground cumin, ½ teaspoon garlic powder, ¼ teaspoon allspice, and ¼ teaspoon ground cloves.

Roasting fresh chiles

Preheat the broiler and place the chiles in a skillet or on a baking sheet. Broil the chiles for about 5 minutes per side. If the chiles need to be peeled, immediately place the chiles in a paper sack or plastic food-storage bag, close it tightly, and let the chiles steam for 20 minutes. To peel the chiles, remove them from the bag and gently rub off the skins.

Roasting and rehydrating dried red chiles

To use dried chiles, you need to rehydrate them first. To do this, simply remove the stems and seeds of the chiles. Then in a dry cast-iron skillet over medium-high heat, cook them for 5 to 10 seconds on each side or until they begin to puff up a bit. Add enough warm water to cover the chiles, turn off the heat, and let the chiles soak for 30 minutes, or until they are soft and plumped. To use the chiles, drain them from the soaking water, which can be bitter, rinse the chiles, and then proceed with the recipe.

SWEET POTATO AND CHIPOTLE TORTILLAS, PAGE 28

CHAPTER 1

BREAKFASTS AND BREADS

In my family, the menfolk were the ones in charge of weekend and special occasion breakfasts. It started with my grandpa flipping pancakes on Saturday mornings, and my dad making us eggs on Sundays before church. Now, my brother has taken on the family mantle, and he's always happy to make breakfast for anyone who asks. Lately, he even has an assistant giving him a hand: his toddler son, Austin Jack, who loves to cook. He'll walk into the kitchen and ask his dad, "Can I help?" My brother will pull him up on a chair, and Austin Jack will stir a bowl or pour ingredients.

Clearly, Austin Jack loves working with food. Though sometimes in his eagerness, he overreaches a bit. One time when I was visiting, my brother, as usual, was making breakfast. And as usual (well, when traveling), I was sitting around doing nothing, when my brother said, "Hey, Sis, please hand me the blueberries."

I went looking for the berries, but they weren't on the counter, nor were they in the refrigerator. Then I saw Austin Jack drinking from a bowl as large as his head. "Have you seen the blueberries?" I asked him.

He put down the bowl. It was empty, but Austin Jack grinned at me with a face covered in blue juice. He didn't answer, but his face told me the story of what had happened. "I think I found your blueberries," I said. My brother laughed and admitted they had a hard time keeping berries on hand when my nephew was around.

Clearly we wouldn't be having blueberries with our breakfast that morning. That said, as my brother is a hospitable Texan and all, there were still plenty of other good things to enjoy.

Bacon-Molasses Breakfast Sausage 16

Sausage and Pepper Breakfast Casserole 19

Green Chile Baked Eggs 20

Chilaquiles in Black Bean Salsa 21

Breakfast Enchiladas 22

Potato-Chorizo Breakfast Tacos 25

Buttermilk Bacon-Fat Flour Tortillas 26

Sweet Potato and Chipotle Tortillas 28

Apple-Jalapeño Dutch Baby Pancake 29

Great-Grandma Blanche's Chocolate Muffins 30

Apricot Bread 31

Pecan-Lime French Toast Casserole 33

Blueberry Granola 34

Cranberry-Gruyère Scones 37

Buttermilk Dinner Rolls 38

Angel Biscuits 39

Bacon-Cheddar-Chipotle Biscuits 40

Klobasnek (Sausage Kolaches) 42

Oatmeal Bread 44

Jalapeño Corn Sticks 47

See, Texans take breakfast seriously. Whether it's whipping up batches of their own breakfast sausage (often using recipes that have been passed down from one generation to the next), or giving their loved ones large bags of homemade granola for Christmas each year (so even quick weekday breakfasts will be a little more special), Texans embrace that first meal of the day with gusto.

Our cuisine has many cultural influences, and you'll find this on display during breakfast, too. For instance, in North and in Central Texas, you may be served a large rumpled skillet pancake known as a Dutch baby—just forget that it actually hails from Germany. Or if you're near the border, you might enjoy a plate of breakfast enchiladas, plump with crisp bacon and melted cheese.

We love casseroles in Texas, so they also make an appearance at our breakfast table. Sometimes they are sweet, in the form of French toast casserole. And sometimes they are savory, in the form of a breakfast strata.

And of course, no Texas table would be complete without a bowl of biscuits or thick slices of crusty, freshly baked bread. In this chapter I've included some of my favorites. Many, like the Bacon-Cheddar-Chipotle Biscuits (page 40), are well suited for the breakfast table; others are just all-around great breads for any time of day.

Whether served at morning, noon, or night, homemade bread is a Texan tradition. In my family, we all enjoy baking, but the person who may have loved it the most was my great-grandma Gibson, who was renowned for her baked breads.

When my grandma used to come home from school, on the counter would be oatmeal bread, a tender sweet loaf still warm from the oven. My great-grandmother would cut off a slice for her and then slather it with freshly churned, creamy butter. It was a fine treat, and always a warm welcome home.

My great-grandma would also bake biscuits to go with fried chicken and make corn sticks to go with fried fish. But the bread she was most famous for was her dinner roll. The rolls were the best. This sentiment, however, is not unusual. If you ask any Texan about their family's dinner rolls, chances are they will reply that *theirs* are the best.

All Texans' dinner rolls start out the same—with flour and yeast. But from there, anything can happen. Some folks use butter, while others use vegetable shortening. Some use water, while others use buttermilk. There might be an egg, and there might be sugar—it's these variables that make each dinner roll similar but different.

These family recipes are usually closely guarded formulas. I was talking to one friend who was shocked to discover that her grandmother had actually published the family's dinner roll recipe in her church's cookbook. "Now everyone knows her secret!" she said.

My great-grandmother did indeed leave behind many bread recipes, but her dinner roll recipe is incomplete, so perhaps she felt the same way. But bread is about sharing. Whether it's baking bread's gorgeous aromas, which delight anyone who happens to come nearby, or it's passing a basket of warm rolls to the person sitting

next to you at the table—bread is meant to be enjoyed with others. So shouldn't we share our bread recipes, too?

We do have a handwritten card with part of my great-grandmother's roll recipe, though it is vague about some ingredients. And because no one got the full recipe before she left this world, for years my family's dinner rolls have not been the same.

Now, my brother has taken to the family tradition and become an ardent baker. He'll spend days on just one bread recipe and usually has a loaf or two going in his oven. Because of his passion, last Christmas we put him on roll duty, and he came up with a batch that was gone from the table in record time. My mom even said they were very close to Great-Grandma Gibson's, which was the highest of praise.

When I returned home, I asked my brother for the recipe, excited that perhaps he'd cracked our family's dinner roll code. Unfortunately, he's a tinkerer with his baking—and not terribly meticulous about writing down his experiments. So although he had eventually found a formula that works, he hadn't recorded it, and neither of us was sure about all that he'd done. I was back where I started. No matter, I took what I knew about my great-grandma's dinner rolls, and I took what I knew from him, and came up with something on my own.

The dinner rolls I bake are very good. At first I was concerned because they weren't exactly like my great-grandmother's or even my brother's, but that's okay. I think in hindsight that perhaps my great-grandmother was vague with her recipe to give future generations the freedom to come up with their own way of doing things. And as we've all enjoyed being creative with our baking, that's not such a bad legacy at all.

BACON-MOLASSES BREAKFAST SAUSAGE

✪

MAKING BREAKFAST SAUSAGE is an old family tradition for us. My grandpa's family used to raise their own hogs, and when it came time for butchering day, they made sure that nothing went to waste. All parts of the animal were used—for hams, bacon, lard, and sausage. My grandpa was in charge of making the breakfast sausage—a tradition he passed on to us.

Breakfast sausage is a loose sausage that hasn't been cured, which makes it appropriate for a home cook. My grandpa's recipe was typically Texan in that it was seasoned with sage. While there is nothing finer than a basic breakfast sausage, I find it's an excellent base for other flavors, such as the smoky notes of bacon and smoked paprika and bittersweet tones of molasses. This isn't exactly my grandpa's breakfast sausage, but I'm sure he would have enjoyed it just fine. MAKES 1½ CUPS; SERVES 4 TO 6

8 ounces ground pork

4 ounces bacon, finely chopped

1 teaspoon molasses

1 teaspoon smoked paprika (pimentón)

½ teaspoon brown sugar

½ teaspoon kosher salt

¼ teaspoon dried sage

¼ teaspoon black pepper

Stir together the pork, bacon, molasses, smoked paprika, brown sugar, salt, sage, and black pepper until well combined.

Heat up a skillet over medium heat and cook a small spoonful of the sausage for a couple of minutes on each side. Taste and adjust the seasonings, if necessary.

Once you're satisfied with the flavor balance, refrigerate the mixture for an hour for the flavors to come together. To cook the sausage, form it into 2-inch-wide, ¼-inch-thick patties and fry over medium-high heat until both sides are brown and crisp, 5 minutes per side.

The sausage will keep in the refrigerator for a week uncooked, and it can also be frozen uncooked for 3 months.

SAUSAGE AND PEPPER BREAKFAST CASSEROLE

★

THE MORNING AFTER my grandma Ashner's funeral, the family met at her home to begin going through her things. We were all exhausted from the day before, and the prospect of dealing with her stuff was a bit daunting. To fortify us for the task at hand, my aunt brought a breakfast casserole, made extra hearty with lots of sausage, bread, peppers, and cheese. As we silently tucked into warm slices of the casserole, we all began to feel a little bit better, and before long, we were sharing stories and recollections.

This type of breakfast casserole, also known as a strata, works well for busy days, as it can be assembled the night before and baked in the morning. And while you certainly don't need a somber occasion to serve it, this substantial breakfast will give your family and friends the strength needed to begin a new day. SERVES 8

In a large, ovenproof skillet, heat 1 teaspoon of the oil over medium-low heat and add the breakfast sausage. (If using breakfast sausage that comes in a casing, remove the casing.) Cook, occasionally stirring and breaking up any large clumps, until lightly browned, 5 to 7 minutes. With a slotted spoon, transfer the sausage into a large mixing bowl.

Leaving the skillet on the heat, add the remaining 1 teaspoon of oil (if there is plenty of grease in the skillet after cooking the sausage, you don't need to add the oil) and then add the jalapeños. Cook, occasionally stirring, until the chiles are softened, about 5 minutes. Add the garlic and cook for 30 seconds more.

Turn off the heat and scrape the vegetables from the skillet into the bowl with the cooked sausage. Add the cubed bread and toss together until well combined. Once the skillet has cooled, about 5 minutes, transfer the bread, sausage, and vegetables into the skillet.

Whisk together the eggs, milk, mustard powder, salt, pepper, and cayenne and pour over the bread. Stir in half of the cheese and then top the casserole with the remaining cheese. Cover and allow the bread to rest, refrigerated, for at least 2 and up to 8 hours, or until the bread has absorbed the milk and egg mixture.

Preheat the oven to 350°F and take the skillet out of the refrigerator.

Bake the casserole, uncovered, for 45 to 50 minutes, until it's puffed and golden brown on top. (The casserole will deflate as it cools.) Serve warm with salsa.

2 teaspoons vegetable oil

1 cup (8 ounces) Bacon-Molasses Breakfast Sausage (page 16), or other breakfast sausage

2 jalapeño chiles, stemmed, seeded, and diced

2 cloves garlic, minced

8 slices (12 ounces) Texas toast bread or French bread, cut into 1-inch cubes

6 eggs, beaten

2 cups whole milk

1 teaspoon powdered mustard

½ teaspoon kosher salt

½ teaspoon black pepper

Pinch of cayenne

1 cup (4 ounces) shredded cheddar cheese

1 cup (4 ounces) shredded pepper Jack cheese

Old-Fashioned Texas Hot Sauce (page 241) or other salsa, for serving

GREEN CHILE BAKED EGGS

★

"WILL YOU BE HERE FOR BREAKFAST?" asked my mom. It was spring, and I had spent the past week driving around Texas looking at wildflowers and would be concluding my trip in Houston where she lives. I told her that I would indeed be there for breakfast. "Great!" she said. "I'll make Sue's eggs."

Sue is a friend of my mom's, and she is famous for her green chile baked eggs. She gave my mom the recipe, and our family has since made it a staple for special occasions. While I tend to associate this dish with Christmas morning, Mom's making it in the spring signaled to me that maybe a simple visit was cause for celebration, too.

Now, about this breakfast dish. It's not complicated—it's just eggs, cheese, flour, and Hatch chiles. It's also very rich; because there's so much cheese in it, one slice will supply you with a week's worth of vitamin D and calcium. This bit of decadence is probably why my family saves it for special days.

But you know what? I've decided that mom had the right idea—spending precious time with loved ones is always cause for celebration. We should cherish every moment we have. SERVES 4 TO 6

4 eggs

¼ cup all-purpose flour

1½ teaspoons powdered mustard

½ teaspoon baking powder

½ teaspoon kosher salt

1 cup (4 ounces) cottage cheese

1 cup (4 ounces) shredded Monterey Jack cheese

1 cup (4 ounces) shredded cheddar cheese

¼ cup (½ stick) unsalted butter, at room temperature

1 Hatch or poblano chile, roasted (see page 9), peeled, stemmed, seeded, and diced

Old-Fashioned Texas Hot Sauce (page 241) or other salsa, for serving

Preheat the oven to 350°F. Lightly grease an 8-inch square casserole dish or baking pan.

In a large bowl, beat the eggs. Stir in the flour, mustard, baking powder, and salt. Stir in the cottage cheese, Monterey Jack cheese, cheddar cheese, butter, and diced chile and mix until incorporated.

Pour the egg mixture into the casserole dish, and bake for 20 to 25 minutes, or until the top is lightly browned and the center is firm. Serve warm with salsa.

CHILAQUILES IN BLACK BEAN SALSA

⭐

CHILAQUILES, WHICH IS A DISH comprised of fried corn tortillas tossed with a salsa and usually a protein—often eggs but occasionally chicken or beef—is sometimes confused with a popular Texan breakfast known as migas, which is eggs scrambled with fried tortilla strips, vegetables, and cheese. The two are similar—they are both clever ways to use up old corn tortillas—but the main difference is that chilaquiles at heart is a salsa-based dish, whereas migas is an egg-based dish.

Typically, chilaquiles are made with a tomatillo- or tomato-based salsa, but I decided to buck tradition and serve them with a creamy black bean salsa. If you're a fan of nachos or bean dip, then this is a dish for you. The crispy fried tortillas are a terrific vehicle for the earthy, smoky black beans; when topped with a fried egg, avocado slices, jalapeños, and cheese, they make for a hearty breakfast. SERVES 4

In a large skillet, heat about ¾ inch oil over medium-high heat until it reaches 350°F. If you don't have a candy thermometer, after 5 minutes of heating, you can stick a wooden spoon into the oil to see if it's ready. If the oil bubbles around the spoon, it should be hot enough. Line a baking sheet with paper towels. In batches, place the quartered tortillas in the hot oil and fry for about 30 seconds per side or until light brown and crisp. Remove the fried tortillas with a slotted spatula and place on the paper towel–lined sheet. Repeat until all the quartered tortillas have been fried.

Carefully discard all but 2 tablespoons of the oil. Return 1 tablespoon of the oil to the skillet and turn the heat down to medium-low. Add the onion and cook until translucent, about 5 minutes. Add the garlic and cook for 30 seconds more.

Transfer the onion and garlic to a blender or food processor. Add to the blender the black beans, broth, chipotle chile, cilantro, cumin, and salt. Puree until smooth. Pour the black bean salsa into the skillet and cook over low heat, occasionally stirring, until the salsa is heated, about 2 minutes. Taste and adjust the seasonings.

Meanwhile, in another large skillet, heat the remaining 1 tablespoon of oil over medium heat. Add the eggs and fry until the whites and yolks are set to your preference. For over easy, it takes about 2 minutes. For over hard, cook for about 2 minutes and then flip the eggs and cook for 1 minute more.

Add the fried tortillas to the black bean salsa, and gently stir until the chips are well coated. Serve immediately, topping each plate with a fried egg, cilantro, cheese, jalapeño, and avocado.

Oil, for frying

12 corn tortillas, cut into quarters

½ yellow onion, chopped

4 cloves garlic, chopped

2 cups cooked or canned black beans

1 cup bean broth or chicken broth

1 canned chipotle chile in adobo sauce

¼ cup chopped fresh cilantro, plus more for serving

¼ teaspoon ground cumin

¼ teaspoon kosher salt

4 eggs

Cotija or feta cheese, crumbled, for serving

1 jalapeño, sliced into rounds, for serving

1 avocado, peeled, pitted, and diced, for serving

BREAKFAST ENCHILADAS

★

THE MORNING AFTER A FAMILY WEDDING, we all met for breakfast at a local Mexican restaurant in downtown Bryan, Texas. Bacon enchiladas were on the menu—and while I was tempted to order them, I decided at the last minute to go with breakfast tacos instead.

The thought of those enchiladas, however, stayed with me. At the time, I thought that enchiladas for breakfast sounded unusual (silly me). But the more I thought about it, the more I felt that a plate of enchiladas in a light chile salsa could be the perfect way to begin the day.

Back in New York, I set about making a batch of breakfast enchiladas, using guajillo chiles for their bright flavor and, of course, crisp slices of bacon to go along with the thick strands of melted cheese. These enchiladas could be eaten at any time of day, but the lighter sauce and bacon makes them especially appropriate in the morning. Enchiladas are a great addition to any weekend table, though you can also make a batch early in the week and then reheat them each morning (or afternoon, or evening!) as needed. SERVES 4

ENCHILADA SAUCE

2 teaspoons vegetable oil

½ yellow onion, diced

4 cloves garlic, chopped

6 dried guajillo chiles, rehydrated, stemmed, and seeded (see page 9)

1 canned chipotle chile in adobo sauce, with a dash of adobo

1 (14.5-ounce) can diced tomatoes, drained

1 cup chicken broth

1 teaspoon ground cumin

½ teaspoon dried oregano

¼ teaspoon ground allspice

Salt

To make the sauce, heat 1 teaspoon of the oil in a skillet over medium-low heat. Add the onion and cook until translucent, about 5 minutes. Add the garlic and cook for 30 seconds more.

Scrape the cooked onion and garlic into a blender or food processor and add the rehydrated guajillo chiles, chipotle chile, tomatoes, chicken broth, cumin, oregano, and allspice. Blend until smooth, about 2 minutes. Heat the remaining 1 teaspoon of oil in a pot over medium-low heat and pour in the sauce. Cook, occasionally stirring, until fragrant and slightly darker in color, 10 minutes. Adjust the seasonings and add salt to taste.

Preheat the oven to 350°F. Grease a large baking dish (9 by 13 inches works well).

To make the enchiladas, pour ½ cup of the sauce along the bottom of the baking dish. In a skillet, heat the oil over medium-low heat. One at a time, heat up the tortillas in the hot oil until soft and pliant and then keep them wrapped in a cloth or tortilla warmer until all the tortillas are heated.

To assemble, lay a tortilla on a plate or clean work surface and add about ¼ cup of cheese, a slice of bacon, and a teaspoon of cilantro. Roll the tortilla and place it in the baking dish, seam side down. Repeat with the remaining tortillas, packing the rolled tortillas next to each other in the baking dish. Evenly pour the rest of the sauce over the enchiladas and top with the remaining shredded cheese.

Bake for 15 minutes, or until cheese is lightly browned and bubbling. Serve warm, topped with the pickled jalapeño, sour cream, and guacamole.

ENCHILADAS

1 tablespoon vegetable oil

12 corn tortillas

4 cups (1 pound) shredded Monterey Jack cheese

12 slices thick-cut bacon, cooked

¼ cup chopped fresh cilantro, plus more for serving

1 whole pickled jalapeño, sliced into rings

Sour cream, for serving

Guacamole, for serving (page 66)

POTATO-CHORIZO BREAKFAST TACOS

★

BREAKFAST TACOS ARE A TEXAS TRADITION, and in the morning you find them all over the state, at taco stands, gas stations, small town cafés, and even in people's homes.

While just about any filling can be used in a breakfast taco, one of my favorites is the combination of chorizo and potatoes. The spicy chorizo wakes you right up, and contrasts nicely with the hearty potatoes. When you scramble in some eggs and fold it all into a warm flour tortilla, such as Buttermilk Bacon-Fat Flour Tortillas (page 26) or Sweet Potato and Chipotle Tortillas (page 28), you have a breakfast that will keep you well filled until the next time you decide to eat. MAKES 8 TACOS; SERVES 4

In a pot, cover the potato with water. Bring to a boil, turn the heat to low, and simmer until the potato cubes are just beginning to soften but are still firm, 3 minutes. (Be sure not to overcook.) Drain and season with the salt and black pepper.

Heat the oil in a skillet over medium-low heat. Add the chorizo, breaking it up into smaller pieces. Cook, occasionally stirring, until brown, about 5 minutes. With a slotted spoon, transfer the chorizo into a bowl.

Leaving the skillet on the heat, add the potatoes and cook until the potatoes are tender with the edges beginning to crisp, 7 to 10 minutes, stirring occasionally.

Meanwhile, beat the eggs with the water. When the potato is cooked, return the chorizo to the skillet and stir until well combined. Pour in the eggs and cook until the eggs are scrambled to your preference (I like mine well done, so I cook them for about 3 minutes), gently stirring two or three times. Add salt and black pepper to taste.

Divide the chorizo, potato, and egg mixture among the tortillas. Top each with shredded cheese, cilantro, and salsa and serve.

1 large (12-ounce) russet potato, peeled and cut into ¼-inch cubes

¼ teaspoon kosher salt, plus more as needed

¼ teaspoon black pepper, plus more as needed

1 tablespoon vegetable oil

½ cup (4 ounces) Mole Chorizo (page 164), or other Mexican chorizo, removed from its casing and crumbled

4 eggs

1 tablespoon water, at room temperature

8 Buttermilk Bacon-Fat Tortillas (page 26), Sweet Potato and Chipotle Tortillas (page 28), or other flour tortillas, warmed

Shredded cheddar cheese, for serving

Chopped fresh cilantro, for serving

Old-Fashioned Texas Hot Sauce (page 241), Tomatillo-Chipotle Salsa (page 242), or other salsa, for serving

BUTTERMILK BACON-FAT FLOUR TORTILLAS

★

WHEN I WAS MAKING TORTILLAS one day, I was out of regular milk so I substituted buttermilk. While I was shaking things up a bit, I also threw in some leftover bacon grease to see what it would add. The result was a fluffy, supple tortilla with just a hint of smoke. It's my new favorite for breakfast tacos, though it's awfully good with just about anything you choose to place inside of it. But even though this flour tortilla works well with others, it's also mighty fine hot off the skillet, served on its own.

MAKES 8 TORTILLAS

2 tablespoons bacon grease (see note)

2 tablespoons unsalted butter

2 cups all-purpose flour

½ teaspoon baking powder

¼ teaspoon kosher salt

¾ cup buttermilk

Combine the bacon grease and butter in a pot and cook over medium-low heat until bacon grease and butter have melted. Remove from the heat.

In a bowl, stir together the flour, baking powder, and salt. Pour in the melted fat mixture and stir until the flour is crumbly. Pour in the buttermilk and stir until a soft dough forms. Place the dough on a floured surface and knead for 2 minutes until the dough is firm and smooth. Cover the dough and let it rest for an hour.

Divide the dough into eight pieces and roll each piece into a ball. One at a time place a dough ball on a floured surface, pat it out into a 4-inch circle, and then roll with a *palote* or rolling pin from the center out until the tortilla is thin and about 8 inches in diameter. Keep the rolled-out tortillas covered, side by side, until you are ready to cook. (I usually have one cooking as I roll out another.)

In a dry cast-iron skillet heated over medium-high heat, cook each tortilla for 30 seconds on one side, flip it, and then cook for 1 minute on the other side. It should start to puff a bit. Flip it again and cook for 30 more seconds. Cover the cooked tortilla with a cloth until you are ready to serve. Repeat with the remaining balls of dough.

NOTE: Bacon grease is what's left over in the skillet after cooking bacon. While our great-grandmothers usually kept theirs in an old coffee can over the stove, to save my bacon grease, I pour it into a glass jar and store it in the refrigerator.

SWEET POTATO AND CHIPOTLE TORTILLAS

⭐

THE INSPIRATION FOR THESE came when I had too much mashed sweet potato left over from a late-fall meal. I'd made sweet potato biscuits before and they had turned out a wonderful shade of light orange with a soft, pliable texture, so I was curious if those qualities would translate to flour tortillas.

My hunch was correct. While you might find these unusual, they are actually very versatile and go well with a host of fillings for tacos, such as eggs or pork. They are also, however, fine on their own, especially when warm, as they are tender and soft with a hint of earthy sweetness from the sweet potato and a little kick from the chile.

One of my ancestors was known as Tater Chambers because he not only grew sweet potatoes, he also adored eating them. It's not documented if he was a fan of Mexican food, as I'm not sure if it had quite made its way to North Texas in the middle of the 1800s. That said, I do reckon he would have appreciated these sweet potato tortillas because they are a terrific way to use up any leftovers you may have. They are also good enough to bake one or two sweet potatoes for this recipe alone.

MAKES 8 TORTILLAS ★ PICTURED ON PAGE 12

2 tablespoons (¼ stick) unsalted butter

¼ cup whole milk

1 cup cooked mashed sweet potato (from 1 or 2 sweet potatoes)

2 cups all-purpose flour

1 teaspoon baking powder

½ teaspoon chipotle chile powder

¼ teaspoon kosher salt

Water (optional)

Melt the butter in a pot over low heat. Turn off the heat and add the milk and the sweet potato; stir until well combined.

In a bowl, stir together the flour, baking powder, chipotle chile powder, and salt. Add the flour mixture to the sweet potato mixture, and stir until a smooth dough forms. If the dough is too dry, add a little water, and if it's too sticky, add a little more flour. You want the dough to be soft and flexible. Cover the dough and let it rest for an hour.

After an hour, divide the dough into eight pieces and roll each into a ball. One at a time, place a dough ball on a floured surface, pat it out into a 4-inch circle, and then roll with a *palote* or rolling pin from the center out, until it is thin and about 8 inches in diameter. Keep the rolled-out tortillas covered, side by side, until you are ready to cook. (I usually have one cooking as I roll out another.)

In a dry cast-iron skillet heated over medium-high heat, cook a tortilla for 30 seconds on one side, flip it, and then cook it for 1 minute on the other side. It should start to puff a bit. Flip it again and cook for 30 more seconds. Cover the cooked tortilla with a cloth until you are ready to serve. Repeat with the remaining balls of dough.

APPLE-JALAPEÑO
DUTCH BABY PANCAKE

⭐

DUTCH BABY PANCAKES ARE NOT DUTCH. Nope, they are from Germany. This, of course, does not make them any less delicious. And as Texas has many folks with German roots, you'll find these pancakes served in North and Central Texas where this cultural influence is most strong.

If you're not familiar with Dutch babies, they are a large skillet pancake that is baked. Though associating them with regular pancakes is a bit of a mistake; Dutch babies are thin, crisp, and delicate on the outside with a creamy, fruit-studded center within.

Traditionally, Dutch babies are made with apples, but I like to throw some jalapeños into mine as well, especially in late summer and early fall when you'll find both fruits in fine form. Good looks and flavor aside, the Dutch baby's simplicity and ability to feed several makes them perfect for mornings when you have guests. SERVES 4 TO 8

Preheat the oven to 425°F.

In a large ovenproof skillet, melt the butter over low heat. Add the apples, granulated sugar, salt, and cinnamon and cook, stirring occasionally, until the apples are soft, about 10 minutes.

Meanwhile, in a blender or food processor, combine the eggs, milk, flour, and vanilla and mix until a smooth batter is formed. Alternatively, you can combine the eggs, milk, flour, and vanilla in a mixing bowl and whisk until smooth.

When the apples are done, sprinkle the diced jalapeños on top of them and then pour the batter over.

Bake, uncovered, in the oven for 15 minutes, or until the Dutch baby is puffy and an inserted knife pulls out clean. Sprinkle with confectioners' sugar and serve.

¼ cup (½ stick) unsalted butter

2 firm cooking apples, such as Granny Smith, peeled, cored, and thinly sliced

¼ cup granulated sugar

½ teaspoon kosher salt

¼ teaspoon ground cinnamon

4 eggs

1 cup whole milk

1 cup all-purpose flour

½ teaspoon vanilla extract

2 jalapeño chiles, stemmed, seeded, and diced

Confectioners' sugar, for serving

GREAT-GRANDMA BLANCHE'S CHOCOLATE MUFFINS

✦

WHEN I WAS GOING THROUGH the pile of handwritten recipe cards that had belonged to my great-grandma Blanche, this recipe for muffins jumped out at me.

Now, my great-grandma was indeed famous for her cakes and her cookies, but these muffins were a mystery. And when I asked my mom about them, she shrugged and said she didn't believe that she'd ever tried them.

It's a shame they haven't received more attention until now. These muffins have a rich, sweet flavor, which I've made even more chocolaty by throwing in some chocolate chips. Beyond the flavor, however, is the texture; they are fluffy with a slightly crisp topping that provides a satisfying contrast to the soft center when you take a bite.

With a cup of strong coffee or cold milk, these are a welcome addition to the breakfast table or for your afternoon snack. And if you share them with your neighbors, you will be very popular. They're so good, though, you might find yourself hoarding them, as I suspect my great-grandma did, which is why no one in the family recalls ever eating these extraordinary chocolate muffins. MAKES 12 MUFFINS

1½ cups sugar

½ cup vegetable oil

2 eggs

½ cup whole milk

1 teaspoon vanilla extract

2 cups all-purpose flour

½ cup unsweetened cocoa powder

1 teaspoon baking powder

¼ teaspoon ground cinnamon

¼ teaspoon kosher salt

½ cup semisweet chocolate chips

Preheat the oven to 400°F. Lightly grease twelve regular muffin cups or line them with paper liners.

Stir together the sugar, oil, eggs, milk, and vanilla. In a separate bowl, whisk together the flour, cocoa, baking powder, cinnamon, and salt until well blended. Add the liquids and stir until a smooth batter forms. Stir in the chocolate chips. Fill the muffin cups three-quarters full.

Bake for 20 to 25 minutes, until lightly browned on top and when a knife inserted into the muffin comes out clean. Serve warm.

APRICOT BREAD

★

APRICOT BREAD has long been a family favorite. My grandma will make a batch and take it to Sunday school to share with her friends.

Apricots have a natural honey-like sweetness that goes well with the crunchy pecans and bright orange zest in this recipe. And while there's enough sweetener involved that you might consider this bread cake-like, it's sturdy enough that it can hold up to a slather of butter or cream cheese, best applied when the bread is fresh out of the oven. Enjoy this bread after church on Sunday morning, in the afternoon as a tea-time snack, or even for dessert, if you're craving something fruity.
MAKES 1 LOAF; SERVES 12

Preheat the oven to 350°F. Lightly grease and flour a 9 by 5-inch loaf pan and line the bottom with parchment paper.

Whisk together the flour, sugar, baking powder, baking soda, cinnamon, and salt until well blended.

Stir together the eggs, buttermilk, vanilla, and melted butter. Combine the wet ingredients with the dry ingredients, and stir until a thick batter forms. Stir in the apricots, pecans, and orange zest. Evenly spoon the batter into the prepared loaf pan.

Bake, uncovered, for 50 to 60 minutes, or until an inserted knife comes out clean. Cool for 15 minutes before removing from the pan. Wrapped tightly, this can be stored at room temperature for 3 days or refrigerated for 1 week.

2 cups all-purpose flour

1 cup sugar

2 teaspoons baking powder

¼ teaspoon baking soda

1 teaspoon ground cinnamon

½ teaspoon kosher salt

2 eggs, beaten

½ cup buttermilk

1 teaspoon vanilla extract

¼ cup (½ stick) unsalted butter, melted and cooled

1 cup dried apricots, chopped

1 cup chopped pecans

1 tablespoon orange zest

PECAN-LIME FRENCH TOAST CASSEROLE

⭐

MY STEPMOTHER CHRIS makes a lemon curd French toast casserole, which I sadly have to admit I've never tried. We've talked about it many times, but it seems whenever I visit we get so busy that we never get around to making it.

Finally, I decided to try my hand at my own version. While Chris's recipe was definitely the inspiration for this French toast casserole, I decided to make it a little more Texan by using limes instead of lemons and pecans instead of poppy seeds. (Although I'm sure if you went the lemon/poppy seed route, it'd be delicious.) This casserole is a little tart and a little sweet, and the crunchy nuts nicely accent the soft bread. You could serve it with syrup, but it's soft and flavorful with just a sprinkling of powdered sugar. The recipe as written feeds a large group, but it can easily be halved—just layer the French toast in a 9-inch square baking dish instead. SERVES 10 TO 12

LIME CURD

¾ cup granulated sugar

2 eggs, beaten

½ cup fresh lime juice (or substitute lemon or Ruby Red grapefruit juice)

1 teaspoon finely grated lime zest

¼ cup (½ stick) unsalted butter, at room temperature

¼ teaspoon kosher salt

CASSEROLE

12 ounces day-old bread, cut into 1-inch thick slices (see note)

2 teaspoons finely grated lime zest

1 cup chopped pecans

4 cups whole milk

4 eggs, beaten

¼ cup granulated sugar

1 teaspoon ground cinnamon

½ teaspoon almond extract

¼ teaspoon kosher salt

Confectioners' sugar, for serving

To make the lime curd, in the top of a double boiler or in a small, heatproof bowl, whisk together the sugar, eggs, lime juice, and zest. Place the top of the double boiler or bowl over a pot of simmering water and, while continually stirring, cook until the curd has thickened, 7 to 10 minutes. Remove from the heat and stir in the butter until it's melted, then add the salt. Refrigerate for at least 2 hours. The curd will keep for a week in the refrigerator, so this can be done in advance.

To make the casserole, lightly grease a 9 by 13-inch baking dish. Spread each slice of bread generously with the lime curd and then lay the slices of bread, curd side up, in the bottom of the dish. (It's okay if some pieces overlap.) You may have to tear some pieces in half to cover the whole bottom of the casserole. Sprinkle on top of the bread the lime zest and pecans.

Whisk together the milk, eggs, granulated sugar, cinnamon, almond extract, and salt. Pour this over the bread. Allow the bread to absorb the milk for at least 2 hours, or overnight. If you're only going to wait 2 hours, you can leave the casserole out at room temperature, but if you are leaving it any longer then that, the casserole should be covered and refrigerated.

Preheat the oven to 350°F. Bake the casserole, uncovered, for 45 to 50 minutes, until it's puffed and golden brown on top. (The casserole will deflate as it cools.) Sprinkle with confectioners' sugar for serving.

NOTE: I measure the bread by weight rather than the number of slices since loaves can vary in width. That said, if using a standard white bread loaf, you'll want about 12 slices. If using a standard baguette, you'll want about 16 slices.

BLUEBERRY GRANOLA

★

EVERY YEAR FOR CHRISTMAS, my uncle Austin makes batch upon batch of his home-made granola, and then shares it with his family and friends. I'm not exaggerating when I say it's probably the best granola that you've ever had. He says the secret ingredient is powdered milk, but I believe there's something more powerful involved.

When I was working on my first book, Austin told me the most important thing was to have fun while I was writing it. If you are having fun, he said, then those who cook from it will have fun, too. Of course, this philosophy applies to everything in life, and clearly Austin gets great joy out of making granola, which is why his is so delicious.

Now, this is the granola you make in March, when your Christmas stash from Uncle Austin has been depleted. While it's not *exactly* his granola, because it wasn't made with his two hands, it's a decent approximation. And if you make it with joy, then chances are it will bring much happiness to others, too. MAKES 4 CUPS

2 cups rolled oats (not instant)

1 cup sliced almonds

1 cup chopped pecans

1 cup unsweetened coconut flakes

1 tablespoon powdered milk

½ teaspoon kosher salt

½ teaspoon ground cinnamon

½ cup canola oil

½ cup honey

1 teaspoon vanilla extract

½ cup dried blueberries

Preheat the oven to 350°F. Lightly grease a 9 by 13-inch baking dish.

In a large bowl, stir together the oats, almonds, pecans, coconut, powdered milk, salt, and cinnamon. In a separate small bowl, stir together the oil, honey, and vanilla extract and then pour over the oats. Stir until well combined. Pour the granola into the baking dish.

Bake, uncovered, for 30 to 35 minutes, or until fragrant and toasted, stirring the granola every 10 minutes. Remove the granola from the oven and stir in the dried blueberries. Allow the granola to cool, then store it in an airtight container for up to a month.

CRANBERRY-GRUYÈRE SCONES

✪

SCONES HAVE LONG BEEN a favorite addition to our family's breakfast table. My mom is quite famous, in fact, for her scones, and she has been known to make up new scone recipes on the spot, depending on what is available.

These cranberry scones stem from one such experiment that she created at my grandma's farm one morning. They were delicious, and I asked her if she could give me the recipe. Unfortunately, my attempts at recreating what she had done were a complete failure.

Not to be deterred, however, I decided to make my own cranberry scone. I kept the cranberries, but decided to go for a more sweet and savory scone, so I threw in some salty and nutty Gruyère cheese, along with a handful of crunchy pecans, two things that go quite well with the tart cranberries. They make a fine addition to any cool-weather holiday breakfast table. While these might not be my mom's cranberry scones, I'm okay with that; even though they're different, they're still just as good.

MAKES ABOUT 8 SCONES

Preheat the oven to 425°F. Lightly grease a baking sheet or a 10-inch cast-iron skillet.

Mix together the flour, sugar, baking powder, salt, and cinnamon. Cut the butter into pieces, and work it into the flour mixture with your hands or a pastry blender, until the flour mixture has the texture of pea-size crumbs.

Add the half-and-half and egg, mixing until the dough is a bit loose and sticky. Stir in the pecans, cranberries, and cheese, and mix until well combined. The dough will be slightly stick and wet.

Turn the dough out onto a floured surface and gently roll out until it's ½ inch thick. With a 3-inch biscuit cutter or a glass, cut out the scones and place ⅛ inch apart on the baking sheet. (You may have to gather the scraps and roll out again.)

Bake until lightly brown, about 15 minutes. Serve warm. They are best on the day they are made, but they can be tightly wrapped and then reheated, up to 2 days after baking. They can also be frozen.

2 cups all-purpose flour, plus more for rolling the scones

¼ cup sugar

2 teaspoons baking powder

½ teaspoon kosher salt

¼ teaspoon ground cinnamon

½ cup unsalted (1 stick) butter, chilled, cut into slices

¼ cup half-and-half

1 egg, beaten

½ cup chopped pecans

½ cup dried cranberries, chopped

½ cup (2 ounces) shredded Gruyère cheese

BUTTERMILK DINNER ROLLS

★

SUNDAY DINNERS AND HOLIDAY MEALS aren't complete without a basket of warm dinner rolls. Every family has their own special recipe, and mine is no different. Here is my version, inspired by Great-Grandma Gibson's mysteriously half-written recipe from years ago, made soft and tender with buttermilk, butter, and eggs. While these are not difficult to make, I'd say their rich flavor lends them more toward special occasions rather than everyday eating. That said, I do always keep a few on hand, and they freeze very well. MAKES 18 ROLLS

1 tablespoon (1 packet) active dry yeast

3 to 3½ cups all-purpose flour

1 tablespoon sugar

1 teaspoon kosher salt

¼ cup vegetable oil

6 tablespoons (¾ stick) unsalted butter, melted and cooled

1 cup buttermilk, at room temperature

1 egg, beaten

Stir together the yeast, 3 cups of the flour, sugar, and salt. Add the oil, 4 tablespoons of the butter, the buttermilk, and beaten egg and stir until the dough comes together, adding more flour if it's too sticky. Turn the dough out on a floured surface and knead for 5 minutes, or until smooth.

Place the dough in a lightly oiled bowl and cover with a damp cloth. In a warm place, allow to rise until doubled in size, 1 to 2 hours.

Lightly grease a 9 by 13-inch baking pan. Punch down the dough and form into eighteen equal-sized balls. Place the balls in the pan so that the sides are touching, cover, and allow to rise until doubled, about 1 hour.

Preheat the oven to 375°F.

Brush the rolls with the remaining 2 tablespoons melted butter and bake, uncovered, for 22 minutes, or until lightly browned. Serve warm. The rolls can also be tightly wrapped and stored at room temperature for up to 3 days or in the refrigerator for up to 1 week. They can also be frozen.

ANGEL BISCUITS

★

A READER ASKED ME if I had a recipe for angel biscuits. She sent me a list of all the recipes her homesick Texan mother in England was wanting, and I had most of them but said biscuits. Some research was in order!

Angel biscuits, so called because they are triple leavened with yeast, baking powder, and baking soda, are a cross between a dinner roll and what you normally think of as a biscuit. They tend to be softer and more airy, and often people will make a double or triple batch of dough on a Sunday and then keep it in the refrigerator all week, pulling off biscuits and baking them as needed. If you like your biscuits fresh and warm, I recommend this approach.

A little asking around led me to a friend's old recipe that she insisted I make. They turned out light and fluffy and indeed live up to their name. So I thank my reader for sharing her love of them with me, as they are a delightful addition to any family's table. Serve these heavenly biscuits with Blueberry-Pecan Jam (page 266) or Plum Jam (page 265) for breakfast, or with a smear of butter as a tasty lunch or dinner accompaniment. MAKES ABOUT 12 BISCUITS

Stir together the flour, yeast, sugar, baking powder, baking soda, and salt. Stir in the room-temperature butter until the flour mixture has the texture of peas. Add the buttermilk and stir until a shaggy dough forms. Cover the bowl and allow to rise until doubled in size, about 1 hour.

Grease a baking sheet or large ovenproof skillet. Turn the dough out onto a floured surface and gently roll out until it's ½ inch thick. With a 3-inch biscuit cutter or glass, cut out the biscuits and place them ⅛ inch apart on the baking sheet. (You may have to gather the scraps and roll out again.) Cover the biscuits and allow to rise again, until almost doubled in size, about 30 minutes.

Preheat the oven to 400°F. Brush the biscuits with the melted butter.

Bake for 12 to 15 minutes, or until lightly browned on top. Serve warm. They are best on the day they are made, but they can be tightly wrapped and then reheated, up to 2 days after baking. They can also be frozen.

2½ cups all-purpose flour

1 tablespoon (1 packet) active dry yeast

2 tablespoons sugar

½ tablespoon baking powder

½ teaspoon baking soda

¼ teaspoon kosher salt

½ cup (1 stick) unsalted butter, at room temperature, plus 1 tablespoon unsalted butter, melted

1 cup buttermilk, at room temperature

BACON-CHEDDAR-CHIPOTLE BISCUITS

☆

WHILE THERE'S NOTHING FINER to me than a basic biscuit, warm from the oven and drizzled in butter, sometimes you want to make them a little more decadent, especially if you have traveling plans.

Such was the inspiration for these. I was returning to New York, and my mom asked me if I had any cravings for the plane. A long time ago, she had made me some bacon-cheddar biscuits, so that's what I asked her to make. She did, but unfortunately I had a terrible cold and couldn't taste a thing. The biscuits she made did not get the proper reception that they should have received.

When I was finally well again, I decided to re-create the biscuits in my New York kitchen. These biscuits are chock-full of bacon and cheese, with a little bit of chipotle chile added to give some smoke and heat. They are hearty enough that they can stand alone for breakfast, especially if you opt to use them as the base for a scrambled egg sandwich. They also go well with soup or chili. If you're traveling, know that they'll hold up well on long journeys, too. MAKES 8 TO 10 BISCUITS

2 cups all-purpose flour

1 tablespoon baking powder

½ teaspoon kosher salt

4 slices bacon, cooked and chopped

½ cup (2 ounces) shredded cheddar cheese

1 canned chipotle chile in adobo, finely diced

½ cup (1 stick) unsalted butter, cold

¾ cup of half-and-half

Preheat the oven to 450°F. Grease a baking sheet or a large ovenproof skillet.

Whisk together the flour, baking powder, and salt. Stir in the bacon, cheddar cheese, and diced chipotle chile. Cut the butter into small pieces and work into the flour mixture with your hands or a pastry blender, until the flour is crumbly. Stir in the half-and-half, mixing until the dough is well combined. It's okay if the dough is a little sticky.

Pour the dough out onto a floured surface and knead for 1 minute, until the dough is smooth and no longer wet. (You can sprinkle more flour on the surface if you find that it's sticking.) Roll out the dough until it's ¼ inch thick and then fold over in half. Using a 3-inch biscuit cutter or a glass, cut out the biscuits. (You may have to gather the scraps and roll out again) Place the cut biscuits next to each other on the greased baking sheet (so they rise up, not out).

Bake for 15 minutes, or until the tops are golden brown. Serve warm. They are best on the day they are made, but they can be tightly wrapped and then reheated, up to 2 days after baking. They can also be frozen.

KLOBASNEK
(SAUSAGE KOLACHES)

⭐

IF YOU MEET A CZECH TEXAN, he or she will politely inform you it's incorrect to use the term *sausage kolache* when referring to a sausage-stuffed kolache. When you scrunch up your face with confusion, the person will then kindly explain that the correct term for this savory pastry is *klobasnek*. But wait, let's back up here for a minute. If you're not familiar with a kolache, then you may be wondering what the heck I'm talking about. Allow me to explain.

A kolache is a sweetened yeast roll that's been stuffed with a fruit, cream cheese, or a poppy seed filling. The roll is either square or round, and there's a well in the center to contain the filling. With a *klobasnek*, the dough is wrapped entirely around the filling, and the only way you can tell what's inside is to take that first bite. You find these pastries all over Texas, though they were first introduced in Central Texan Czech communities, such as the small towns of West and Caldwell.

While the origin of the term *klobasnek* for the sausage-stuffed version is a little vague, The Village Bakery in downtown West has claimed provenance for the term. What's interesting, however, is that these Czech pastries are more associated with Southeast Texas than with Central Texas.

The two pastries are different things, but some people still insist on calling them sausage kolaches. This doesn't bother me, but I can see how it could upset some linguistic purists. No matter what you call them, however, they are good. I like to eat them for breakfast, warm from the oven when the cheese is still melted and the sausage juicy with a snap. Though they are still good a few hours later at room temperature and can easily be reheated, too. MAKES 8 PASTRIES

Over medium heat, warm the milk and 4 tablespoons of the butter until the milk is just beginning to steam, but is not boiling, and the butter is melted. Remove from the heat.

In a large mixing bowl, whisk together the yeast, sugar, salt, and 1½ cups of the flour. Pour in the warm milk mixture and stir until a sticky dough has formed. Cover the dough and let it rest for 30 minutes.

Meanwhile, beat together the oil and egg yolks. Pour the eggs into the flour mixture and blend until fully incorporated.

Slowly stir in enough of the remaining 2 to 2½ cups flour until the dough comes together and is soft but not sticky. Turn the dough out onto a floured surface and knead for about 10 minutes, or until it is smooth.

Place the kneaded dough in a lightly oiled bowl and cover. Allow to rise until doubled in size, about 1 hour.

Grease or line a baking sheet with parchment paper. After the dough has risen, punch it down and divide into 8 even-size pieces. In your hands, roll the pieces of dough into balls and then flatten them into disks 4 inches in diameter. In the center of each piece of dough, place ½ tablespoon of the cheddar cheese, 2 slices of jalapeño, and a piece of sausage. Fold one side of the dough over the other and roll, then seal by pinching on all sides. Place on the baking sheet 1 inch apart, seam side down. Cover and allow to rise for 45 more minutes.

Preheat the oven to 375°F.

Melt the remaining 4 tablespoons of butter. Brush the tops of the klobasneks with half the melted butter. Bake, uncovered, for 15 to 18 minutes, or until lightly browned. After you remove them from the oven, brush each klobasnek with the remaining melted butter. Serve warm. They are best on the day they are made, but they can be tightly wrapped and then reheated, up to 2 days after baking. They can also be frozen.

1 cup whole milk

8 tablespoons (1 stick) unsalted butter

1 tablespoon (1 packet) active dry yeast

¼ cup sugar

½ teaspoon kosher salt

3½ to 4 cups all-purpose flour

2 tablespoons vegetable oil

2 egg yolks

½ cup (2 ounces) grated cheddar cheese

2 whole pickled jalapeños (page 258), cut into 16 slices (optional)

1 pound smoked kielbasa sausage, cut into 8 (2-inch) pieces

OATMEAL BREAD

★

ONE SUMMER while I was visiting my grandma, she pulled out her recipe box and began sharing with me her cards. Every dish came with a story, but Grandma especially lit up when we came across the card for Great-Grandma Gibson's oatmeal bread. "That's my favorite," said Grandma.

Great-Grandma Gibson's oatmeal bread wasn't an everyday thing—she only baked it about once a week. But when Grandma would wake up and see a loaf cooling in the kitchen, she knew it was going to be a great day. She recalled one time when she came home from college, and Great-Grandma Gibson had just pulled a loaf out of the oven. "I was so hungry, and it smelled so good, I probably ate most of the loaf with some butter," she said.

While this is a yeast bread, kneading the dough isn't necessary for success. And after you pull your first loaves out of the oven and take your first bite of this slightly sweet and nutty soft bread, you'll understand why my grandma almost ate a whole loaf in one sitting as you'll be inclined to do the same, too. MAKES 2 LOAVES

2 cups whole milk

1 cup rolled oats (not instant)

2 tablespoons (2 packets) active dry yeast

½ cup warm water

2 teaspoons kosher salt

1 large egg, beaten

½ cup honey

¼ cup vegetable shortening or unsalted butter (½ stick), at room temperature

5 to 6 cups all-purpose flour

OAT TOPPING

1 tablespoon whole milk

1 tablespoon water

1 tablespoon rolled oats (not instant)

Over medium heat, bring the milk to a boil in a large pot and then immediately remove from the heat. Stir in the oats and let stand for 2 hours until well moistened.

Grease two 9 by 5-inch loaf pans or one baking sheet, depending on if you want the bread to be in a loaf shape or a ball shape.

Dissolve the yeast in the warm water. Stir the yeast mixture, salt, egg, honey, and shortening into the oats. Working 1 cup at a time, stir in the flour until the dough is stiff.

Form the dough into two loaves and place in the loaf pans. Alternatively, you can form into two equal-sized balls and bake on a sheet. Cover with a clean cloth and let rise in a warm place until doubled in size, about 1 hour.

Preheat the oven to 350°F. To make the wash, stir the milk with the water and brush evenly over the loaves. Sprinkle the oats on top.

Bake for 40 to 45 minutes, until browned and hollow sounding when you tap the bottom of the bread. Serve warm. The bread can also be tightly wrapped and stored at room temperature for up to 3 days or refrigerated for up to 1 week. It can also be frozen.

JALAPEÑO CORN STICKS

★

WHEN MY FRIENDS JOHN AND MONICA were married, they had a fish fry in Austin's Zilker Park for all of their family and friends. While the fish was crisp, and the pies abundant, perhaps my favorite thing on the menu that day was the corn sticks, something that you don't see on the Texas table nearly enough.

Corn sticks are individual servings of cornbread that have been baked in a special pan. Because we're Texan, our corn sticks are made without sugar (after all, it's bread not cake), and many times we'll throw in some jalapeños for heat and flavor, as well.

The traditional cornstick pan is cast iron with seven corn-shaped grooves for each stick. My cornstick pan belonged to my great-grandmother, which I think makes the corn sticks taste especially fine, as a little bit of history goes into each one. But even if you're starting from scratch with a new pan, that's okay, as new memories can be made and passed down to your loved ones someday. MAKES 14 CORN STICKS

Preheat the oven to 450°F. Lightly grease two cornstick pans. (If you only have one, you can make the corn sticks in batches. You can use a large cast-iron skillet instead of cornstick pans, too.)

Mix together the cornmeal, flour, baking powder, baking soda, salt, and jalapeños. Whisk together the egg, buttermilk, and bacon grease and pour into the dry ingredients. Stir until well combined. The batter will be very thick. Spoon the batter evenly into the cornstick pan, filling each indention to the rim.

Bake for 15 to 17 minutes, or until the top is lightly brown and an inserted knife comes out clean. If you are baking in a skillet, bake for 15 to 18 minutes. Serve immediately as they will dry out after a few hours.

NOTE: Cornstick pans traditionally come with slots for seven corn sticks, and that's what this recipe makes. If your pan has more or less slots, you may have to increase or decrease the ingredient quantities proportionally.

1½ cups yellow cornmeal

½ cup all-purpose flour

2 teaspoons baking powder

½ teaspoon baking soda

1 teaspoon kosher salt

2 jalapeños, stemmed, seeded, and diced

1 egg, lightly beaten

1 cup buttermilk

¼ cup bacon grease, melted, or vegetable oil

SPINACH, BACON, AND ARTICHOKE DIP, PAGE 53

CHAPTER 2

STARTERS AND SNACKS

Y ou brought oyster crackers? Now it's really a holiday!" my
cousin told me, when he saw the bowl of spiced oyster
crackers I made. It was Thanksgiving, and we were in New
York City for the holiday—a rare occurrence for both of us, since
we'd spent almost every Thanksgiving in our lives at the family
farm in North Texas.

Thanksgiving at the farm is not a fancy affair, but it is a lot of
fun. We fly in from all over the country—me from New York, my
brother's family from Oregon, and my cousins from Virginia—and
it's the only time many of us will see each other all year. It's always
a splendid occasion for rejuvenation and reconnection.

Now, our Thanksgiving menu may change from year to year, and
different people may attend, but there is always one constant at my
grandma's Thanksgiving gathering: spiced oyster crackers. These
buttermilk, herb, and garlic-flavored crackers, which she makes in
large batches, have long been a family favorite. Sure, she makes
them year-round, but for some reason they are most associated with the holidays,
and their appearance is a given from Thanksgiving until New Year's Day.

What I've failed to mention, however, is how crazy we all are for these crackers.
The minute you walk into her house, after a few hugs and brief exchange of pleas-
antries, people then make a beeline for the cracker bowl and start stuffing handfuls
into their mouths.

Newcomers to our Thanksgivings will look at us in wonder, because on the surface
the crackers don't appear all that special. Of course, because we're friendly Texans,
we'll pass the bowl to the newcomers and insist they try them. Without fail, after that
first bite they will nod their heads and agree. "Why, yes! These *are* the best crackers

Spinach, Bacon, and
Artichoke Dip **53**

Pico de Gallo
Deviled Eggs **54**

Jalapeño Pimento Cheese **56**

Bacon-Jalapeño
Cheese Ball **57**

Fired-Up Wings **58**

Pigs in Jalapeño-Cheddar
Blankets with Jalapeño
Dipping Sauce **61**

Choriqueso **62**

Crazy Nachos **65**

Roasted Pumpkin Seeds **67**

Orange-Cinnamon
Candied Pecans **68**

Chipotle Ranch–Spiced
Oyster Crackers **71**

I've ever had!" they'll say. (And as there is now another fan of the crackers in our midst, Grandma will then duck out of the room and return with more from her secret stash she keeps hidden away.)

I've thought a lot about these crackers, and while they are indeed delicious, what makes them so dear to our hearts is that they are that first bite you eat when you arrive at the farm. When you're handed the bowl after walking through the door, it's a sign that you are now in a warm and welcoming place.

Texans are a generous people, and when you are a guest in their home, they will always offer you something to eat. For instance, you might be presented with a bowl of spinach and artichoke dip, made smoky and fiery with a hearty dose of bacon and chipotle chiles. Or you might be led to a platter laden with pigs in jalapeño cheddar blankets, little sausages wrapped in a flaky, buttery pastry laced with chiles and cheese. And no gathering of Texans is complete without a bowl of queso, though I suppose pimento cheese would be welcome, as well.

If we are watching football, we will pass around large plates stacked tall with fiery wings or nachos loaded with beans, meat, guacamole, and cheese. Though sometimes we'll keep it simple and just offer crunchy candied pecans, pumpkin seeds, or, of course, spiced oyster crackers as you walk into the door. But no matter what you're served, these little bites are meant to make you feel comfortable in our homes. After all, Texans would have it no other way.

SPINACH, BACON, AND ARTICHOKE DIP

★

WHO HASN'T ENJOYED the pleasures of a creamy spinach and artichoke dip, often served in a hollowed-out bread bowl? Of course, the original is hard to beat. Though trust me when I say that if you opt to add lots of salty, smoky bacon and warm, earthy spices, such as cumin and chipotle chile powder, your family and friends will agree: sometimes a classic can indeed be improved. Or as one guest of mine said when she took her first bite, "Oh, heck yeah!" SERVES 8 ★ PICTURED ON PAGE 50

Preheat the oven to 350°F.

In a 4-cup baking dish, stir together the artichoke hearts, bacon, chipotle chile powder, cumin, garlic, cream cheese, mayonnaise, lime juice, spinach, and Cotija cheese until well combined. Adjust the seasonings and add salt and pepper to taste. Sprinkle the Monterey Jack on top of the dip.

Bake for 25 to 30 minutes, or until lightly browned and bubbling. Serve warm with tortilla chips, crackers, or a sliced baguette.

1 (14-ounce) can artichoke hearts, drained and chopped

10 slices bacon, cooked and chopped

½ teaspoon chipotle chile powder

¼ teaspoon ground cumin

2 cloves garlic, minced

8 ounces cream cheese, at room temperature

¼ cup mayonnaise

1 tablespoon fresh lime juice

1 cup frozen chopped spinach, thawed and drained

½ cup (2 ounces) Cotija or feta cheese, crumbled

Salt and black pepper

1 cup (4 ounces) shredded Monterey Jack cheese

Tortilla chips, crackers, or a sliced baguette, for serving

PICO DE GALLO
DEVILED EGGS

✪

IT'S NOT A CELEBRATION unless you have a plate of deviled eggs. This stuffed hard-boiled egg has a long history in Texan cuisine, and there are as many variations of it as there are wildflowers in a field in the middle of spring.

My family makes them the traditional way, with lots of mustard and mayonnaise. I've taken that basic recipe but livened it up with some pico de gallo, a fresh tomato salsa that provides a cool and refreshing contrast to the richness of the eggs.

SERVES 4 TO 6

2 ounces grape tomatoes, diced, or 1 (3- to 4-ounce) ripe tomato, cored, seeded, and diced

1 jalapeño, stemmed, seeded, and diced

1 tablespoon diced red onion

1 clove garlic, minced

2 tablespoons chopped fresh cilantro

¼ teaspoon ground cumin

Pinch of cayenne

2 teaspoons fresh lime juice

Salt

6 hard-cooked eggs, peeled and halved lengthwise

¼ cup prepared yellow mustard

2 tablespoons mayonnaise

To make the pico de gallo, stir together the tomatoes, jalapeño, onion, garlic, cilantro, cumin, cayenne, and lime juice. Taste and add salt.

Scoop out the yolks from the eggs into a bowl and mash with a fork or spoon until smooth with the mustard and mayonnaise. Reserving 2 tablespoons of the pico de gallo for garnish, pour the rest into the bowl with the mashed yolks, and gently stir until well combined. Taste and adjust the seasonings.

Spoon the mixture into the halved eggs, and then garnish the eggs with the reserved pico de gallo.

JALAPEÑO PIMENTO CHEESE

⭐

PIMENTO CHEESE IS A POPULAR orange and red spread that's served all over the South. Like most Texans, I grew up eating it on sandwiches or spooned into celery stalks. Traditionally, pimento cheese is made with cheddar or American cheese, mayonnaise, a hint of onion, and a healthy dose of jarred red pimento peppers. This is fine eating. Texans, however, are known to like their heat, so I liven up my pimento cheese with pickled jalapeños. And while those jarred red pimentos impart a certain familiar flavor, I've decided that using pickled red jalapeños or Fresno chiles adds the expected vibrant colors but also a lot more punch. MAKES 3 CUPS

4 pickled red jalapeño or Fresno chiles (page 258), stemmed, seeded, and diced

2 pickled green jalapeño chiles (page 258), stemmed, seeded, and diced

3 cups (12 ounces) shredded sharp yellow cheddar cheese

1 tablespoon grated yellow onion

¾ cup mayonnaise

2 teaspoons prepared yellow mustard

1 teaspoon chile pickle juice or vinegar

Salt

Celery sticks and crackers, for serving

Stir together the red chiles, green chiles, cheese, onion, mayonnaise, mustard, and pickle juice until well combined, then season with salt to taste. Chill for 2 hours. Serve with celery sticks and crackers.

BACON-JALAPEÑO CHEESE BALL

⭐

WHEN I WAS GROWING UP, it was the mark of a very grown-up party when there was a pecan-covered cheese ball on the table. While the kids would get their cheese fix by dipping chips into the pot of chile con queso, the adults would nibble on wheat crackers topped with the nutty, creamy spread.

Then, cheese balls went out of style. Whenever you'd mention them in chic company, there would inevitably be giggling and eye rolling. Heck, the term *cheese ball* even began to connote an over-the-top, slightly out-of-touch buffoon.

But all things retro eventually return, and cheese balls have been making their way back into polite company. This is very happy news for me, as I never stopped liking them, even if presenting them at a party meant I might not be considered the most sophisticated hostess. But what's not to love about a cheese ball? It looks festive and tastes terrific.

Of course, good looks and flavor aside, the best thing about a cheese ball is its infinite variety. Most cheese balls start with a base of cream cheese, but from there you can add just about anything you want—goat cheese, blue cheese, herbs, spices, dried fruit, and nuts. In the recipe below, I've punched up the classic cheese ball with bacon, jalapeños, and pecans. But you should know that with a cheese ball, the only limit is your good taste. SERVES 12

Mix together the cream cheese, cheddar cheese, cilantro, garlic, cumin, cayenne, lime juice, Worcestershire sauce, half of the diced jalapeños, and half of the bacon. Taste and adjust the seasonings as needed, adding salt to taste.

Place the pecans and remaining diced jalapeños and bacon on a plate. Stir together until well mixed. With your hands, roll the cheese mixture into a ball, then place on the plate and roll in the jalapeños, bacon, and pecans until covered.

Chill, covered, for 1 hour before serving. Serve with crackers.

8 ounces cream cheese, at room temperature

½ cup (2 ounces) shredded cheddar cheese

2 tablespoons chopped fresh cilantro

1 clove garlic, minced

¼ teaspoon ground cumin

Pinch of cayenne

1 teaspoon fresh lime juice

½ teaspoon Worcestershire sauce

2 jalapeños, stemmed, seeded, and diced

6 slices bacon, cooked and crumbled

Salt

¼ cup chopped pecans, roasted

Crackers, for serving

FIRED-UP WINGS

★

THERE'S A SMALL TOWN in Texas called Buffalo. It's located between Dallas and Houston, and the town's name has always stuck with me when thinking about fiery wings, which are often called Buffalo wings. When I was young, because said wings are spicy, I assumed they were named after this small Texas town. But no, they're named after a town in upstate New York on the Canadian border, a place that is decidedly *not* known for its spicy cuisine.

To eliminate any confusion, I simply call my wings Fired-Up Wings. I make them with my homemade Red Chile Salsa Picante (page 246), which packs plenty of heat, and serve them with a chipotle–blue cheese dressing, which is both smoky and cool.

These red chile hot wings are a perfect party food, and they always go fast—so if you're serving a crowd you might want to double the recipe. And while the dish's origins may be in the Northeast, with my addition of red chile salsa, there's no question that this version has its roots firmly planted in Texas—Buffalo and beyond. SERVES 4

Salt

2 pounds chicken wings, wingtips removed and separated into flats and drumettes

1 cup Red Chile Salsa Picante (page 246) or other vinegar-based hot sauce (such as Cholula, Tapatío, or Frank's RedHot)

Chipotle–Blue Cheese Dressing (page 82)

Preheat the oven to 375°F. Lightly grease a baking sheet.

Lightly salt the wings and then toss them with ½ cup of the sauce. Place the wings on the baking sheet and bake, uncovered, for 45 minutes, turning once after about 25 minutes.

Remove the wings from the oven and turn on the broiler. With tongs, place the wings in a bowl and toss with the remaining ½ cup of sauce. Drain the fat from the baking sheet and return the wings to the sheet. Place under the broiler and cook for 1 to 2 minutes, until brown spots begin to appear.

Serve warm with Chipotle–Blue Cheese Dressing for dipping (and lots of napkins).

PIGS IN JALAPEÑO-CHEDDAR BLANKETS WITH JALAPEÑO DIPPING SAUCE

⭐

IF YOU DIDN'T GROW UP eating pigs in blankets, then I feel awfully bad for you. This party classic, where you take miniature hot dogs and wrap them in pastry, is an iconic, festive dish, and always the first thing to be gobbled up from the table.

While it's traditional for most folks to make these with canned dough, because I'm difficult, I suggest you make them with a homemade dough instead. But trust me, the dough comes together easily, and because it's homemade, you can improve it with fun additions like diced jalapeños and a handful of cheddar cheese.

After that, the procedure is just as simple as using the canned stuff, and these will taste so much better. I've also given you a jalapeño dipping sauce, which will add even more flavor and heat. Your family and friends will thank you. SERVES 6 TO 8

To make the dough, mix together the cream cheese and butter until smooth. Stir in the flour, salt, cayenne, cheese, and jalapeño until a soft dough forms. Divide the dough in half, shape each piece into a ball, wrap in plastic wrap, and refrigerate for 30 minutes.

Preheat the oven to 375°F. Lightly grease two baking sheets or line with parchment paper.

On a lightly floured surface, roll a ball of dough into an 11-inch circle. With a sharp knife or a pizza cutter, cut the circle into 16 equal-sized wedges, like slicing a pie.

To assemble the pigs, gently lift one of the dough triangles, and starting at the wider end opposite the point, roll the dough around one of the wieners. Place the wiener on the baking sheet and repeat with the remaining dough. Repeat with the remaining dough and remaining wieners.

Bake, uncovered, for 20 to 25 minutes, or until the crust is lightly browned.

Meanwhile, as the pigs are baking, make the dipping sauce by stirring together the mayonnaise, mustard, jalapeño, garlic, cilantro, and cumin. Add salt to taste and chill until serving.

Serve the pigs warm with the dipping sauce.

DOUGH

8 ounces cream cheese, at room temperature

½ cup (1 stick) unsalted butter, at room temperature

1½ cups all-purpose flour

½ teaspoon kosher salt

¼ teaspoon cayenne

½ cup (2 ounces) shredded sharp cheddar

1 jalapeño, stemmed, seeded, and minced

32 cocktail-size wieners

JALAPEÑO DIPPING SAUCE

½ cup mayonnaise

¼ cup prepared yellow mustard

1 jalapeño, stemmed, seeded, and finely diced

1 clove garlic, finely minced

1 teaspoon chopped fresh cilantro

¼ teaspoon ground cumin

Salt

CHORIQUESO

★

THE CLASSIC CHILE CON QUESO that Texans like to serve is made with spicy canned tomatoes and a brick of processed cheese. While it may sound a little scary, it's actually very good. All that said, this is *not* a recipe for that type of queso, delicious though it may be.

Choriqueso is a combination of chorizo, a spicy, loose Mexican sausage, and *queso*, which is simply the Spanish word for cheese. It's a skillet dish that can be served either with crisp tortilla chips for dipping or with soft, warm tortillas for wrapping. I like to serve it when I have taco night, as it makes for a fine starter, though it's equally welcome on Fridays before the big game or even as a simple weeknight dinner with a salad on the side. SERVES 8

1 cup (8 ounces) Mole Chorizo (page 164) or other Mexican chorizo, removed from its casing and crumbled

½ cup heavy cream

2 cups (8 ounces) shredded Monterey Jack cheese

2 tablespoons chopped fresh cilantro

Tortilla chips and/or corn tortillas, warmed for serving

In a skillet over low heat, brown the chorizo until cooked through, 5 to 7 minutes. With a slotted spoon, remove the chorizo from the skillet and place in a bowl, then drain off any excess grease.

Return the skillet to the stove. With the heat on low, pour the heavy cream into the skillet and then immediately stir in the Monterey Jack. Continue to stir until the cheese completely melts, 2 to 5 minutes. Turn off the heat and gently stir in the cooked chorizo. Top with the chopped cilantro and serve warm with tortilla chips or warm corn tortillas.

CRAZY NACHOS

★

WHEN I WAS YOUNG and growing up in Dallas, our favorite Mexican restaurant was a family-owned hole-in-the wall called Herrera's. It's now expanded to a much larger location, but in the 1970s it was in an old adobe building that had ten tables and to reach the dining room, you had to walk through the kitchen. Dallas went crazy for its soulful cooking, and the waits to get in were often long, but it was worth it.

We all had our favorite things to order: for my dad, it was the enchiladas, I loved the tamales, and my mom always went for the crazy nachos. Now, it always surprised me that my mom would order nachos since she ate them at home almost every single day for her lunch. However, she explained that while hers were good, Herrera's Crazy Nachos were the best.

In those days—before nachos became a sloppy stack of "chips and stuff"—nachos were a refined, simpler dish, with each individual tortilla chip topped with just cheese, beans, and jalapeños. So when Herrera's added taco meat, guacamole, and sour cream to their crazy nachos, it was considered quite daring and wild. That said, Herrera's crazy nachos were still elegant: each chip was a self-contained bite of all these fantastic flavors.

I admit that the name may seem a bit dated to some, as there's really nothing crazy about these nachos at all. But no matter what you call them, they're a fully loaded treat that is great to enjoy when watching games or sitting around and visiting with family and friends. And, if you're like my mom, they make a fine meal, too. SERVES 4

To make the chipotle taco meat, in a large skillet, heat the oil over medium-low heat. Add the beef and onion and cook, stirring occasionally, until the beef is lightly browned and the onion is translucent, about 10 minutes. Add the garlic and cook for 30 seconds more. Add the tomato, chili powder, cumin, oregano, cayenne, and chipotle chile. Stir until the spices are well distributed, turn down the heat, and simmer for 15 minutes, stirring occasionally. Stir in the masa harina until well combined, then taste and adjust the seasonings. Add salt and black pepper to taste. Stir in the lime juice and remove from the heat.

CONTINUED

CHIPOTLE TACO MEAT

1 teaspoon vegetable oil

1 pound ground beef

½ yellow onion, diced

2 cloves garlic, minced

1 ripe plum tomato (about 2 ounces), seeded, cored, and diced

1 tablespoon chili powder

2 teaspoons ground cumin

1 teaspoon dried oregano

¼ teaspoon cayenne

1 canned chipotle chile in adobo, minced, or ½ teaspoon chipotle chile powder

1 teaspoon masa harina or cornmeal

Salt and black pepper

1 tablespoon fresh lime juice

To make the guacamole, mash the avocado until smooth. Stir in the jalapeño, cilantro, garlic, cumin, and lime juice. Adjust seasonings and add salt to taste.

Preheat the oven to 375°F.

To make the nachos, pour ½ inch of oil into a heavy skillet and heat to 350°F. If you don't have a candy thermometer, after 5 minutes of heating, you can stick a wooden spoon into the oil to see if it's ready. If the oil bubbles around the spoon, it should be hot enough. In batches, fry the tortillas for 1 minute, until golden brown, turning once. Drain on a paper towel and sprinkle lightly with salt.

Place the chips close together but not overlapping on a baking sheet or cast-iron skillet, and top each with 1 teaspoon refried beans, 2 tablespoons chipotle taco meat, and 2 tablespoons cheddar cheese.

Bake for 5 minutes, or until the cheese is melted. After removing the nachos from the oven, top each with 1 tablespoon guacamole, 1 tablespoon sour cream, and 1 pickled jalapeño slice. Serve warm, with salsa on the side.

GUACAMOLE

1 avocado, peeled and pitted

1 jalapeño, stemmed, seeded, and finely diced

2 tablespoons chopped fresh cilantro

1 clove garlic, minced

Pinch of ground cumin

1 teaspoon fresh lime juice

Salt

CRAZY NACHOS

Vegetable oil, for frying

4 corn tortillas, quartered

Salt

⅓ cup refried beans

2 cups (8 ounces) shredded cheddar cheese

1 cup sour cream

2 whole pickled jalapeños, cut into 16 slices (page 258)

Old-Fashioned Texas Hot Sauce (page 241), Tomatillo-Chipotle Salsa (page 242), or other salsa, for serving

ROASTED PUMPKIN SEEDS

★

WHEN I WAS GROWING UP, when we had our Halloween pumpkin party, we'd always bake up the seeds inside for a nutty, crunchy snack. While the hull can be a little tough, boiling the seeds first does help make the seeds more pleasantly crisp after you bake them in the oven. And while pumpkin seeds are like a blank slate and can take on many different flavors, both savory and sweet, I prefer to spice them up with smoked paprika and cayenne, for a pungent, fiery bite.

These make for a fantastic snack and if you are making Pumpkin Pasilla Soup (page 128), you'll definitely want to serve these alongside. MAKES 1½ CUPS

Rinse the seeds until they're clean and free of any pumpkin. Place the seeds in a pot and cover with 4 cups of water and the salt. Bring to a boil, turn down the heat, and simmer for 10 minutes. Drain the seeds and pat dry with a clean towel.

Preheat the oven to 375°F. Line a baking sheet with parchment paper.

Toss the seeds with the melted butter and then stir in the smoked paprika and cayenne until well coated. Taste and adjust the seasonings, adding more salt if needed.

Spread out the seeds on the baking sheet in a single layer.

Bake for 20 minutes or until lightly browned. Allow to cool for 15 minutes before serving. Stored in an airtight container at room temperature, these will keep for 1 week.

1½ cups raw pumpkin seeds

1 tablespoon kosher salt

2 tablespoons (¼ stick) unsalted butter, melted

¼ teaspoon smoked paprika

Pinch of cayenne

ORANGE-CINNAMON CANDIED PECANS

★

CANDIED NUTS ARE VERY POPULAR during the holidays. These pecans, made with a host of warming spices such as cinnamon, ginger, clove, and allspice also get a little sweetness and brightness from lime zest and orange juice.

These have become a favorite holiday gift of mine, with many recipients clamoring for the recipe. In the past, I've demurred but decided to share it with you as these pecans are just too good to keep to myself. And when you hand over a jar of these nuts to your family and friends, they'll be sure to thank you, too. MAKES 4 CUPS

¼ cup (½ stick) unsalted butter

4 cups pecans

3 tablespoons sugar

1 teaspoon fresh lime juice

2 tablespoons fresh orange juice

2 tablespoons finely grated orange zest

2 teaspoons ground cinnamon

½ teaspoon ground ginger

¼ teaspoon ground cloves

¼ teaspoon ground allspice

Salt

Preheat the oven to 350°F. Line a baking sheet with aluminum foil or parchment paper.

Melt the butter in a large skillet over low heat. Add the pecans and stir until they are well coated with the butter. Turn off the heat, and add the sugar, lime juice, orange juice, orange zest, cinnamon, ginger, cloves, and allspice. Stir to coat. Spoon out the pecans onto the sheet in one layer, and then evenly drizzle over them any remaining butter that's in the skillet.

Bake for 10 minutes and then rotate the pan. Continue to bake for 5 to 10 more minutes, or until the nuts are dark in color and fragrant. Allow to cool for 30 minutes on the sheet and then sprinkle with salt to taste. Store in an airtight container at room temperature.

CHIPOTLE RANCH–SPICED OYSTER CRACKERS

★

WHEN YOU VISIT our family farm at Thanksgiving, as you walk in the door you will be greeted with a bowl of spiced oyster crackers. We all clamor for the bowl, and because they're such a family favorite, my grandma has been known to hide some of these crackers away for later nibbling, lest we all eat the whole stash in one go. Yes, they are that good.

Traditionally, the crackers have been prepared with a packaged ranch dressing powder, but I decided to make a homemade version, which not only has fewer ingredients, but has a fresher flavor, too. And while I was shaking things up, I decided to go ahead and throw in some chipotle chile powder for smoke and heat.

These tangy, spicy little snacks, while seemingly innocent, can be dangerously addictive. While you may be tempted to reach into the bowl again and again, you might want to save room for dinner. Consider yourself warned. MAKES 2 CUPS

Preheat the oven to 250°F.

Stir together the buttermilk powder, dried onion flakes, dill weed, parsley, garlic powder, chipotle chile powder, and salt.

Toss the oyster crackers evenly with the canola oil and then stir in the chipotle-buttermilk powder. Taste and adjust the seasonings. Spread the crackers evenly in a 9 by 13-inch pan.

Bake for 30 minutes, stirring once. Allow to cool for 15 minutes before serving. Stored in an airtight container at room temperature, this will keep for 1 week.

NOTE: Buttermilk powder can be found in the baking aisle at most grocery stores. If it's not available, dried milk powder can be substituted, but the crackers won't be as tangy.

¼ cup buttermilk powder (see note) or dried milk powder

2 teaspoons dried onion flakes

2 teaspoons dried dill weed

2 teaspoons dried parsley

1 teaspoon garlic powder

1 teaspoon chipotle chile powder

½ teaspoon kosher salt

1 (8-ounce) box oyster crackers

¼ cup canola oil

CHAPTER 3

SALADS AND SIDES

I have a confession to make. If I'm going to a backyard barbecue, chances are I will prefer the side dishes to whatever pig or ribs or burgers are actually being billed as the main event. I'm not sure why I feel this way, though it probably has something to do with my upbringing. See, at my family's table—being farm folks and all—sides have always been the true stars.

When my family gets together, there will be colorful salads, slaws, casseroles, beans, potatoes, and more. Sure, there will also be some sort of meat dish, but it's that abundant array of sides that adds life to the table and makes a meal interesting.

Of course, I realize you might not agree with me. For instance, take a look at how we announce what we're having for dinner. People will say, "We're having roasted whole fish," or "We're having ham." With so much emphasis on the meaty center of the meal, I find that people seldom question what else might be on the plate.

And, while no one invites anyone over to their house for sides, you still need these dishes to round out the meal. This is where the other guests come into play. Texans are not able to arrive at any function—be it indoors or out—with empty hands. If you ask a Texan to sit at your table, know that they will bring something, as they love to share. For instance, if I'm attending a backyard gathering where the star of the show is being prepared by my host, then I'm happy to bring a side player, such as a big bowl of ambrosia or creamy macaroni and cheese.

Now, this is where it gets interesting. When you arrive at the gathering, the main dishes are the known commodity. After all, this

Guacamole Salad **77**

Apple-Walnut Salad **78**

Tomato, Cucumber, and Peach Salad **81**

Chipotle–Blue Cheese Wedge Salad **82**

Frito Salad **85**

German Potato and Green Bean Salad **86**

Spicy Pea Salad **89**

Macaroni Salad **90**

Sauerkraut Salad **93**

Mustard Coleslaw **94**

Ambrosia Salad **95**

Ancho Chile Applesauce **96**

Chipotle-Cheddar Scalloped Potatoes **99**

Oyster Casserole **100**

Bacon and Chipotle Corn Pudding **101**

Smoky Collard Greens **102**

Green Chile Hominy Casserole **103**

Creamy Macaroni and Cheese **104**

Cowboy Beans **107**

Ranch-Style Beans **108**

Refried Black Beans **109**

Spanish Rice **110**

is why your friend invited you over in the first place. Sure, that brisket the host has smoked all day is indeed delicious and you're very happy to have the opportunity to eat it with such good company. But ever since you received your invitation, you've been curious about what the other guests might bring.

It's this anticipation of the unknown that has made arriving at the party an exciting moment. If you're mad about side dishes like me, when you walk into the kitchen and see your family and friends peeling back the foil or lifting the lids from their trays and bowls, your heart just might beat a little faster. Then you and the other guests will gather around all the side dishes and talk about all the offerings to the feast.

"Oh, look! It's my favorite apple-walnut salad!" one might say, while another asks, "Is that your aunt's coleslaw you were telling me about? I was hoping you'd bring that." Sure, there may be some showing off and bragging involved, but at heart, everyone is simply pleased to have the opportunity to share a beloved dish.

Of course, I mean no disrespect to the host, who has been up since before dawn working the smoker to provide us with a main dish. But that table laden with colorful salads, slaws, casseroles, beans, potatoes, and more, is proof that side dishes are also a very important part of the meal. I'm sure you now agree.

GUACAMOLE SALAD

⭐

ONE DAY A NON-TEXAN FRIEND asked if I could tell him the difference between guacamole and guacamole salad. That's easy, I replied. Guacamole salad is always served on a bed of lettuce, preferably iceberg. What's more, guacamole salad involves not only the standard mashed avocados and jalapeños you'd associate with guacamole, but also cream cheese or mayonnaise.

These days, you seldom see guacamole salad outside the state. But back in Texas, when you have guacamole at a more old-fashioned Tex-Mex joint, more often than not, it will be this version of the avocado dip. Likewise, this is how some of my older relatives still prefer to have it served.

If you browse through old Texan cookbooks from the mid-nineteenth century, you'll find plenty of recipes for guacamole salad, though it's fallen out of favor lately. Admittedly, my guacamole is usually not made in this fashion either, but there is still a place in my heart for this creamier, more American version of guacamole, and whenever it's served, I'm a kid back in Dallas again. Sure, guacamole salad may not be "authentic" in that it's not a traditional Mexican preparation—but to those of us who grew up eating it, it's as genuine as can be. SERVES 4 TO 6

Mash the avocado and mayonnaise until smooth. Stir in the tomato, jalapeño, onion, garlic, and lemon juice. Add salt to taste. Serve in scoops over iceberg lettuce leaves and, if you like, with tortilla chips on the side.

2 avocados, peeled and pitted

1 teaspoon mayonnaise or cream cheese, at room temperature

1 (2-ounce) plum tomato, seeded and finely diced

1 jalapeño, stemmed, seeded, and finely diced

¼ yellow onion, finely diced

1 clove garlic, minced

1 tablespoon fresh lemon juice

Salt

Iceberg lettuce leaves, for serving

Tortilla chips, for serving (optional)

APPLE-WALNUT SALAD

★

DURING ONE TRIP TO TEXAS, I spent most of my time driving around South Texas taking pictures. It was enjoyable, but since I didn't know too many people along my route, I ended up eating every single meal in a restaurant.

As someone who rarely goes out to eat, dining exclusively in restaurants was a lark at first. But after a while, I began craving something homemade. So when I finally arrived in Houston, my mom could have cooked anything, and it would have tasted good. That night we ate this apple-walnut salad. It was crisp, refreshing, and cool—a tonic after the heavier fare I'd been eating on the road. However, what also made this salad so good was the fact it had been made with love. And after a week of eating food coming from impersonal kitchens, that was just what I needed. SERVES 4 TO 6

1 teaspoon kosher salt, plus more as needed

2 crisp red apples, such as Gala

2 crisp green apples, such as Granny Smith

2 celery ribs, diced

1 jalapeño, stemmed, seeded, and diced

1 cup toasted walnuts

1 cup (4 ounces) blue cheese crumbles

¼ cup extra-virgin olive oil

2 tablespoons white wine vinegar

1 clove garlic, minced

¼ teaspoon dried dill weed

In a large bowl, stir together the salt with 4 cups of water. Dice the apples, leaving on the peels, and as you cut them add them to the salted water. This will keep them from turning brown.

Once all the apples have been cut, drain and rinse them. Return the apples to the bowl, and toss with the celery, jalapeño, walnuts, and blue cheese crumbles. Whisk together the olive oil, vinegar, garlic, and dill weed and stir into the salad. Add more salt to taste. Serve immediately.

TOMATO, CUCUMBER, AND PEACH SALAD

★

TOMATO AND CUCUMBER SALAD makes frequent appearances in Texas during the summer months. It's a refreshing dish as the cool cucumber is a terrific partner to soft, ripe tomatoes. Also abundant during this time are peaches, and I've found they play well with the tomatoes and cucumbers, bringing a bit of tart sweetness to the mix.

While big round beefsteak tomatoes are perfect for this salad, it's just as good with a variety of heirloom tomatoes, or plum tomatoes, too. To keep it simple, I don't bother peeling anything, though feel free to peel your fruit if you prefer.

The time frame for this is limited—you only want to make it when the fruit is ripe and in season as they are the stars of the dish. When my counter is overflowing with tomatoes and peaches, however, I find myself enjoying it several times a week. And I believe that after you try it, you'll find yourself doing the same. SERVES 4 TO 6

In a large bowl, whisk together the olive oil, lime juice, red onion, garlic, salt, and cumin. Add the tomatoes, peaches, cucumber, jalapeño, and cilantro and toss. Taste and adjust the seasonings. Top with the crumbled cheese and serve immediately. The salad can be refrigerated and served later, but note that it will begin to get soggy after about 2 hours.

¼ cup extra-virgin olive oil

3 tablespoons fresh lime juice

¼ red onion, finely diced

1 clove garlic, minced

½ teaspoon kosher salt

¼ teaspoon ground cumin

1 pound ripe tomatoes (heirloom, beefsteak, or plum), seeded, cored, and chopped

1 pound ripe peaches, pitted and chopped

1 cucumber, diced

1 jalapeño, stemmed, seeded, and diced

¼ cup chopped fresh cilantro

4 ounces queso fresco or ricotta salata, crumbled

CHIPOTLE–BLUE CHEESE WEDGE SALAD

★

WHENEVER MY DAD GIVES ME A RECIPE, chances are he'll say, "And it should be served with a blue cheese wedge salad." This is his favorite side dish, though admittedly I spent most of my life avoiding it—most bottled blue cheese dressings are too sweet or have a strange, rubbery texture.

Then a friend introduced me to his homemade recipe, and it was a revelation. The balance between the salty cheese and the tangy dressing was perfect. I had no idea blue cheese dressing could be so good, and I've been a convert ever since.

I've tinkered with his recipe a bit by adding chipotle chile powder for smoke and heat. It works as a dipping sauce or a topping, but my favorite vehicle is an iceberg wedge salad.

Some may associate iceberg lettuce with a time when people sacrificed flavor for convenience, but in the summer, it's one of my favorite things to eat. The thick, crisp leaves may lack strong flavor, but they work terrifically with a robust, heavier topping. Throw in some crumbled bacon and a ripe, juicy tomato, and you have a refreshing, filling dish. My dad would be very pleased. SERVES 4

CHIPOTLE–BLUE CHEESE DRESSING

1 cup (4 ounces) crumbled blue cheese

½ cup mayonnaise

2 tablespoons buttermilk, plus more if needed

1 clove garlic, chopped

½ teaspoon chipotle chile powder, or 1 canned chipotle chile in adobo sauce

¼ teaspoon paprika

2 teaspoons white wine vinegar

½ cup sour cream or thick Greek-style yogurt

Salt and black pepper

SALAD

1 head iceberg lettuce

8 slices bacon, cooked and crumbled

1 cup diced red, ripe tomato

To make the dressing, combine ½ cup the blue cheese crumbles with mayonnaise, buttermilk, garlic, chipotle chile powder (or canned chipotle chile), paprika, and vinegar in a blender or food processor, and blend until smooth. Stir in the sour cream and remaining ½ cups of blue cheese crumbles. Add salt and black pepper to taste. (If you want a thinner dressing, stir in more buttermilk until it's the desired thickness.)

To make the salad, cut the iceberg lettuce into four wedges, lengthwise. Place each wedge on a plate and top each with crumbled bacon, diced tomatoes, and ¼ cup of the dressing. (Any remaining dressing can either served on the side or refrigerated for 1 week). Serve immediately.

FRITO SALAD

★

AT LEAST ONCE A WEEK at my house, we ate a dish that my mom called bean salad when I was growing up. It was beans, lettuce, tomatoes, and cheese tossed with a red wine vinaigrette and served on Fritos or tortilla chips. I hated it.

Now, I'm not sure why I had such a strong dislike for this satisfying dish, as it was comprised of many of my favorite elements, including beans, cheese, and chips. On paper, it sounds like something every kid can get behind. I reckon it was the salad element that made me think it was worse than it was, but as I got older and started making it myself, I realized what a fine light supper it was.

Most recipes for this salad call for bottled salad dressing, though it's far easier and tastier to make one from scratch. This makes for a good, weeknight supper, though it also travels well, too. Just be sure if you're taking it to a potluck to add the chips and dressing right before serving, otherwise they'll get soggy. SERVES 4 TO 6

To make the dressing, whisk together the vinegar, lime juice, olive oil, garlic, cilantro, and chili powder until well combined. Add salt to taste.

To assemble the salad, toss together the greens, tomatoes, jalapeños, bell pepper, cilantro, beans, and Cotija cheese. If serving immediately, add the chips and dressing. If serving later, toss with the chips and dressing when ready to serve.

DRESSING

¼ cup red wine vinegar

1 tablespoon fresh lime juice

¾ cup extra-virgin olive oil

2 cloves garlic, minced

2 teaspoons finely chopped fresh cilantro

2 teaspoons chili powder

Salt

SALAD

4 cups mixed greens

2 cups grape tomatoes, quartered

2 jalapeños, stemmed, seeded, and diced

1 green bell pepper, stemmed, seeded, and diced

½ cup chopped fresh cilantro

2 cups Ranch-Style Beans (page 108) or other cooked pinto beans, rinsed and drained

½ cup (2 ounces) Cotija or feta cheese, crumbled

2 cups Fritos or other thick corn tortilla chips

GERMAN POTATO AND GREEN BEAN SALAD

✪

TEXANS TAKE GREAT PRIDE in their potato salads, serving them year-round. While there are many variations on potato salads, one popular rendition is German potato salad, which is a warm dish comprised of cubed new potatoes that have been cooked with bacon and mustard. It is brighter and a bit lighter than the mayonnaise-y versions you might be familiar with—and a perfect accompaniment for a summer picnic.

Another popular Texan side dish is cubed new potatoes tossed with green beans. This dish is usually seasoned with only salt and pepper, and while it's good, I was curious what would happen if you took that dish and gave it the smokiness and tang found in German potato salad. My hunch was correct, and combining the two dishes into one makes for a tremendous salad.

This was conceived as a warm side dish, as both of its predecessors were usually served that way. Though if you prefer to chill it first, there will be no loss of impact or flavor. SERVES 8

2 pounds new red potatoes, cut into ½-inch cubes (do not peel)

1 tablespoon kosher salt

2 cups green beans

¼ cup white vinegar

2 tablespoons prepared yellow mustard

8 ounces bacon, diced

¼ yellow onion, diced

2 cloves garlic, minced

¼ cup chopped fresh parsley

2 tablespoons chopped fresh dill, or 1 teaspoon dried dill weed

Pinch of cayenne

Salt and black pepper

In a pot large enough to hold both the potatoes and the green beans, put in the potatoes (you'll be adding the green beans later). Cover with water by 2 inches and add the salt. Over medium heat, bring the pot to a boil, then cook the potatoes for 5 minutes.

Add the green beans and continue to cook until the potatoes are fork tender and the green beans are bright green, about 5 more minutes. Drain and run cool water over the potatoes and the green beans to stop them from cooking any longer. With the heat off, return the green beans and potatoes to the pot and toss with the vinegar and mustard while still warm.

Meanwhile, in a large skillet, cook the bacon over medium-low heat, turning once, until crisp, about 10 minutes. Transfer the cooked bacon to a paper towel. Drain the skillet of the bacon grease, leaving 2 tablespoons (reserving the rest for another use).

With the skillet still over medium-low heat, add the onion and cook until translucent, about 5 minutes. Add the garlic to the skillet and cook for 30 seconds more. Turn off the heat and add the cooked potatoes, green beans, bacon, parsley, dill, and cayenne. Stir until everything is well combined and add salt and pepper to taste. Serve warm or chilled.

NOTE: For an extra tangy salad, substitute Dilly Green Beans (page 254) for the fresh green beans. You won't need to cook the Dilly Green Beans, so toss them with the potatoes after the potatoes are cooked and drained.

SPICY PEA SALAD

★

FOR ME, PEA SALAD WAS always the odd-looking dish holding court next to the congealed salad at the church potluck or in the cafeteria line. I was not a fan. But when I learned that it was a favorite of not only my esteemed aunt but also many friends, I decided it was time to revisit this classic dish.

For the uninitiated, this combination of peas, aromatics, and cheese may seem a little strange. (Trust me, I was once a reluctant eater of it, as well.) But once you take your fist bite of this creamy and refreshing salad, I predict you'll be a convert, too.

Research has led me to believe that it may have its roots in an Eastern European salad also comprised of peas and cheese, though I have also found American recipes for pea salad going back to the 1800s that are similar to the ones we eat today. No matter its origin, this salad makes a fine addition to any spring or summer gathering, when the English peas are crisp, juicy, and sweet.

The fun thing about pea salad, however, is that much like Texas weather in the spring, you never know quite what you'll get, as folks are fond of taking the basic form and making it their own. My version veers from the traditional recipe because I've replaced the Longhorn cheddar with smoked cheddar cheese, and the cucumber pickles with jalapeño pickles. I've also thrown in some cilantro, a dash of cumin, smoked paprika, and lime juice. But no matter how you make this classic dish, remember it's the peas that are the true stars, so you may use frozen peas but don't ever use canned. SERVES 8

Stir together the peas, onion, cilantro, pickled jalapeños, smoked paprika, cumin, and smoked cheddar cheese. Gently stir in the mayonnaise and lime juice. Taste and adjust the seasonings, then add salt to taste.

Chill for 1 hour before serving.

NOTE: If you like, you can also add crumbled cooked bacon, diced Texas dried sausage, diced hard-cooked egg, and/or pickle relish. As I said, with pea salad, anything goes!

3 cups (12 ounces) fresh or frozen English peas, thawed

¼ red onion, diced

¼ cup chopped fresh cilantro

1 or 2 pickled jalapeños (page 258), stemmed, seeded, and diced

¼ teaspoon smoked paprika

¼ teaspoon ground cumin

4 ounces smoked cheddar cheese, cubed

¼ cup mayonnaise

2 teaspoons fresh lime juice

Salt

MACARONI SALAD

★

MOST TEXAN MACARONI SALADS are made with sweet pickles, peas, peppers, and mayonnaise, and it's the rare potluck, barbecue, or church supper that doesn't have a bowl of this dish. While I enjoy the classic rendition, after reading *The First Texas Cookbook*, which was indeed the first cookbook published in Texas back in 1883, I decided to make a few changes.

According to the book, more than one hundred years ago, almost every salad included a combination of shredded raw cabbage and boiled eggs. I followed suit with my macaroni salad, but brought it back to the twenty-first century by throwing in some cilantro and chipotle chile. I got rid of the peas, but I kept the sweet pickles and mayonnaise, also adding mustard and lime juice for a tangier, brighter bite.

If you're a fan of coleslaw and egg salad, this is the macaroni salad for you. But what I appreciate the most is how including elements from an 1883 recipe made this old standby feel fresh and new. SERVES 8

2 cups shredded red cabbage

1 teaspoon kosher salt

8 ounces elbow macaroni

4 hard-cooked eggs, peeled and diced

½ cup grated carrot

2 cloves garlic, minced

¼ red onion, finely diced

½ cup chopped fresh cilantro

½ cup Sorghum Mustard Pickles (page 259) or other sweet cucumber pickle, diced

¼ cup mayonnaise

1 tablespoon fresh lime juice

1 tablespoon prepared yellow mustard

1 canned chipotle chile in adobo sauce, diced

¼ teaspoon ground cumin

Put the cabbage in a strainer and then place the strainer in a bowl. Toss the cabbage with the salt and refrigerate for 1 hour. This step will drain the cabbage of its excess water and keep it crisp in the salad.

Meanwhile, cook the macaroni according to the package instructions, drain, rinse, and refrigerate for at least 1 hour.

After an hour, take the cabbage from the strainer and place in a large mixing bowl. Add the eggs, carrot, garlic, red onion, cilantro, pickles, and macaroni.

Whisk together the mayonnaise, lime juice, mustard, chipotle chile, and cumin. Spoon the dressing over the salad, and stir until well combined. Taste and adjust the seasonings. While it should be chilled enough to eat immediately, it will be even better if refrigerated for at least an hour before serving.

SAUERKRAUT SALAD

✪

SAUERKRAUT SALAD ORIGINALLY HAILS from Eastern Europe, so in Texas it's most often found in the central part of the state, where the population of Eastern European descendants is highest. That said, your family certainly doesn't have to hail from that part of the world to appreciate this refreshing sweet-and-sour salad.

Usually, sauerkraut salad in Texas is comprised of sauerkraut, celery, bell peppers, and sugar, but I found a German recipe that called for sausage, which seemed like an inspired addition. While I was changing things, I decided to use my Sorghum Mustard Pickles (page 259) for a touch of sweetness instead of granulated sugar, and I threw in some pickled jalapeños for heat, too.

For the sauerkraut, I used prepared since I've never made a batch. (My great-grandma made it all the time, but apparently those sauerkraut-making genes skipped me.) If you also don't ferment your own, please feel free to do the same.

This tangy dish is an excellent foil for heartier meat dishes, such as Peppery Ribs (page 160) or Coffee-Chipotle Pork Chops (page 152), though it can certainly work as a light dish on its own. SERVES 8

Drain and lightly squeeze the sauerkraut. Toss it in a large bowl with the salami, sweet pickles, pickle juice, pickled jalapeño, green onions, and caraway seeds. Add salt, if you think it needs it, and black pepper to taste. Chill for 1 hour. Serve cold.

6 cups (32 ounces) sauerkraut

4 ounces salami, thinly sliced and cut into strips

½ cup diced Sorghum Mustard Pickles (page 259) or other sweet cucumber pickle

2 tablespoons sweet pickle juice

1 pickled jalapeño (page 258), stemmed, seeded, and diced

4 green onions, green part only, chopped

Pinch caraway seeds

Salt and black pepper

MUSTARD COLESLAW

★

MY DAD'S SIDE OF THE FAMILY always had a tangy, mustardy coleslaw at their summertime gatherings. Many coleslaws can fall into the sweet category, but this one was decidedly savory. Its sharp acidity paired perfectly with any rich, fatty meat that was smoked or cooked on the grill.

This coleslaw isn't the exact duplicate of what we ate growing up as a key ingredient for that is not available in New York stores (Durkee's Famous Sauce, in case you're wondering). But this is a fine substitute, with plenty of vinegar and pickle juice, mustard, and mayonnaise, along with some green peppers for added crunch. And, while it may not be the centerpiece of your summertime party, this tangy Texas coleslaw will definitely be a very welcome guest. SERVES 8

6 cups (about 10 ounces) shredded green cabbage

½ yellow onion, diced

2 cloves garlic, minced

1 green bell pepper, stemmed, seeded, and diced

1 cup diced Sorghum Mustard Pickles (page 259) or other pickled cucumber

1 jalapeño, stemmed, seeded, and diced

¼ cup chopped fresh cilantro

¼ cup mayonnaise

2 tablespoons prepared yellow mustard

1 tablespoon pickle juice or white vinegar

Salt and black pepper

Toss the shredded cabbage with the onion, garlic, bell pepper, pickles, jalapeño, cilantro, mayonnaise, mustard, and pickle juice. Add salt and pepper to taste. Chill for 1 hour. Serve cold.

AMBROSIA SALAD

★

"WILL YOU BE SERVING FIVE-CUP SALAD?" asked my grandma. I was having Christmas in New York, and this concoction, so named as it contains five cups of several ingredients, such as marshmallows, oranges, pineapple, and coconut, was a Christmas tradition in my family. "It's not the holidays without it," she said.

This fruit salad is a potluck and holiday standard in many Texan families, and yet I could never get into it because I can't stand marshmallows. Their soft, squishy texture to me always seemed just wrong. Five-cup salad, however, has a connection to another fruit salad known as ambrosia, which, even though it's also served with marshmallows, has been known to take on a more refined air.

My version of ambrosia skews toward the latter; it contains all the fruit and coconut, but I've replaced the marshmallows with pecans for their nutty crunch. I've also added a squirt of lime juice and a pinch of cayenne to the sour cream dressing, which are decidedly nontraditional, but do add a piquant touch. Another tradition of five-cup salad is that all of its components usually come from a can. If you're serving this in the winter, however, I highly suggest using fresh satsuma oranges, a small, seedless orange that is easy to peel and is full of juicy, sweet flavor. SERVES 4 TO 6

In a large bowl, stir together the oranges, pineapple, coconut, and pecans. Whisk together the sour cream, brown sugar, lime juice, and cayenne, then stir into the fruit mixture until well combined. Refrigerate for 1 hour before serving.

8 ounces satsuma or clementine oranges, peeled and sliced

1 cup cubed pineapple

1 cup shredded unsweetened coconut

1 cup pecans, chopped

1 cup sour cream

1 tablespoon brown sugar

1 teaspoon fresh lime juice

Pinch of cayenne (optional)

ANCHO CHILE APPLESAUCE

★

ONE AUTUMN, my mom was on a business trip in the Northeast, and we decided to meet halfway at a Connecticut farm and go apple picking. It was a crisp, beautiful day and, while there are apple trees on my grandma's farm, it was fun picking them in a region that is known for its vibrant fall color and fruit.

Loaded with bags of apples and little storage space when I returned to New York City, I knew that I'd have to find a dish that would use some of them. Applesauce seemed like a good choice. I've always preferred cinnamon applesauce and decided to make that. And I threw in some ancho chile powder to give it added color, depth, and spice.

This is a wonderful fall dish that pairs well with meat, such as Coffee-Chipotle Pork Chops (page 152), or can be spooned into yogurt for breakfast, as well. Though for me, the best thing about this applesauce is that it reminds me of an enjoyable day with my mom. SERVES 4 TO 6

1½ pounds red baking apples (about 4), peeled, cored, and diced

1 teaspoon ancho chile powder

1½ teaspoons ground cinnamon

Pinch of ground nutmeg

Pinch of ground cloves

Pinch of cayenne

1 teaspoon finely grated lemon zest

½ cup water

½ cup packed brown sugar

¼ teaspoon vanilla extract

¼ teaspoon kosher salt

Combine the apples, ancho chile powder, cinnamon, nutmeg, cloves, cayenne, lemon zest, and water in a pot. Cook over medium-low heat, stirring occasionally, for 15 to 20 minutes, until the apples are cooked down to a soft substance, depending on how ripe they are. Gently mash out any lumps. Stir in the brown sugar, vanilla extract, and salt. Taste, adjust the seasonings, and cook over low heat for 5 minutes. This dish is delicious served warm or chilled.

CHIPOTLE-CHEDDAR SCALLOPED POTATOES

⭐

EVERY SPRING I MAKE A POINT of returning home to see the famous Texas bluebonnets. This is our state flower, and from the end of March to the middle of April, the fields of Texas are carpeted by this beautiful blue bloom. It's one of the things I miss most living in New York, which is why I make my yearly trip back home. One year, though, there was an awful drought—and when I got home I saw no bluebonnets. But I'd flown all the way from New York to Texas for these flowers—and I wasn't going to give up easily. I drove for hours and finally reached the North Texas town of Ennis. As I turned down a country road, my persistence was rewarded. Suddenly every field was bathed in blue. I'd spent half the day thinking I *missed* the bluebonnets that season—so when I finally did find them, I appreciated their beauty even more.

Around dinnertime, I ended up outside of a small-town café where I ordered the daily special. Now, I don't even remember what the main dish was that day, but I *do* remember it included a side dish of scalloped potatoes—sliced potatoes cooked in cream. The potatoes were simple and good—it was solid, everyday fare.

That said, bluebonnets are not an everyday occasion. So when I returned to New York, I decided to make a more celebratory version of scalloped potatoes—in honor of our state flower—by enlivening the old-fashioned dish with some chipotle chiles, cheddar cheese, and bacon. These potatoes are rich and slightly decadent—you certainly don't want to eat them at every meal. But if you have a special happening, these scalloped potatoes will make a fine addition to your family's table. SERVES 8

Preheat the oven to 400°F. Lightly grease a large baking dish (9 by 13 inches works well) or large ovenproof skillet.

Pour the half-and-half into a blender or food processor, and add the garlic, chipotle chile, salt, black pepper, and nutmeg. Blend until smooth. Pour the blender contents into a bowl. Add the heavy cream and whisk the two together.

Arrange half the sliced potatoes on the bottom of the baking dish. Pour half of the chipotle cream mixture over the potatoes. Layer the remaining potato slices on top. Pour the rest of the cream mixture over the potatoes. Cover the baking dish with aluminum foil.

Bake for 40 minutes. Remove the dish from the oven, take off the foil, and evenly sprinkle on top the shredded cheddar and the crumbled bacon. Bake, uncovered, for 20 more minutes, or until the top is brown and bubbling and the potatoes are soft. Serve immediately.

½ cup half-and-half

2 cloves garlic, chopped

1 canned chipotle chile in adobo sauce

½ teaspoon kosher salt

½ teaspoon black pepper

Pinch of ground nutmeg

2½ cups heavy cream

2 pounds russet potatoes, peeled and cut into ⅛-inch rounds

2 cups (8 ounces) shredded sharp white cheddar cheese

4 slices bacon, cooked and crumbled

OYSTER CASSEROLE

★

ONE CHRISTMAS many years ago, my great-grandpa Gibson asked my grandma to make oyster casserole for Christmas dinner. We ate it growing up, he said, and it's been a long time since I've had it with the holiday meal. My grandma then prepared a classic Texan oyster casserole comprised of crackers, cream, and oysters. And my great-grandpa was very pleased.

Now, that's perhaps the last time she made this dish, and it happened before I was born. As she was telling me this story, I asked why we didn't serve it more often. She didn't really have an answer, so I decided to take matters into my own hands and make my own. Of course, I fiddled with the original old-fashioned recipe, and while the oyster, cracker, and cream combination is excellent on its own, it's even better when you throw in some bacon, aromatics, and jalapeños, too.

This is typically a side dish, much like a dressing, though it's rich enough that it could be a main dish. Typically it's only served at the holidays, but I find it's satisfying whenever it's chilly outside, and oysters are still in season. SERVES 6 TO 8

1 pint raw oysters

6 slices bacon, cooked and crumbled

4 cloves garlic, minced

2 jalapeños, stemmed, seeded, and diced

¼ cup chopped fresh cilantro

¼ teaspoon cayenne

1 tablespoon fresh lemon juice

Salt

2 cups crushed saltine crackers

½ cup (1 stick) unsalted butter, thinly sliced

1 cup cream

Preheat the oven to 400°F. Lightly grease a large ovenproof skillet.

Drain the oysters, reserving the liquid. Stir together the oysters, bacon, garlic, jalapeños, cilantro, cayenne, and lemon juice. Add salt to taste.

In the skillet, sprinkle 1 cup of the crushed saltines along the bottom. Layer the oysters on top of the crackers. Place half of the butter slices on top of the oysters and then top with the remaining 1 cup crushed saltines. Layer on top of the saltines the remaining butter slices.

Stir together the reserved oyster liquid and cream. Evenly pour over the oysters.

Bake, uncovered, for 20 to 25 minutes, or until lightly browned and bubbling. Allow to rest for 10 minutes, then serve warm.

BACON AND CHIPOTLE CORN PUDDING

✪

CORN PUDDING IS AN OLD Texan favorite that makes appearances on the summer-time barbecue table, but is equally welcome in the colder months as well. Most folks have a similar basic recipe of corn, cream, and eggs, but then liven them up a bit with their own special twists.

Here's my version of corn pudding, made a bit smoky and spicy with chipotle chiles and bacon. I also add a bit of brightness to the pudding with lime juice. Then after baking, I finish it off with cilantro and a sprinkle of salty Cotija cheese. It's a fine side, though it's hearty enough that with a salad or vegetable it could work as a main, too. And if you want to go the nontraditional route, you can sneak a few cold slices for breakfast, too, as I have been known to do. SERVES 4 TO 8

Preheat the oven to 350°F.

In a large ovenproof skillet, preferably cast iron, over medium-low heat, cook the bacon, turning once, until crisp, about 10 minutes. Place the cooked bacon on a paper towel–lined plate and pour off all but 1 tablespoon of the bacon grease in the pan. (Reserve the rest for another use.)

Add the corn and chipotle chiles to the skillet and cook, occasionally stirring, until the corn is fragrant and warm, 3 to 5 minutes. Add the garlic and cook for 30 seconds more. Turn off the heat and stir in the cumin, cayenne, nutmeg, cornmeal, and baking powder. Adjust the seasonings and add salt to taste.

Whisk together the eggs, half-and-half, and cooked bacon, and then pour over the corn, stirring until well blended. Top the casserole with the Monterey Jack, and bake, uncovered, for 25 to 30 minutes, or until top is lightly golden brown in spots, and the pudding is set.

Before serving, pour over the baked pudding the lime juice, and garnish with the chopped cilantro and Cotija cheese. Serve warm.

6 ounces bacon, cut into 1-inch pieces

2 cups fresh corn kernels or 2 cups frozen corn kernels, thawed

2 canned chipotle chiles in adobo sauce, diced

2 cloves garlic, minced

¼ teaspoon ground cumin

Pinch of cayenne

Pinch of ground nutmeg

½ cup cornmeal

1 teaspoon baking powder

Salt

3 eggs, beaten

1 cup half-and-half

2 cups (8 ounces) shredded Monterey Jack cheese

1 teaspoon fresh lime juice

Chopped fresh cilantro, for garnishing

Cotija or feta cheese, crumbled, for garnishing

SMOKY COLLARD GREENS

★

I LOVE MY COLLARD GREENS soft and smooth, lightly dressed in a broth rich with flavor. There's no instant gratification with collard greens because you're looking at cooking them for at least an hour and a half to get them as soft as I like them. How soft? Well, as my grandma said when I once made greens at her farm, "Goodness, you've cooked those to the point of no nutrition!"

To which I reply, that's why God invented pot liquor, which is the delicious cooking liquid. It's super healthy, as all the vitamins that are no longer in the vegetables will have leached into it. So drink up, and you'll be just fine. Though, truth be told, collard greens are remarkably hardy and actually retain much of their nutritional value even after cooking for hours on end.

The common way to cook collard greens is with lots of smoked meat, be it bacon, ham, or even turkey. But if you're looking to make your greens a bit healthier and vegetarian, why not give the greens a smoky flavor boost from fiery chipotle chiles, smoked paprika, and peanut butter? Heck, they're so good you might not even miss the meat at all! SERVES 4 TO 6

3 bunches collard greens (about 3 pounds)

2 tablespoons vegetable oil

1 yellow onion, diced

4 cloves garlic, minced

1 (14.5-ounce) can diced tomatoes, preferably fire roasted

2 canned chipotle chiles in adobo sauce, chopped

4 cups water

1 tablespoon apple cider vinegar

¼ cup smooth peanut butter

¼ teaspoon ground cumin

½ teaspoon smoked paprika

Salt and black pepper

Red Chile Salsa Picante (page 246), for serving

Thoroughly clean each collard leaf, removing the ribs and stems. Tear each leaf in half. In a large pot or Dutch oven, heat the oil over medium heat and sauté the onion until lightly brown, about 10 minutes. Add the garlic and cook for 30 seconds more. Add the tomatoes and chipotles. Add the torn leaves to the pot and add the water.

Bring the water to a boil and then turn heat down to a simmer. Stir in the vinegar, peanut butter, and cumin. Cook the greens, uncovered, until they are the texture you prefer, about 1½ hours. Stir in the smoked paprika and adjust the seasonings, adding salt and black pepper to taste. Serve with Red Chile Salsa Picante.

NOTE: If you want to add meat, you can add 8 ounces diced smoky ham or smoked turkey to the pot when you add the collard greens.

GREEN CHILE HOMINY CASSEROLE

✪

HOMINY CASSEROLE, which is essentially hominy with sour cream and cheddar cheese, is an old-fashioned Southern side dish you don't see much anymore. In the 1950s and 1960s, my grandma loved bringing this hearty, portable dish to potlucks. But when she shared her recipe with me, she suggested I throw in some chile peppers, saying "I bet that would make this recipe even better."

Hominy, which is corn that's been treated with the mineral lime, is the foundation for both grits and masa, making this grain both distinctly Southern and Southwestern. It has a chewy soft texture and a toasted nutty flavor, a combination that can be unusual but one I find strangely addictive.

Grandma's hominy casserole is the classic rendition of the dish, though she also shared a recipe that was a bit more gussied up with olives and pimentos. For my version of hominy casserole, I decided to do a bit of a hybrid, adding roasted poblano chiles, jalapeños, cilantro, and garlic to the standard sour cream and cheese base. I also threw in some chorizo, which elevates this casserole to a main dish if you like, though it can work quite well as a decadent side dish, too. SERVES 4 TO 6

Preheat the oven to 350°F.

Heat the vegetable oil in a large ovenproof skillet over medium-low heat. Add the chorizo and cook, occasionally stirring, until brown, 8 to 10 minutes. With a slotted spoon, remove the chorizo and drain any excess grease from the skillet, leaving 1 teaspoon. Add the onion and jalapeños and cook, occasionally stirring, until the onion is translucent, about 5 minutes. Add the garlic and cook for 30 seconds more.

Remove the skillet from the heat and add the chorizo, hominy, diced poblanos, sour cream, cumin, cayenne, cilantro, lime juice, and 1 cup of the cheddar cheese. Stir until well combined, adjust the seasonings, and add salt and black pepper to taste. Top with the remaining 1 cup cheddar cheese.

Bake, uncovered, for 30 minutes or until brown and bubbling. Serve immediately.

1 teaspoon vegetable oil

1 cup (8 ounces) Mole Chorizo (page 164), or 8 ounces other Mexican chorizo, removed from its casing and crumbled

½ yellow onion, diced

2 jalapeños, stemmed, seeded, and diced

4 cloves garlic, minced

2 (15-ounce) cans hominy, drained

2 poblano chiles, roasted (see page 8), peeled, seeded, and diced

8 ounces sour cream

½ teaspoon ground cumin

¼ teaspoon cayenne

½ cup chopped fresh cilantro

2 teaspoons fresh lime juice

2 cups (8 ounces) shredded cheddar cheese

Salt and black pepper

CREAMY MACARONI AND CHEESE

★

WHEN I WAS YOUNG, I used to think that enjoying macaroni and cheese from a box was good eating. It was smooth and simple, a dish you didn't have to think too much about. That said, it was something my mother would never buy as she (rightfully so) preferred to serve her homemade macaroni and cheese instead.

Her homemade macaroni and cheese involved all sorts of stirring and baking and chopping and such. It was very good as it was topped with a lid of blistered cheese and the soft pasta was studded with garlic and bacon. But, because of its complexity, it wasn't something you'd make too often.

Then as I was browsing through a Texas Junior League cookbook one day, I learned a trick. If you stir cheese into heated heavy cream and toss it with cooked pasta, you will soon have a creamy macaroni and cheese that has the ease of the boxed version but with a million times more flavor.

This isn't a baked macaroni and cheese, so you won't get that chewy layer of melted cheese on top. But this undemanding dish can be made a bit more complex if you toss in some cooked bacon for a smoky crunch, though it certainly doesn't need that to succeed. SERVES 8

8 ounces elbow macaroni (2 cups)

1½ cups heavy cream

3 cups (12 ounces) shredded white cheddar cheese

1 cup (4 ounces) shredded Gruyère cheese

Pinch of cayenne

Pinch of ground nutmeg

Salt and black pepper

4 slices bacon, cooked and crumbled (optional)

Bring a large pot of salted water to a boil and add the macaroni. Cook according to the package directions and drain.

Return the pasta to the pot and pour in the heavy cream. Turn the heat on low and, while stirring, slowly add the cheddar and Gruyère. Continue to stir until the cheese is melted and well combined, which should take a couple of minutes. Add the cayenne, nutmeg, salt, and pepper. Stir in the bacon and serve immediately.

NOTE: It's the fat in the cream that makes this recipe work, yet be so simple to make. Unfortunately, there's not a good substitute that will yield the same results. But feel free to experiment with different melting cheeses. For instance, you can substitute 1 cup of smoked Gouda for the Gruyère. Or use pepper Jack instead of cheddar.

COWBOY BEANS

★

COWBOY BEANS, a popular staple in Texas, is a dish fashioned from pinto beans and meat. Recipes usually call for ground beef, which has always seemed a little silly to me as I doubt that the cowboys' chuck wagon was stocked with perishable meat while out on the trail. However, they would have had on hand ample supplies of dried beef. With that in mind, I make my cowboy beans with beef jerky instead.

These slow-cooked beans are spicy, sweet, and savory, with the beef jerky adding both texture and a rich flavor. The beans make a good side dish for barbecues and potlucks, or you can serve them with a salad and biscuits and make them the main course of a meal. Though no matter how you offer them, when you close your eyes you can imagine you're eating them by the fire under the stars, as you live your life on the trail. SERVES 8

In a large pot, cover the beans with 1 inch of water and bring to a boil. Turn the heat to low and simmer for 15 minutes, uncovered. Drain the beans and rinse.

Preheat the oven to 250°F. Return the beans to the pot and add the onion and garlic. Cover with water by 1 inch and bring to a boil. Remove the pot from the burner, cover the pot, and bake in the oven for 1 hour.

Remove the pot from the oven and stir in the beef jerky, coffee, molasses, mustard, and chili powder. Return the pot to the oven, turn up the oven temperature to 350°F, and continue to cook, uncovered, until the beans are tender and the liquid is reduced and thickened, 1½ hours to 2½ hours, depending on the age of the beans. (If the beans are tough and don't soften within this time frame, you may need to add a bit more water to the pot to keep the beans from becoming too dry.) The final consistency should be like a slightly soupy pot of baked beans.

Once the beans are done, add salt and pepper to taste. Serve immediately.

1 pound dried pinto beans

½ yellow onion

2 cloves garlic

Water

3 ounces beef jerky, diced

½ cup brewed coffee

2 tablespoons molasses

2 tablespoons prepared mustard

1 tablespoon chili powder

Salt and black pepper

RANCH-STYLE BEANS

★

RANCH-STYLE BEANS are a Texas classic. These soupy beans aren't fiery, but they do have a depth and brightness that can be very addictive. When I lived in Texas, we ate them often—in bowls topped with cheese, as a base to salads, or as a side to enchiladas or baked ribs.

In Texas, you can buy these beans at the store, and it's the rare Texas pantry that doesn't have a can or two waiting to be opened for a quick and easy side dish for a weeknight meal. But when I moved to New York, those beloved beans that had been a staple back home could not be found.

This was difficult, and it took a lot of experimenting to come up with a similar-tasting recipe. Then a wise friend clued me into the fact that he believed that the beans were simply pintos swimming in a chili gravy. Once I had that in mind, making my own ranch-style beans was a snap. SERVES 8

1 pound dried pinto beans

Water

1 tablespoon vegetable oil

1 yellow onion, diced

4 cloves garlic, minced

4 ancho chiles, rehydrated, stemmed, and seeded (see page 9)

1 (14.5-ounce) can diced tomatoes, drained

1 teaspoon brown sugar

1 teaspoon apple cider vinegar

1 teaspoon paprika

1 teaspoon ground cumin

½ teaspoon dried oregano

Salt and black pepper

In a large pot, cover the beans with water by 1 inch and bring to a boil. Turn the heat to low and simmer for 15 minutes, uncovered. Drain the beans and rinse.

Return the beans to the pot, add enough water to cover by about 1 inch and bring to a boil. Turn the heat down to low and simmer, covered, until the beans are soft and tender, 1 to 2 hours. (The cooking time will be determined by the age of the beans.)

Meanwhile, in a skillet, heat the oil over medium-low heat and add the onion. Cook, stirring occasionally, until the onion is translucent, about 5 minutes. Add the garlic and cook for 30 seconds more. Turn off the heat and transfer the onion and garlic into a blender or food processor. Add the ancho chiles, diced tomatoes, brown sugar, apple cider vinegar, paprika, cumin, and oregano. Blend until smooth. Taste and adjust the seasonings and add salt and pepper.

Once the beans are soft and tender, stir in the ancho-chile puree. Continue to cook the beans, uncovered, over low until the broth has darkened and the beans are flavorful, about 1 hour. You want these beans to be a little soupy, so add water if the liquid gets too low while cooking. Once done, taste and adjust the seasonings. Serve immediately.

REFRIED BLACK BEANS

★

WHEN I FIRST MOVED to New York, my quest for good-quality Mexican food became obsessive. While I may have occasionally found a decent taco or a plate of serviceable nachos, the one dish that eluded me was a proper serving of refried beans.

Ever since I can remember, refried beans have been my ultimate comfort food. Sure, beans taste great on their own—but when you add a boost of pork flavor, well, beans go from good to sublime.

While I typically make my refried beans with pinto beans, when I'm feeling a little wild, I will use black beans instead. Refried black beans are not as common in Texas (though you do see them occasionally, especially in Austin), but this certainly doesn't mean they are any less good. I prefer to start with dried beans, as I find they're more flavorful than canned. To save time, however, you can substitute canned beans, though I recommend simmering them with the aromatics so they'll be more lively. SERVES 8

If you are using dried beans, in a large pot, cover the beans with water by 1 inch and bring to a boil. Turn the heat to low and simmer for 15 minutes, uncovered. Drain the beans and rinse.

Return the beans to the pot, add the garlic, onion, cilantro, and jalapeño, and cover the beans with water by 1 inch. Bring the pot to a boil, turn the heat down to low, cover, and simmer for 1½ hours.

Remove the lid and add salt to taste. Continue to simmer, uncovered, until the beans are tender, anywhere from 30 minutes to 2 hours, depending on the freshness of the beans.

If you are using canned beans, pour the beans into a pot with the garlic, onion, cilantro, and jalapeño, add 1 cup of water, and simmer, uncovered, for 30 minutes.

Once the beans are cooked, allow them to cool in their liquid, about 15 minutes. When they are cool enough to handle, scoop out 1 cup of the cooking liquid and put it in a blender or food processor. Drain the beans (reserve the rest of the liquid), and add the beans to the blender. Puree until smooth, adding some of the reserved liquid, if needed. (Any additional liquid can be reserved for another use, such as thickening stocks.)

In a large skillet, melt the bacon grease over low heat. Pour in the bean puree and cook, occasionally stirring, until the beans have reduced and are darker in color, 5 to 10 minutes. Add salt to taste. Serve immediately.

1 pound dried black beans, or 3 (15-ounce) cans black beans

½ yellow onion

2 cloves garlic

2 sprigs cilantro

1 jalapeño, stemmed, seeded, and halved lengthwise

Salt

1 tablespoon bacon grease, lard, or vegetable oil

SPANISH RICE

★

BEANS AND RICE. Do any two foods go better together? Okay, maybe, peanut butter and jelly, but if you give me a serving of beans, I'm going to want a serving of rice right beside it.

This recipe came from a friend of mine from Austin. For years, I had been struggling with my Spanish rice method, even going so far as to dump a whole jar of hot sauce into the rice, which simply resulted in a soupy mess. My friend was bragging about what a good cook her Mexican grandma had been, so I asked if she'd mind sharing her recipe for rice.

"It's very simple," she said. She didn't speak in exact measurements—instead she gave me a broad set of guidelines. That's also how I cook, so I understood her language, though sometimes when you're preparing a recipe for the first time you want more specific instruction. I was a bit nervous.

Fortunately, the recipe came together with great success. When the rice was done, I sautéed some diced onion, added some minced garlic, cumin, and tomato paste and then stirred it into the cooked rice. It certainly looked right—golden brown—and it certainly smelled right—fragrant with cumin and garlic. I took a bite, and it was a revelation—this was the Mexican rice I had been searching for. If you're looking for a good Spanish rice recipe, it may indeed be the one that you've been seeking, too.

SERVES 4 TO 6

1½ cups long-grain rice
1 tablespoon vegetable oil
½ yellow onion, diced
4 cloves garlic, minced
1 tablespoon tomato paste
½ teaspoon ground cumin
1 tablespoon fresh lime juice
½ cup chopped fresh cilantro
Salt

Cook the rice according to its package directions and then remove from the heat. You should have about 3 cups of cooked rice.

Heat the oil in a skillet over medium-low heat. Add the onion and cook until translucent, about 5 minutes. Add the garlic and cook for 30 seconds more. Stir in the tomato paste and cumin and cook for 1 minute. Turn off the heat.

Add the cooked rice to the skillet and stir until well combined with the tomato paste and spices. Stir in the lime juice and cilantro. Add salt and adjust the seasonings. Serve immediately.

CHAPTER 4

CHILIS, SOUPS, AND STEWS

A black-and-white photo of a sheep with a lamb hangs in my grandma's living room. My uncle Austin took that photo on the day of my great-grandfather's funeral. Apparently, when the family returned to the house after the funeral, the ewe had just given birth.

"We were struck by the circle of life and all that," Grandma said. "It's timeless."

While I was at that funeral, I was very young, so I don't remember too much about it. I also don't remember too much about my great-grandfather, except that he liked to sit on the front porch and smoke a pipe. He also loved to eat. I assume he ate very well: he was a cattleman and a farmer, so there was always plenty of fresh food on hand. And because he loved a good meal, I believe he would have appreciated the potluck we held in his honor.

In my collection of family recipes, I have the record of food donations from the potluck held after the burial. It's a booklet that the funeral home gave to families so they could keep track of who brought what, so they could not only write a thank-you card but also return the correct dish to the proper person. The cover states, "This booklet will enable you to keep a record of friends who bring food to the home."

It's a fascinating document, as it illuminates what people brought to gatherings back in the 1970s. Popular dishes included deviled eggs, potato salad, pea salad, congealed salads, fried chicken, ham, hominy casserole, pecan pie, and lemon pie, among many other comfort-food dishes. What's even more interesting is these are the same dishes that made appearances at my grandfather's funeral, thirty years later.

Much like the circle of life, Texan comfort food is also timeless.

Black-Eyed Pea and Mexican Chorizo Soup 117

Venison Chili 118

Pork Chili Verde 121

Buttermilk Potato Soup with Bacon and Jalapeño 122

Chipotle Chicken and Dumplings 125

Sopa de Lima (Mexican Lime Soup) 127

Pumpkin Pasilla Soup 128

Squash Blossom Soup with Zucchini-Corn Salsa 131

Southeast Texas Gumbo 132

That said, one thing did surprise me about the array of dishes that were brought to my grandfather's and great-grandfather's funerals: the absence of soups. Sure, pickles, appetizers, main dishes, side dishes, and desserts are all well represented, and one person did bring chicken and dumplings, and another a pot of beans—but that was as close to soup as it got. I found this odd, as soups can be the most comforting dishes of all.

For instance, hearty chilis made with venison or green chile peppers will warm you up on cold winter days. If you're not feeling your best, soups such as creamy potato or a lively sopa de lima can be the best medicine. And when you've been away from family and friends for too long, there's nothing like a pot of Southeast Texas gumbo or black-eyed pea and chorizo soup simmering on the stove to say, "Welcome home."

Perhaps people didn't bring soups to the potluck because they're hard to transport or keep warm. Or perhaps people were operating under the (incorrect, I think) assumption that soups weren't fancy or impressive enough fare for a large group. But even if they weren't the first choice for this particular gathering, it doesn't mean that Texans don't love their soups, chilis, and stews. Nope, quite the contrary. And when Texans desire a delicious, heart-warming meal, often it will be bowls of soup that you'll find on the family table. I know that when I've had a long day or need a little comfort, a big bowl of soup is soothing and just what I need—and I reckon others might feel the same.

BLACK-EYED PEA AND MEXICAN CHORIZO SOUP

⭐

MY MOM ONCE MADE a soup from a recipe she'd been given by our family friend Mary Jo. It was full of chicken, salsa, cheese, and beans and was just the thing you needed on a cold night.

Back in my kitchen in New York, I thought about recreating it, but I opted to make it with the ingredients that I had on hand. So instead of chicken, I used Mexican chorizo. And since New Year's Day was approaching I used black-eyed peas instead of beans. (They are traditionally eaten on this day for good fortune, as their golden color is said to represent coins.) The soup takes little time to come together, but is full of flavor and warmth. Mary Jo had told my mom, "Make this soup, and your kids will thank you." And while I may have changed the original recipe a bit, this adaption has made me pretty thankful as well. SERVES 8

In a large pot, cover the black-eye peas with water by 1 inch and bring to a boil. Turn the heat to low and simmer, uncovered, for 1½ hours or until black-eyed peas are tender. Drain the peas, reserving 1 cup of the cooking liquid, and rinse. (If using canned black-eyed peas, simply drain the cans, reserving 1 cup of liquid.)

Over medium-low heat, heat the oil in a skillet and add the chorizo. Cook for 10 minutes or until browned, breaking up any large pieces. With a slotted spoon, transfer the cooked chorizo from the skillet to a large soup pot. Add the onion to the oil left in the skillet and cook over medium-low heat until translucent, about 5 minutes. Add the garlic and cook for 30 seconds more.

Transfer the onions and garlic to a blender or food processor, and add the tomatoes, chipotle chiles, cumin, oregano, and allspice. Blend until smooth. Pour into the soup pot with the chorizo. Add the black-eyed peas and their liquid, the chicken broth, and cilantro.

Bring to a boil, turn the heat down to low, and gently simmer for 15 minutes. Add the shredded cheese and continue to cook until the cheese has melted, about 5 minutes, occasionally stirring. Stir in the crushed tortilla chips and simmer for 10 more minutes. Add the lime juice and then adjust the seasonings, adding salt and black pepper.

To serve, top each bowl with sour cream and cilantro.

1 pound dried black-eyed peas or 3 (15-ounce) cans black-eyed peas

1 teaspoon vegetable oil

2 cups (1 pound) Mole Chorizo (page 164) or other Mexican chorizo, removed from its casing and crumbled

½ yellow onion, chopped

4 cloves garlic, chopped

1 (14.5-ounce) can diced tomatoes, preferably fire-roasted, drained

2 canned chipotle chiles in adobo sauce

½ teaspoon ground cumin

½ teaspoon dried oregano

¼ teaspoon ground allspice

4 cups chicken broth

¼ cup chopped fresh cilantro, plus more for garnishing

2 cups (8 ounces) shredded pepper Jack cheese

½ cup finely crushed tortilla chips

2 tablespoon fresh lime juice

Salt and black pepper

Sour cream, for garnish

VENISON CHILI

★

VENISON CHILI IS A popular cold-weather dish in Texas, as people who go deer hunting every year are looking for ways to use up their abundance of meat. You'll see it served at church suppers, informal dinner parties—really, just about everywhere—since during the season, there's always plenty of venison to go around.

Venison has a pleasing yet strong flavor with echoes of beef and lamb. It's also very lean, which gives it a good chew—although when it's stewed for too long, it can become overly tough and stringy. Now, I have to admit I am not a hunter. So when I was trying to come up with a recipe, I turned to a cousin who's both an avid outdoor sportsman and cook. "Add pork," he advised, explaining that the fat from pork would add both flavor and moisture to the pot.

While today's Texan chili purists typically keep pork away from their bowls of red (and I include myself here), when doing research on chili recipes from the 1800s, I learned that adding pork was a common practice back then, so I didn't feel inauthentic about it after all. (In case you're wondering, yes, beans were still absent from those early recipes.) My venison chili is much like my beef chili—it has some of the same chiles and spices—but the use of venison with the addition of pork results in an earthier flavor. If you can't get your hands on any venison, you can substitute four pounds of beef chuck or brisket for the venison and pork, which still makes for an excellent bowl of red. SERVES 8

4 slices bacon

3 pounds venison, chopped into ¼-inch cubes

1 pound pork shoulder, chopped into ¼-inch cubes

Salt and black pepper

1 yellow onion, diced, plus more for serving

4 cloves garlic, minced

1 tablespoon ground cumin

¼ teaspoon ground cinnamon

¼ teaspoon ground allspice

Pinch of cloves

1 cup brewed coffee

1 (12-ounce) bottle dark Texan beer

In a large pot, cook the bacon over medium-low heat, turning once, until crisp, about 10 minutes. Transfer the cooked bacon to a paper towel. Drain the skillet of the bacon grease, leaving 2 tablespoons (reserving the rest for another use).

Add the venison and pork to the pot and cook, occasionally stirring, until the meat is lightly browned, 5 to 7 minutes. (You may have to do this in batches, depending on the size of your pot.) Remove the meat from the pot. Lightly season with salt and black pepper.

Add the onion to the pot and cook until translucent, about 5 minutes. Add the garlic and cook for 30 seconds more. Return the venison and pork to the pot, crumble in the bacon, and add the cumin, cinnamon, allspice, cloves, coffee, beer, and 2 cups of the water. Turn the heat up to high to bring it to a boil.

Meanwhile, combine the ancho, pasilla, and chipotle chiles in a blender or food processor with the remaining 1 cup of water. Blend until a smooth puree forms and pour this into the pot. Add salt and black pepper to taste.

Once the pot comes to a boil, turn the heat down to low and simmer, uncovered, for 1½ hours, occasionally stirring, or until the venison is tender and the broth has reduced a bit. (You want the chili to be thick, but while cooking, if it appears it's becoming too dry, feel free to add a bit more water.) Taste and adjust the seasonings. To thicken the chili, scoop out ¼ cup of the chili and combine it the masa harina. Stir the mixture back into the pot and continue heating the chili until thickened.

Serve with onions, cheddar cheese, jalapeños, and tortilla chips or saltines.

3 cups water, plus more as needed

6 ancho chiles, rehydrated, stemmed, and seeded (see page 9)

2 pasilla chiles, rehydrated, stemmed, and seeded (see page 9)

2 canned chipotle chiles in adobo sauce

1 tablespoon masa harina or cornmeal

Shredded cheddar cheese, for serving

Jalapeño slices, for serving

Tortilla chips or saltines, for serving

PORK CHILI VERDE

★

WHILE I ENJOY MAKING CHILI with beef and red chile peppers—that thick concoction folks call "Texas red"—sometimes I make a less-orthodox chili with pork and green chile peppers instead. This chili verde was inspired by New Mexican green chili, though my interpretation is nothing like that dish.

When I served a friend from Albuquerque my green chili, he laughed and said it had nothing to do with what he ate in New Mexico. "You've made a *Texan* green chili," he said. He then insisted I not call it green chili, lest other New Mexicans think this was related to their state dish, which is not only made with New Mexican green chiles instead of the poblano and jalapeños I used, but also has potatoes added. So I've named it pork chili verde to avoid any confusion. But no matter its provenance, when you serve it people will ask for seconds and perhaps even thirds, and it will be a true hit. SERVES 6 TO 8

In a large soup pot or Dutch oven, heat 1 tablespoon of the bacon grease over medium-low heat. Lightly salt and pepper the pork and add to the pot, browning on each side, 2 to 5 minutes per side. You may have to do this in batches. Once browned, transfer the pork to a large bowl, pouring the pan juices into the bowl.

Return the pot to the stove and heat the remaining 1 tablespoon of bacon grease over medium-low heat. Add the onion and cook until translucent, about 5 minutes. Add the garlic and cook for 30 seconds more.

Return the pork and its juices to the pot. Add the poblano chiles, jalapeño chiles, tomatillos, chicken broth, Mexican lager, cumin, oregano, allspice, cayenne, and ½ cup of the cilantro. Turn the heat to high and bring to a boil; then turn the heat down to low and gently simmer, uncovered, for 2 hours, stirring occasionally and skimming any fat from the surface.

Taste and adjust the seasonings, adding salt and pepper to taste. Continue to cook, uncovered, until the pork is tender, anywhere from 30 to 60 minutes more. To thicken the chili, in a bowl mix together the masa harina with 2 tablespoons of the chili liquid. Stir this back into the pot, along with the remaining ½ cup cilantro and the lime juice. Cook until the chili has thickened, 10 more minutes. Serve with sour cream and shredded Monterey Jack cheese.

2 tablespoons bacon grease or vegetable oil

Salt and black pepper

4 pounds boneless pork shoulder, cut into 1-inch cubes

1 yellow onion, diced

6 cloves garlic, chopped

4 poblano chiles, roasted (see page 9), peeled, seeded, and diced

4 jalapeño chiles, stemmed, seeded, and diced

1 pound tomatillos, husked and halved

2 cups chicken broth

1 cup Mexican lager

2 tablespoons ground cumin

2 tablespoons dried oregano

½ teaspoon ground allspice

Pinch of cayenne

1 cup chopped fresh cilantro

2 tablespoons masa harina or cornmeal

1 tablespoon fresh lime juice

Sour cream, for serving

Shredded Monterey Jack, for serving

BUTTERMILK POTATO SOUP WITH BACON AND JALAPEÑO

⭐

MY GRANDMA CALLS ME her good cook. She'll say to her friends when I visit, "I don't have to be in the kitchen because my good cook is here!" Usually, she lets me cook whatever I want.

But one time I visited she wasn't feeling well, and she requested that I make her one thing—potato soup. She told me that her mom used to make potato soup when she was young, and she had a craving. I asked if she had my great-grandmother's recipe and she said no. "You're my good cook," she said. "I know you can do it."

With no recipe, I looked through her refrigerator for inspiration. Most soups start with a base of aromatics, such as celery and onions, so I threw those into a pot and cooked them in bacon grease left over from breakfast. I also added garlic, chicken broth, and a mess of peeled and cubed potatoes. After I brought everything to a boil, I let it simmer for a while until the potatoes were soft. Later, after pureeing the potatoes, I stirred in some buttermilk and added bacon and jalapeños, too.

The potato soup tasted pretty darn good to me, but, of course, the real test was if Grandma liked it. I ladled it into bowls, set the table, and told her lunch was ready. She came into the dining room, sat down, and said the blessing. "It smells wonderful in here!" she said.

"Is this what you had in mind?" I asked after she took her first bite. She paused, took another and said, "Thank you. This is just what I needed. You're my good cook."

SERVES 4 TO 6

6 slices bacon, diced

1 celery stalk, chopped

½ yellow onion, chopped

4 cloves garlic, chopped

4 cups chicken or vegetable broth, plus more as needed

2 pounds russet potatoes, peeled and cut into 1-inch cubes

Pinch of ground cumin

Pinch of cayenne

In a large skillet, sauté the bacon over medium heat until crisp and the fat has rendered, about 5 minutes. Remove the bacon from skillet and place on a paper towel–lined plate.

Pour 1 tablespoon of the bacon grease into a large pot, reserving the rest for another use. Add the celery and onion and cook over low heat, stirring occasionally, until soft, about 8 minutes. Add the garlic and cook for 30 seconds more. Add the chicken broth, potatoes, cumin, and cayenne. Turn the heat to high and bring to a boil; then turn the heat to low and simmer, uncovered, for 30 minutes, or until the potatoes are fork tender.

Turn off the heat and let the soup cool for 10 minutes. Pour into a blender or food processor, and puree. (You may have to do this in batches. Alternatively, you can use an immersion blender in the pot.)

Return the soup to the pot and stir in the bacon, jalapeños, cilantro, buttermilk, and half-and-half. (This is a thick soup; so if you prefer it thinner, add water, more broth, more buttermilk, or half-and-half.) Turn the heat to low and cook for 5 minutes. Adjust the seasonings and add salt and black pepper to taste. Serve with sour cream and Monterey Jack.

2 jalapeño chiles, roasted (see page 9), stemmed, seeded, and diced

2 teaspoons chopped fresh cilantro

½ cup buttermilk, plus more as needed

½ cup half-and-half, plus more as needed

Salt and black pepper

Sour cream and shredded Monterey Jack cheese, for serving

CHIPOTLE CHICKEN AND DUMPLINGS

★

ONE OF THE BEST THINGS about small Texas towns is that they usually have a café that specializes in classic Texan cooking. You know the kind of joint I'm talking about—it's a place where you can get a cheese enchilada to go with your chicken-fried steak, the beans are dripping with a bacon-rich broth, the iced tea is served in a bottomless glass, and the toughest decision you'll make that day is whether to order the pie or the cobbler for dessert.

And, of course, these cafés always serve chicken and dumplings.

When making my own chicken and dumplings, I took some liberties with the classic version of this dish, like spicing it up with chipotle chiles and cilantro. After one bite, you'll agree these are definitely not your grandmother's chicken and dumplings. But don't worry, these chicken and dumplings still fulfill the original dish's mandate, which is that after eating, it you will feel cozy and satisfied. And sometimes, that's just what you need. SERVES 4 TO 6

To make the soup, put the chicken in a large pot, breast side down, and pour in the chicken broth along with enough water to cover the chicken by 1 inch, 10 to 12 more cups. Add the garlic, onion, carrot, celery, peppercorns, and bay leaf. Bring the pot to a boil; then turn the heat down to low. Simmer, uncovered, for 1 hour.

Remove the chicken with tongs and place in a large bowl and allow to cool for 20 minutes. Meanwhile, strain the broth, discarding the vegetables, then remove the fat from the broth with a gravy separator. If you don't have a separator, you can take a quart-sized plastic storage bag and pour some broth into it. Snip a bottom corner of the bag and drain the broth, stopping when you get to the fat layer that is on top. (You will probably have to remove the fat in batches.) Return the broth to the pot; you should have 10 to 12 cups. Bring the broth to a boil, and then cook until the broth has reduced to 6 cups, which will take 15 to 20 minutes.

While the chicken cools and the broth reduces, make the dumplings. Stir together the flour, baking powder, salt, cilantro, oil, egg, and milk until a dough forms. It's okay if it's a little sticky. Pour the dough out onto a generously floured surface (you should use about 2 tablespoons flour), and knead for a minute, until the dough is smooth. Make sure there's enough flour covering your surface, then roll out the dough into a rectangle that measures about 12 inches by 8 inches and is about 1/8 inch thick. (Don't fret if it's not perfect; mine never is.) With a sharp knife or pizza cutter, cut the dumpling dough into 1-inch squares.

CONTINUED

CHICKEN SOUP

1 (3-pound) chicken or the equivalent in chicken parts

2 cups chicken broth

Water

2 cloves garlic, smashed

1 yellow onion, cut into quarters

1 carrot, chopped

2 celery ribs, halved

1 teaspoon peppercorns

1 bay leaf

½ teaspoon kosher salt, plus more as needed

½ teaspoon black pepper

¼ teaspoon ground allspice

¼ teaspoon ground cumin

1 tablespoon fresh lime juice

1 canned chipotle chile in adobo sauce, finely minced

1 cup half-and-half

Chopped fresh cilantro, for garnish

DUMPLINGS

1¼ cups all-purpose flour, plus more for dusting

1 teaspoon baking powder

¼ teaspoon kosher salt

1 teaspoon finely chopped fresh cilantro

1 tablespoon vegetable oil

1 egg, beaten

¼ cup whole milk

After 20 minutes, the chicken should be cool enough to handle. Remove the meat from the skin and the bones; chop the meat and discard the rest. You should have about 4 cups of meat. Toss the chicken with the salt and pepper and return the meat to the pot of broth. Stir in the allspice, cumin, lime juice, and chipotle chile. Add salt to taste.

If the pot is not already boiling, bring it back to a boil over medium heat. Drop the dumpling squares into the boiling liquid and continue to boil, for 10 minutes, without stirring. (They will expand a bit as they cook.) After 10 minutes, gently stir in the half-and-half, turn the heat down to medium-low, and continue to cook for 15 more minutes. Taste and adjust the seasonings.

Pour evenly into bowls and garnish with chopped cilantro.

NOTE: Traditionally, chicken and dumplings is served, as the name implies, with simply the chicken, broth, and dumplings. As some have said, "It's not called chicken, peas, carrots, and dumplings!" That said, if you prefer a more loaded soup base, you can add frozen peas, diced carrots, and/or celery to the broth. I would do about a cup of each. If adding celery and carrots, use freshly cut vegetables, not the ones used to make the broth, and add them when you reduce the broth, because they'll take longer to get soft. Peas, however, can be added any time.

SOPA DE LIMA (MEXICAN LIME SOUP)

······································ ✪ ······································

ON A RECENT VISIT to a friend's house, he served me a flavorful chicken soup that was topped with fried tortilla strips, Monterey Jack cheese, lime slices, and avocado. It was a bit like tortilla soup, but tangier and lighter. "Is this Texan?" I asked. "Sort of," he said. He then explained that this soup—which is called *sopa de lima* or Mexican lime soup—originally hails from the Yucatán region of Mexico. But he used to eat it growing up in San Antonio, and it reminded him of home.

If, like me, you're a big fan of limes, you'll appreciate this bright, refreshing soup. Now, apparently the limes in the Yucatán have a different flavor than the limes we eat in the US. But even if this soup isn't completely authentic to its source material, it has that Tex-Mex flavor that I love. And whether you're serving it to guests or eating it for its more salubrious effects, I think you'll love it, too. SERVES 8

···

Heat ½ cup of the vegetable oil in a large skillet over medium heat until a candy thermometer reads 350°F. Line a baking sheet with paper towels.

Slice the tortillas into strips ¼ inch thick. Add tortilla strips to the hot oil and cook until crisp, about a minute. Drain on the paper towels.

Place the quartered onion and garlic under the broiler. Cook until blackened, about 10 minutes, turning once. Combine the onion and garlic in a blender or food processor along with 1 cup of the broth. Puree until smooth, then pour into a large pot.

Add the remaining 7 cups of chicken broth to the pot, and stir in the oregano, allspice, cinnamon, cumin, cayenne, cilantro, and lime zest. Bring to a boil, turn down the heat, and simmer, uncovered, for 10 minutes. Add the shredded chicken and cook for 5 more minutes. Add salt and black pepper to taste. Adjust the seasonings, then stir in the lime juice.

Garnish each bowl with tortilla strips, Monterey Jack, jalapeños, cilantro, avocado, and lime slices.

Oil, for frying

6 corn tortillas, preferably stale

1 yellow onion, quartered

10 cloves garlic

8 cups chicken broth

½ teaspoon dried oregano

¼ teaspoon ground allspice

¼ teaspoon ground cinnamon

¼ teaspoon ground cumin

Pinch of cayenne

½ cup chopped fresh cilantro

2 teaspoons lime zest

2 cups shredded cooked chicken

Salt and black pepper

¼ cup fresh lime juice

GARNISHES

½ cup (2 ounces) shredded Monterey Jack cheese

2 jalapeños, stemmed, seeded, and diced

½ cup chopped fresh cilantro

1 avocado, pitted, peeled, and cubed

1 lime, cut into slices

PUMPKIN PASILLA SOUP

★

WHILE MOST FOLKS ASSOCIATE pumpkins with colder climes, they grow in Texas, as well. In the fall, you'll see people plopping their children down in pumpkin patches for that classic photo opportunity. Likewise, they are a staple of Mexican cooking, and as Texas and Mexico were once united, I feel that the pumpkin should be considered Texan, too.

As it's a fall fruit, I like to make something warm with my pumpkins, such as this creamy soup that's been livened up with perfect autumn spices, such as allspice and ginger, and the earthy heat of pasilla chiles. While you could make this with canned pumpkin puree, working with a whole pumpkin is not difficult. You'll want to use a sugar or cooking pumpkin, which is smaller and rounder than the ones used for carving or photo opportunities. You can find these at the grocery store or at farmers' markets during the fall. Plus, when you use a whole pumpkin, you can roast the seeds, which makes for a fine, healthy snack. SERVES 8

1 (3-pound) sugar pumpkin, or 2 (15-ounce) cans unseasoned pumpkin puree

1 tablespoon unsalted butter

¼ yellow onion, chopped

4 cloves garlic, chopped

4 cups chicken or vegetable broth

2 pasilla chiles, rehydrated, stemmed, and seeded (see page 9)

¼ cup fresh cilantro, plus more for serving

¼ teaspoon ground cumin

¼ teaspoon ground allspice

Pinch of ground ginger

Pinch of cayenne

2 tablespoons fresh lime juice

Salt

Sour cream, for serving

Roasted Pumpkin Seeds (page 67), for serving

If you are using a fresh pumpkin, preheat the oven to 375°F and line a baking sheet with aluminum foil.

With a sharp knife, cut the pumpkin in half lengthwise, starting at the stem. Remove the stringy bits and seeds from the pumpkin, reserving the seeds for roasting. Place the pumpkin, skin-side up, on the baking sheet and cover with foil.

Bake for 1½ hours, or until the flesh is tender. Let cool, then scoop out the pumpkin flesh—you should have about 4 cups. If using canned pumpkin puree, skip this step.

In a large pot, melt the butter over medium-low heat. Add the onion and cook until translucent, about 5 minutes. Add the garlic and cook for 30 seconds more. Add the pumpkin, chicken broth, pasilla chiles, cilantro, cumin, allspice, ginger, and cayenne. Bring to a boil, turn the heat down to low, and gently simmer for 20 minutes, occasionally stirring.

Turn off the heat and allow the soup to cool for 5 minutes. Working in batches, transfer the soup to a blender or food processor, and puree until smooth. Return the pureed soup to the pot. Stir in the lime juice, taste and adjust the seasonings, and add salt. Reheat the soup on low for serving.

Serve topped with dollops of sour cream and cilantro, with roasted pumpkin seeds on the side.

SQUASH BLOSSOM SOUP WITH ZUCCHINI-CORN SALSA

★

IF YOU'VE EVER GROWN ZUCCHINI in your garden, then you are well aware of how prolific they can be. One way to curb the plant's production is to go out early in the morning and gather its blossoms, which my uncle enjoys doing when he's visiting the family farm.

The squash blossoms are not only beautiful, but they're edible, too. There are several different ways to eat these blossoms, but my uncle's favorite preparation is to puree them into a delicate creamy soup. I also like to add some zucchini-corn salsa to each bowl, which not only gives the smooth soup a flavorful crunch but, with an extra blossom for garnish, makes for a beautiful bowl.

If you don't grow your own squash, you should be able to find zucchini blossoms during the summer and early fall in some supermarkets, Mexican grocery stores, and farmers' markets. SERVES 4

To prepare the squash blossoms, remove the stamens, pistils, and stems and gently rinse. Reserve four blossoms for the garnish and coarsely chop the remaining twelve blossoms.

In a large pot, heat the butter over medium-low heat. Add the onion and cook until translucent, about 5 minutes. Add the garlic and cook for 30 seconds more. Add the chopped squash blossoms and chicken broth, and continue to cook until the blossoms wilt, 2 to 3 minutes. Turn off the heat and allow to cool for 5 minutes.

Meanwhile, to make the zucchini-corn salsa, in a bowl stir together the zucchini, corn, diced poblano chile, serrano chile, garlic, cilantro, cumin, Cotija cheese, and lime juice. Add salt to taste.

After the soup has cooled, transfer it to a blender or food processor and blend until smooth. Pour the soup back into the pot and add the cream. Over low heat, warm the soup but do not let it boil. Add salt to taste.

To serve, place a squash blossom into each of four bowls and pour warm broth over the top. Serve with the zucchini-corn salsa on the side.

16 squash blossoms

2 tablespoons (¼ stick) unsalted butter

½ yellow onion, chopped

3 cloves garlic, chopped

2 cups chicken or vegetable broth

2 cups heavy cream

Salt

ZUCCHINI-CORN SALSA

1 zucchini, diced

2 cups fresh corn kernels

1 poblano chile, roasted (see page 9), peeled, seeded, and diced

1 serrano chile, stemmed, seeded, and diced

1 clove garlic, finely minced

¼ cup chopped fresh cilantro

½ teaspoon ground cumin

½ cup (2 ounces) Cotija or feta cheese, crumbled

2 teaspoons fresh lime juice

Salt

SOUTHEAST TEXAS GUMBO

★

SOMETIMES WHEN YOU get together with old friends for dinner, you become so involved with the conversation that you forget to clean up the kitchen. Such was the case when I spent an evening with my dear friends Mark and Wendy.

Mark is from the Southeast Texas town of Silsbee, which is close to the Louisiana border. He insisted on cooking for us, and he graciously made us a large pot of his family's signature gumbo, which is full of smoked sausage, shrimp, and crab. It was a fine meal, and all of us had several bowls before retiring to the backyard to enjoy a cool evening under the stars.

The next morning we realized, much to our dismay, that we had accidentally left the gumbo on the stove overnight. "I can't believe we forgot the gumbo!" said Mark. I couldn't, either. But instead of tempting fate and eating day-old seafood, I decided to develop my own version for this book. This makes a lot of gumbo—so don't forget to store leftovers in the refrigerator, so you can enjoy it again and again and again.

SERVES 8 TO 12

ROUX

½ cup bacon grease or vegetable oil

1 cup all-purpose flour

GUMBO

¼ cup (½ stick) unsalted butter

1 yellow onion, diced

1 green bell pepper, stemmed, seeded, and diced

8 ounces okra, thinly sliced

6 cloves garlic, minced

1 pound smoked sausage, thinly sliced

2 tablespoons Worcestershire sauce

7 cups chicken broth

1 tablespoon kosher salt

1 tablespoon black pepper

1 pound large shrimp, peeled and deveined

1 pound lump crabmeat

Cooked white rice, for serving

Filé powder, for garnishing

To make the roux, heat the bacon grease over medium-high in a cast-iron skillet. Add the flour, a little bit at a time, stirring continuously, for 30 to 35 minutes, until the roux is a dark praline brown. Remove from the heat.

In another skillet, melt the butter over medium-low heat. Add the onion and bell pepper and cook until soft, about 10 minutes. Stir in the okra and cook for 5 more minutes, then add the garlic and cook for 30 seconds more. Remove from the heat.

While the vegetables are cooking, in a large soup pot over medium-low heat, cook the sausage. When the sausage begins to get crisp, pour in the Worcestershire sauce and 1 cup of the chicken broth. With a wooden spoon, scrape the bottom of the pot to incorporate all the cooked sausage into the broth.

Stir in the roux, and then pour in the remaining 6 cups of chicken broth, along with the sautéed vegetables, salt, and pepper. Simmer over low heat for 1 hour, then add the shrimp and crabmeat and cook for 15 more minutes.

Serve over white rice and garnish with filé powder. Leftovers can be stored in the refrigerator for up to 3 days.

SHREDDED BEEF ENCHILADAS WITH THREE-CHILE SAUCE, PAGE 142

CHAPTER 5

THE MAIN EVENT

In my family, the table has long been a gathering place for spending time with those we love. When I was young, at least once a week my extended family would get together for a meal. Perhaps it would be a Saturday in late spring, when after picking peas in my great-grandmother's field, we'd find she had a glazed ham waiting for us to go with our harvest. Or it might be crispy taco night with my dad's family, and the kitchen would be crowded with aunts and uncles frying up tortillas before stuffing them with spicy beef, lettuce, tomatoes, and cheese.

On Sunday afternoons, we'd often visit my grandparents and walk into a house fragrant with the rich, savory aroma of a slow-cooked brisket. And sometimes the relatives would come to our house, and we'd tuck into plates of saucy enchiladas and bowls of beans.

As I grew older, and we moved farther away from each other, meals with nearby friends replaced meals with extended family. So on a chilly New York afternoon, my fellow Texans and I might crowd around the table and roll out tamales to celebrate the holiday season. Or in the summer, I might throw shrimp, potatoes, and corn into a tall pot and have the neighbors over for a proper seafood dinner.

There has never been much formality to these gettogethers, as anyone who wants to join us is welcome.

Michelada Flank Steak Tortas with Poblano-Buttermilk Dressing 139

Shredded Beef Enchiladas with Three-Chile Sauce 142

Sunday Brisket 145

Steak Fingers with Jalapeño Cream Gravy 146

Brisket Tacos, Dallas Style 148

Crispy Tacos 151

Coffee-Chipotle Pork Chops 152

Jalapeño Pesto–Stuffed Pork Roast 155

Cochinita Pibil 157

Peppery Ribs 160

Balsamic-Tarragon Glazed Ham 163

Mole Chorizo 164

Chicken Spaghetti 167

Jalapeño Fried Chicken 168

Turkey Enchiladas with Sweet Potato–Chipotle Sauce 171

Chicken Fajitas 172

Pollo Asado 175

Chicken Tamales with Tomatillo-Guajillo Salsa 176

Beer-Battered Catfish Tacos 179

Tortilla-Crusted Tilapia 183

Tuna with Avocado and Red Pepper Baked in Parchment 184

Roasted Whole Fish 187

Fried Oysters with Chipotle-Lime Dipping Sauce 188

Ancho Chile Shrimp Quesadilla 189

Shrimp Boil 190

Sausage and Shrimp Jambalaya 193

Stacked Jalapeño-Cheese Enchiladas 194

Black Bean Sopes with Chipotle Crema 196

Fortunately, I've found most Texan main dishes can easily accommodate an extra person or two. Whether it's fried catfish nestled in warm tortillas; sticky, peppery slabs of ribs; or a large dish full of cheesy chicken spaghetti, there always seems to be enough food to go around.

Texas is cow country, so beef features prominently. Texas also borders the Gulf Coast, which means seafood is often on hand. And, of course, Texans also enjoy chicken, pork, and vegetarian main dishes. These classics I'm sharing here are based on old family favorites that have graced our table since before I was born. And, while I may be slightly sentimental, I do enjoy making changes, so it's no surprise that I add jalapeños to my fried chicken and sometimes drape enchiladas with a smoky sweet potato sauce.

There are some showstoppers in my main event rotation that might seem natural for savoring on weekends, such as a jalapeño pesto–stuffed pork roast or flank steak sandwiches with a poblano buttermilk dressing. However, I've found these dishes can be equally at home on a weeknight, as Texan food is flavorful but not too fussy, suitable for any occasion, large or small.

My great-grandma Blanche used to say: "You will stay for dinner." It was an offer made because Texans are hospitable and love feeding others, though it was also an invitation to enjoy each other's company and reconnect with loved ones. Because of my memories, these Texan main dishes have great power over me. And no matter where I may find myself in the world, whenever I savor these favorites, I am taken back to my old family table and feel instantly at home.

MICHELADA FLANK STEAK TORTAS WITH POBLANO-BUTTERMILK DRESSING

ON A TRIP TO THE PANHANDLE to stay at a friend's ranch, we were treated to a quickly assembled large torta (a Mexican-style sandwich) when we arrived. It was restorative after a long day of traveling. We sliced off individual portions, grabbed a cold drink, and then sat eating at a picnic table outside under a clear blue big sky. It was good to be in Texas.

When I returned to New York, the concept stayed with me, and since a sandwich can be made with just about anything, I decided to do a version of the sandwich that involved flank steak and poblano buttermilk dressing.

The Michelada flank steak is so-named because of the ingredients found in the marinade—beer, Worcestershire, and lime juice—all of which are ingredients in a beer cocktail called the Michelada. This tender, flavorful flank steak is terrific on its own but when combined with poblano buttermilk dressing, along with the jalapeños, avocados, and red onions, this sandwich becomes extraordinary. It tastes just as good after a long day of traveling as it does on game day or for dinner, too. SERVES 4 TO 8

To prepare the steak, first make the Michelada marinade. In a large, nonreactive container or food-storage bag, mix together the jalapeños, garlic, salt, pepper, brown sugar, lime juice, cilantro, Worcestershire sauce, and beer. Place the flank steak in the container and then add cold water until the steak is covered. Place the container in the refrigerator, and let the steak marinate for at least 4 but no longer than 24 hours.

While the steak is marinating, make the dressing. Combine the buttermilk, roasted poblano, cilantro, garlic, green onions, cumin, and cayenne in a blender or food processor. Blend until well combined. Pour the buttermilk mixture into a bowl and stir in the mayonnaise and sour cream until well combined. Add salt to taste and refrigerate until serving.

An hour before cooking the steak, remove it from the refrigerator, drain, and rinse. Pat the steak dry, line a plate with paper towels, and place the steak on the towels so any excess surface liquid can drain off the steak.

CONTINUED

STEAK

4 jalapeños, halved lengthwise

6 cloves garlic, chopped

2 tablespoons kosher salt

1 teaspoon black pepper

1 tablespoon brown sugar

2 tablespoons fresh lime juice

1 sprig fresh cilantro

1 teaspoon Worcestershire sauce

1 (12-ounce) bottle Mexican lager

1 flank steak (1½ to 2 pounds)

Water

1 tablespoon unsalted butter

POBLANO BUTTERMILK DRESSING

½ cup buttermilk

1 poblano chile, roasted (see page 9), peeled and seeded

½ cup fresh cilantro

2 cloves garlic

4 green onions, green part only

¼ teaspoon ground cumin

Pinch of cayenne

½ cup mayonnaise

½ cup sour cream

Salt

TORTA

1 baguette (about 20 inches long)

6 ounces Muenster cheese or Monterey Jack cheese, sliced

½ red onion, cut into rings

2 cups mixed salad greens

1 avocado, pitted, peeled, and cut into wedges

2 pickled whole jalapeños (page 258), stemmed, seeded, and sliced into rounds

When the steak is dry and at room temperature, preheat the broiler and heat a large ovenproof skillet over high heat. (If your steak doesn't fit into the skillet, feel free to cut it in half and work in batches.) When the skillet is hot, add the butter, then add the steak. It should hiss when it hits the skillet. Cook for 2 minutes on one side. With tongs, flip the steak and cook it for another 2 minutes. Place the skillet under the broiler and cook it for 1 minute for medium-rare and 2 to 3 minutes for medium. Remove it from the oven and allow it to rest for 10 minutes. Slice the steak against the grain.

To assemble the sandwiches, slice the baguette in half. Spread some of the dressing on both sides of the loaf. Layer on the steak, cheese, onion, greens, avocado, and jalapeños. Cut the sandwich into 4 to 8 servings and serve.

NOTE: The steak can be served either warm or cold, if you want to make it ahead of time. And if you prefer, the flank steak easily can be grilled.

SHREDDED BEEF ENCHILADAS WITH THREE-CHILE SAUCE

⭐

THE FIRST TIME I HAD beef enchiladas made with shredded beef, I was surprised. I was very young, and the shredded beef tucked into the corn tortillas was a shock to me. Until then, the only beef enchiladas I'd seen were stuffed with ground beef instead.

The long strands of beef in this particular plate of enchiladas presented itself as a challenge, as the meat definitely had more chew than pebbly ground beef. Yet it was still tender, and because the beef had more body, it carried more flavor.

While at first I was wary, as I ate my enchiladas, I decided that these were beef enchiladas for grown-ups; since I was eight years old at the time, it made me feel more grown up, too. SERVES 4 TO 6 ★ PICTURED ON PAGE 136

BEEF

2 pounds chuck roast, cut into 2 equal-size pieces (make sure there's some fat on the roast)

Salt and black pepper

1 tablespoon bacon grease, lard, or vegetable oil

1 yellow onion, chopped

4 cloves garlic, chopped

½ cup brewed coffee

2 tablespoons Worcestershire sauce

2 tablespoons apple cider vinegar

2 canned chipotle chiles in adobo sauce

2 teaspoons ground cumin

¼ teaspoon ground cinnamon

1 cup water

Preheat the oven to 275°F.

Sprinkle the roast with salt and pepper. In a large ovenproof pot, heat the bacon grease over medium-low heat, add the meat, and brown on both sides, about 5 minutes per side. Remove the roast from the pot and add the onion. Cook, occasionally stirring, until the onion begins to brown, about 5 minutes. Add the garlic and cook for 30 seconds more.

Return the roast to the pot along with the coffee, Worcestershire sauce, vinegar, chipotle chiles, cumin, and cinnamon, and water. (The meat will not be completely covered, but don't worry; it will produce plenty of liquid as it cooks.) Bring the pot to a boil; cover the pot and place in the oven. Cook the roast, covered, for 3 to 3½ hours, or until the roast practically falls apart when you poke it with a fork. (Be careful of escaping steam when removing the pot's lid.)

Remove the meat from the pot, leaving the broth in the pot to cool. Shred the meat with two forks until it's in long strands. Add salt and pepper to taste.

To make the sauce, pour the broth from the pot into a blender or food processor, along with the onions, garlic, and chipotle chiles also in the pot. Add the rehydrated pasilla and ancho chiles and water. Blend until smooth, about 1 minute. You should have 2 to 2½ cups of sauce.

In a medium pot, heat the oil over medium-low heat. Whisk in the masa harina or flour until it's well incorporated and fragrant, about 30 seconds. Pour the sauce from the blender into the pot, stirring until it's well combined. Stir in the cumin, oregano, and allspice, and add salt and pepper to taste. Cook over low heat (be careful, because it will probably splatter out of the pot as it cooks) for 5 to 10 minutes, stirring occasionally, until the sauce is smooth and the flavors are balanced. Taste and adjust the seasonings. Toss the shredded beef with 2 tablespoons of the sauce, leaving the rest for the enchiladas.

Preheat the oven to 350°F. Grease a large baking dish (9 by 13 inches works well).

To make the enchiladas, in a medium skillet, heat the lard over medium-low heat. One at a time, heat the tortillas in the hot oil until soft and pliant, and then keep them wrapped in a cloth or tortilla warmer until all the tortillas are heated.

Lay a tortilla on a plate or clean surface and add about ¼ cup of beef. Roll the tortilla and place in the greased baking dish seam-side down. Repeat with the remaining tortillas. Evenly pour the sauce over the enchiladas and top with the grated cheese and diced onion. Bake for 15 minutes, or until cheese is lightly browned and bubbling. Serve immediately.

SAUCE

2 dried pasilla chiles, rehydrated, stemmed, and seeded (see page 9)

2 dried ancho chiles, rehydrated, stemmed, and seeded (see page 9)

1 cup water

1 tablespoon vegetable oil

2 tablespoons masa harina or all-purpose flour

1 teaspoon ground cumin

1 teaspoon dried oregano

Pinch of ground allspice

Salt and black pepper

ENCHILADAS

1 tablespoon lard or vegetable oil

12 corn tortillas

2 cups (8 ounces) shredded cheddar cheese

¼ yellow onion, diced

SUNDAY BRISKET

⭐

WHEN I WAS YOUNG, after church on Sundays we'd head to my grandparents for Sunday dinner. Before church, my grandma would have put into the oven a pot roast, and as we entered the house a few hours later, we'd be greeted by its enticing, savory aroma.

This recipe is inspired by those Sunday dinners of my youth. My family's roast was seasoned simply with salt and pepper, but I also slather my brisket with a paste made with garlic, molasses, and mustard, which gives the brisket a deep, gorgeous flavor. And taking a nod from my dad who likes to serve beef with a horseradish cream sauce, I've followed suit, though I've also added a pickled jalapeño for additional fire and spice. Even if you choose not to add the jalapeño, the horseradish cream sauce adds a tangy brightness that goes well with the rich meat. SERVES 4 TO 6

To make the brisket, mince two of the garlic cloves and combine with the salt, pepper, cayenne, molasses, and mustard in a small bowl; stir until a paste forms. Rub this all over the brisket, and allow the brisket to rest, unrefrigerated, for 1 hour. Meanwhile, coarsely chop the remaining 6 cloves of garlic and cut the onion into slivers.

Preheat the oven to 250°F.

In a large ovenproof pot or Dutch oven that can easily hold the brisket, heat the oil over medium heat. Add the onion and cook until the pieces just begin to brown at the tips, about 5 minutes, stirring occasionally. Add the garlic and cook for 30 seconds more. Turn off the heat and pour in the broth, scraping along the bottom to loosen all of the pan drippings.

Place the brisket in the pot, fat side up, spooning some of the onions and garlic from the bottom of the pot on top of the brisket. Cover the pot and transfer to the oven. Cook the brisket, covered, for 5 to 6 hours, or until fork tender. While each brisket is different, I usually allow 1½ hours per pound to cook. Be sure not to overcook it, though. While brisket is a forgiving meat, if left to cook for too long they can become dry.

While the brisket is cooking, make the horseradish sauce. Stir together the horseradish, sour cream, garlic, and jalapeño. Add salt to taste. Refrigerate, covered, until you are ready to serve the brisket.

When the brisket is done, allow it to rest in the pot, uncovered, for at least 30 minutes before serving. Top the brisket with the pan juices and serve with the horseradish sauce on the side.

BRISKET

8 cloves garlic

1 tablespoon kosher salt

1 tablespoon black pepper

¼ teaspoon cayenne

2 tablespoons molasses

2 tablespoons prepared yellow mustard

1 (3- to 4-pound) brisket, from the flat cut, preferably with a bit of fat on it

1 yellow onion

1 tablespoon vegetable oil

1 cup beef broth

HORSERADISH CREAM SAUCE

1 teaspoon horseradish, prepared or freshly grated

1 cup sour cream

1 clove garlic, minced

1 pickled jalapeño, stemmed, seeded, and diced (optional)

Salt

STEAK FINGERS WITH JALAPEÑO CREAM GRAVY

★

STEAK FINGERS, if you're not familiar with them, are simply pounded, breaded, and fried strips of beef. Yep, it's basically chicken-fried steak made into finger food, which is probably how they got the name—instead of the meat resembling a certain part of the body. (At least, that's what I like to think; it seems a bit more appetizing.)

My version is based on my dad's chicken-fried steak recipe and to complete my meal, I serve it with jalapeño cream gravy.

Cream gravy has long been touted as the fourth Texan food group, after Tex-Mex, barbecue, and chicken-fried steak. In my family, it often made an appearance on the family table. (It also made an appearance on the front porch, because my great-grandma Blanche was famous for whipping up batches of gravy to feed her dog and cats.)

At my house, whenever my mom fried meat in the cast-iron skillet, she'd add flour, milk, and a good shake of black pepper to the pan drippings in order to craft a thick, flavorful gravy. Pan drippings are the preferred fat for cream gravy since they add tons of flavor, but in their absence it's perfectly fine to make gravy with bacon grease or vegetable oil.

While cream gravy is traditionally seasoned with black pepper, I find that it takes well to additions such as jalapeños and garlic. Now, my great-grandma (and her dogs and cats) may have found this cream gravy a bit exotic, but I believe you'll find the gravy both tasty and good. SERVES 4

JALAPEÑO CREAM GRAVY

2 jalapeños, stemmed, seeded, and halved lengthwise

2 cloves garlic

2 tablespoons bacon grease or vegetable oil

2 tablespoons all-purpose flour

1½ cups whole milk

¼ teaspoon ground cumin

Salt

To make the cream gravy, place the halved jalapeños skin-side up and the garlic on a baking sheet and place under the broiler for 5 minutes, or until the jalapeños and garlic are blackened. Remove from the broiler. Rub off the blackened jalapeño skin and then dice. Mince the roasted garlic.

In a large heavy skillet, heat the bacon grease over medium-low heat. Whisk in the flour and cook until fragrant and lightly browned, about 1 minute. Slowly pour in the milk and stir until thickened, which should take a couple of minutes.

Turn off the heat and stir in the diced jalapeños and garlic. Add the cumin and salt to taste. If the gravy is too thick, add more milk. It will keep in the refrigerator for 5 days. Reheat on low for serving.

If you are using top round steak, you'll need to pound it with a meat mallet until flattened and doubled in size. If you are using cube steak, you can skip this step. Cut the tenderized steak into sixteen strips.

Mix together the flour with ½ teaspoon salt, 1 teaspoon black pepper, and cayenne on a plate. Whisk together the eggs with the buttermilk in a shallow bowl.

Lightly sprinkle the steak strips with salt and pepper. Dredge each strip in the seasoned flour. Dip the flour-coated steak into the eggs, and then dredge again in the flour.

Preheat the oven to 200°F.

In a large heavy skillet, such as a cast-iron skillet, heat up ½ inch of oil to 350°F over medium-high heat. If you don't have a candy thermometer, after 5 minutes of heating, stick a wooden spoon into the oil. If the oil bubbles around the spoon, it should be hot enough.

Place four strips into the skillet and cook until you see red juices bubbling on top of the meat, 2 to 3 minutes. With tongs, turn over the fingers and cook for another 2 to 4 minutes, until lightly browned. Drain on a paper towel and place in the oven while you fry the remaining strips.

Serve with the jalapeño cream gravy.

STEAK FINGERS

2 pounds top round steak or cube steak

1½ cups all-purpose flour

Kosher salt and black pepper

¼ teaspoon cayenne

2 eggs

1 cup whole milk or buttermilk

Oil, for frying

BRISKET TACOS, DALLAS STYLE

★

DALLAS-STYLE BRISKET TACOS are soft tortillas stuffed with succulent strands of brisket, pulled from a roast that has been braised for a long time. The brisket isn't smoky nor is it fiery—but it's tender and juicy, with a rich depth of flavor that can only come from cooking the meat low and slow.

Another hallmark of Dallas's brisket tacos is that there's always melted Monterey Jack on the tortillas, and each taco is topped with strips of sautéed onions and poblano chiles. Some places also include a small bowl of the pan juices, turning the brisket taco into a Tex-Mex beef sandwich au jus.

What's interesting, however, is that you don't usually find this style of brisket taco in other Texas cities. I'm not sure why this is the case, but Tex-Mex cuisine has many region-specific dishes, so it certainly doesn't surprise me. The Dallas–Fort Worth area has long been associated with cattle, so it makes sense that a big, beefy taco would be an integral part of this town's Tex-Mex scene. SERVES 4 TO 6

BRISKET

1 (3- to 4-pound) brisket, from the flat cut, preferably with a bit of fat still on it

Salt and black pepper

1 tablespoon vegetable oil or bacon grease

1 yellow onion, cut into quarters

8 cloves garlic

¼ cup red wine vinegar

2 cups beef broth

1 teaspoon ground cumin

2 jalapeños, stemmed, seeded, and halved lengthwise

2 leafy stems cilantro

1 bay leaf

Preheat the oven to 250°F.

Sprinkle the brisket with salt and black pepper. In a large ovenproof pot, heat the oil over medium-low heat, add the brisket, and brown on both sides, about 5 minutes per side.

Remove the brisket from the pot and add the onion. Cook, occasionally stirring, until it begins to brown, about 10 minutes. Add the whole garlic cloves and cook for another 2 minutes. Turn off the heat and pour in the red wine vinegar, scraping along the bottom to loosen all of the pan drippings.

Return the brisket (and any juices) to the pot, fat side up. Pour in the beef broth and add the cumin, jalapeños, cilantro, and bay leaf. Cover the pot and place in the oven. Cook the brisket, covered, for 5 to 6 hours, until fork tender. While each brisket is different, I usually allow 1½ hours per pound to cook. Be sure not to overcook it, though. While brisket is a forgiving meat, if left to cook for too long, it can become dry.

Take the brisket out of the oven and let it rest in the pot, uncovered, for 30 minutes.

To make the tacos, heat the vegetable oil in a skillet over medium-low heat and add the onion slivers. While occasionally stirring, cook until softened, about 10 minutes. Add the poblano strips and cook for 1 more minute.

After the brisket has rested, remove it from the pot, cut off the fat cap, and shred the meat with two forks until it's in long strands. To make the gravy, strain the solids and discard and remove the fat from the cooking liquid. Add 2 tablespoons of the gravy to the shredded brisket, reserving the rest for serving. Taste the brisket and adjust the seasonings.

Heat up the broiler. Working in batches, place 6 tortillas on a baking sheet and top each tortilla with 2 tablespoons of Monterey Jack. Slide the tortillas under the broiler for 30 seconds or until the cheese is melted. Repeat for the remaining tortillas. Fill the tortillas with shredded brisket and top with some of the onions and poblano strips. Serve with the pot juices and salsa on the side.

TACOS

1 teaspoon vegetable oil

1 yellow onion, cut into slivers

2 poblano chiles, roasted (see page 9), peeled, seeded, and cut into strips

1½ cups (6 ounces) shredded Monterey Jack cheese

12 Buttermilk Bacon-Fat Tortillas (page 26) or flour tortillas

Old-Fashioned Texas Hot Sauce (page 241), Tomatillo-Chipotle Salsa (page 242) or store-bought salsa, for serving

CRISPY TACOS

★

IN THE OLD DAYS, when Texans thought of tacos, it was the crispy version they had in mind. But thanks to fast-food chains and prepackaged taco shells that taste more like cardboard then corn, crispy tacos have fallen out of favor with many people, and if they're eating tacos, they are more likely to reach for soft tortilla tacos instead. Sure, soft tortilla tacos are how it's done in Mexico, but the crispy taco is a Texan approach to a Mexican dish, and there's no reason why it should be shunned or ignored. It is, after all, true Tex-Mex.

That said, there's no reason why they should be bad, either. The key to a good crispy taco is to make the shells yourself. Yes, it takes a little bit of time, but once you take that first, satisfying bite, you'll be convinced that crispy tacos are just as delicious as soft tacos, and are long overdue their proper praise. SERVES 4 TO 6

To make the filling, in a large skillet, heat the oil over medium-low heat. Add the beef, onion, and jalapeño. Cook, stirring occasionally, until the beef is lightly browned and onions are translucent, about 10 minutes. (If there is a lot of grease in the skillet, drain off some of the grease.) Add the garlic, chili powder, cumin, oregano, cayenne, cilantro, and tomato paste. Stir until the spices are well distributed, turn the heat down, and simmer for 15 minutes, stirring occasionally. Taste and adjust the seasonings and add salt and black pepper. Stir in the lime juice and remove from heat.

To make the tacos, line a baking sheet with paper towels and heat 2 inches of oil to 350°F in a heavy skillet. If you don't have a candy thermometer, after 5 minutes of heating, you can stick a wooden spoon into the oil to see if it's ready. If the oil bubbles around the spoon, it should be hot enough.

Take a tortilla and fold it in half into a "U" shape, holding it with tongs in the center. Using the tongs, dip one half of the tortilla, lengthwise, into the hot oil, leaving the other half out of the oil. Fry the first side until crisp, about 10 seconds, and then repeat for the other side, holding the already-cooked side out of the oil. Drain the taco shell on a paper towel–lined sheet and repeat until all the shells are fried.

To assemble the tacos, take each shell and fill it with the ground beef, lettuce, tomatoes, onion, and cheddar cheese. Serve with salsa.

FILLING

1 teaspoon vegetable oil

1½ pounds ground beef

½ yellow onion, diced

1 jalapeño, stemmed, seeded, and diced

2 cloves garlic, minced

2 tablespoons chili powder

1 teaspoon ground cumin

1 teaspoon dried oregano

¼ teaspoon cayenne

½ cup chopped fresh cilantro

1 tablespoon tomato paste

Salt and black pepper

2 tablespoons fresh lime juice

TACOS

Oil, for frying

12 corn tortillas

2 cups shredded iceberg lettuce

2 plum tomatoes (4 ounces), seeded and diced

½ yellow onion, diced

2 cups (8 ounces) shredded yellow cheddar cheese

Old-Fashioned Texas Hot Sauce (page 241) or store-bought salsa, for serving

COFFEE-CHIPOTLE
PORK CHOPS

★

THERE ARE MANY DIFFERENT regional styles of Texas barbecue, one of which is "cowboy style," which means that instead of smoking the meat with indirect heat (in a smoker, for example), the meat is smoked directly over the coals, much like a cowboy used to cook his food on the range. You find this type of barbecue in Hill Country towns, such as Llano and Macon, with Cooper's being the most-famous place to get your cowboy-style barbecue fix. On early weekend afternoons, you'll see lines of folks waiting by the pits to get their meat. And after you're served, you take a seat at a long communal table where all types mingle together, sharing a fine smoked-meat feast.

While Texas barbecue is known for its brisket, another way the cowboy style differs from the others is its emphasis on the pork chop. My version is definitely inspired by the cowboy tradition; it results in a smoky, juicy, and slightly sweet slab of meat, which goes well with fresh jalapeños and slices of raw onion. Because I live in a small apartment with no outdoor space, I can't smoke my pork chops as it's done in Llano. So instead I rest my chops overnight in a coffee-chipotle rub, which after cooking leaves the meat tender, smoky, and bittersweet. And when I take a bite, I can just about see myself sitting at a Hill Country table, rubbing elbows with church folk, bird-watchers, and weekend riders alike. SERVES 4

2 tablespoons kosher salt

2 tablespoons brown sugar

1 tablespoon black pepper

1 tablespoon finely ground dark-roasted coffee beans

1 tablespoon paprika

1½ teaspoons chipotle chile powder

½ teaspoon granulated garlic

½ teaspoon ground cinnamon

½ teaspoon ground cumin

½ teaspoon ground allspice

4 (5- to 6-ounce) bone-in pork chops, cut ¾ to 1 inch thick

1 tablespoon vegetable oil

Mix together the salt, brown sugar, black pepper, ground coffee, paprika, chipotle powder, granulated garlic, cinnamon, cumin, and allspice. Coat each pork chop with the rub, covering both sides generously. Reserve any leftover rub for another use. Place the pork chops in a plastic food-storage bag, and refrigerate for 8 hours.

To cook the pork chops, remove them from the refrigerator and allow to come to room temperature, about 30 minutes. Preheat the oven to 350°F.

In a large ovenproof skillet, heat the vegetable oil over medium-low heat. Add the pork chops, and cook on each side for 5 minutes. Place the skillet in the oven and cook the pork chops for 15 minutes, uncovered, or until a meat thermometer reads 145°F. Allow to rest for 10 minutes before serving.

JALAPEÑO PESTO–STUFFED PORK ROAST

⭐

ONE SUMMER, MY FAMILY HAD A POTLUCK at my cousin's house. She likes to claim she can't cook, but she surprised us all with a homemade pesto-stuffed pork roast that was the hit of the party.

The roast takes a little bit of effort, especially if you choose to cut the meat yourself. But putting together the jalapeño pesto is not difficult, and after you bake the meat, you and your guests will appreciate slices of tender pork swirled with the nutty, spicy green stuffing. As my cousin would say, if she can do it, anyone can. SERVES 4 TO 6

First, you'll need to roll cut the pork roast to open it up for stuffing. You can either have your butcher do this, or you can do it at home. To roll cut the roast, remove any strings around the pork roast and then lay the roast on a cutting board, with a shorter side facing you. With a sharp knife make an incision along the length of the meat parallel to the cutting board, one-third of the way up the height of the meat, as if you were using the knife to open a book. Cut into the meat, gently pulling it back as you cut, making sure not to cut all the way through. Once done, spread the cut meat until it looks like an open book, with the side on the left thicker than the other.

With the meat now open, place the knife at the top of the center crease or "spine," and cut along the length of the meat parallel to the cutting board, like you did for the first cut, this time halfway up the height of the crease, again pulling back as you cut. At this point, as the meat opens it will be more like unrolling a roll of paper towels. Continue to cut in and unroll until you've reached the end and the meat is flat. Cover the flattened meat with plastic wrap, and then gently pound with the flat side of a meat mallet until the meat is ½ inch thick, if it's not already. If it's not a perfect rectangle, that's okay.

Preheat the oven to 350°F. Line a roasting pan with aluminum foil.

To make the jalapeño pesto, combine the jalapeños, cilantro, garlic, pecans, cumin, 2 tablespoons of the Cotija cheese, 3 tablespoons of the olive oil, and the lemon juice in a blender or food processor and blend until smooth, scraping down the sides as you blend, if necessary. Add salt and black pepper to taste.

CONTINUED

1 (2- to 2½-pound) boneless pork loin roast

2 jalapeño chiles, stemmed, seeded, and halved lengthwise

2 cups chopped fresh cilantro

1 clove garlic, chopped

¼ cup roasted pecans, chopped

¼ teaspoon ground cumin

¼ cup (1 ounce) Cotija or feta cheese, crumbled

¼ cup olive oil

1 tablespoon fresh lemon juice

Salt and black pepper

Spread the jalapeño pesto in the center of the flattened pork loin, leaving a ½-inch border around the edges, and then sprinkle on top of the pesto the remaining 2 tablespoons cheese. Starting from the short end, roll the pork roast and then secure with kitchen string at 1-inch intervals. Rub the outside of the rolled roast with the remaining 1 tablespoon olive oil and lightly sprinkle with salt and pepper. (And if any pesto oozed out of the roast as you rolled, you can rub it over the outside, too.) Place the rolled roast in the roasting pan.

Roast, uncovered, for 40 to 45 minutes, or until a meat thermometer reads 145°F. Allow the roast to rest for 15 minutes before slicing and serving.

COCHINITA PIBIL

★

TEXANS ARE NOT REALLY KNOWN for making pulled pork. That's a specialty found more often in other parts of the South. But there is a dish that some folks refer to as Mexican pulled pork, which has the more proper name of *cochinita pibil*.

Cochinita, which means little pig, and *pibil,* which refers to a cooking technique of wrapping the meat in leaves, is a dish that hails from the Yucatán peninsula. While the cooking technique of this dish is significant, what gives it its unique flavor is the marinade, which is made with ground annatto seeds. Ground annatto, which is also known as achiote, has a subtle nutmeg-like flavor and vibrant red color. You can usually find it at most Mexican groceries, spice shops, and some specialty groceries. Combined with citrus juices, garlic, and spices, it makes an outstanding source of flavor for the pork.

Traditionally, this dish was cooked in a pit in the ground. But before you go grab your shovel, read on. I've made it a little easier, and you can approximate that experience by wrapping the meat in either banana leaves or foil and roasting it in the oven. Banana leaves can be found in Latin specialty markets, and while they do impart some flavor to the dish, if you can't find them, don't fret; it's just as good if you simply wrap the pork in foil.

After the pork has baked, pull it into strands and serve it with corn tortillas and Pickled Red Onions (page 256). It's a time-consuming dish to prepare, which makes it better suited for weekends or special occasions. Leftovers also reheat well.

SERVES 6 TO 8

To make the achiote marinade, combine the olive oil, orange juice, lime juice, vinegar, garlic, guajillo chiles, chipotle chiles, annatto, salt, black pepper, oregano, cumin, allspice, and cloves in a blender or food processor. Blend until smooth.

Transfer the marinade to a nonreactive container and toss the pork with the marinade. Cover and refrigerate it for 8 hours. Before roasting the pork, remove it from the refrigerator and allow it to come to room temperature, about 30 minutes. If you are using frozen banana leaves, take them out of the freezer and allow them to thaw at this time.

Preheat the oven to 325°F. Line the bottom of a roasting pan with either aluminum foil or the banana leaves.

CONTINUED

ACHIOTE MARINADE

¼ cup extra virgin olive oil

½ cup fresh orange juice

¼ cup fresh lime juice

2 tablespoons white vinegar

8 cloves garlic, chopped

4 guajillo chiles, rehydrated, stemmed, and seeded (see page 9)

2 canned chipotle chiles in adobo sauce

¼ cup ground annatto seeds (see note, page 158)

1 tablespoon kosher salt

1 teaspoon black pepper

1 teaspoon dried oregano

1 teaspoon ground cumin

1 teaspoon ground allspice

¼ teaspoon ground cloves

PORK

4 pounds pork shoulder, cut into 2-inch cubes

Fresh or frozen banana leaves (optional)

½ cup water

Corn tortillas, warmed, for serving

Pickled Red Onions (page 256), for serving

Place the pork in the roasting pan and add the water. If using the banana leaves, cover the pork with more banana leaves and then cover the entire pan with foil. If you are not using the banana leaves, just cover the pan tightly with foil. Roast for 3 hours, or until the meat is fork tender. (Be careful of the escaping steam when you remove the foil.)

Remove the pork from the oven and allow it to rest for 30 minutes.

With tongs, transfer the meat to a large bowl and shred with two forks, adding some of the pan juices if it seems too dry. (You can either discard or save the rest of the pork juices for another use.) Serve with warm tortillas and pickled red onions.

NOTE: Annato seeds can usually be found in the spice aisle. If your regular grocery store doesn't carry them, you will be able to find them at a Mexican market or a specialty shop.

PEPPERY RIBS

★

RIBS ARE A TEXAN BARBECUE STAPLE. While traditionally they're smoked, I live in a small apartment without an outdoor space, so I slowly bake my ribs so the meat will be tender, and then finish them under the broiler slathered with a peppery barbecue sauce.

Some folks believe that Texans don't like barbecue sauce, but this is not true. Yes, in Central Texas where the meat-market style of barbecue reigns supreme, sauce has traditionally been regarded as an insult to the meat, because it masks the natural smoky flavor. However, in other parts of the state, such as East Texas, you'll find barbecue slathered with sauce. Not to mention that many folks enjoy using barbecue sauce as a condiment on hamburgers or with fries.

The inspiration for these ribs came from my friend's husband. He likes to enter barbecue competitions, and his ribs have won many accolades. When I asked him for his recipe, however, he was coy, even though I told him my cooking method would be in an oven. He did concede, however, that he was generous with the black pepper, so when making my ribs I followed suit.

Some may insist that these are not *true* Texan ribs as they haven't spent time in a smoker. That said, I've never had leftovers when serving these, because that time under the broiler caramelizes the sauce on these ribs, making them smoky, spicy, and sweet. SERVES 4 TO 6

RIBS

2 tablespoons kosher salt

2 tablespoons black pepper

1 tablespoon brown sugar

1 teaspoon smoked paprika

½ teaspoon chipotle chile powder

2 slabs St. Louis–cut ribs (about 2 pounds each), see note, page 161

Cracked black pepper, for garnish

To make a rub, mix together the salt, pepper, brown sugar, smoked paprika, and chipotle chile powder. Sprinkle each slab of ribs evenly with the rub and then double wrap with aluminum foil, making note of which side is the meat side. Refrigerate the ribs for 2 to 8 hours. (They're good after 2 hours, but even better after 8 hours.)

Preheat the oven to 275°F. Line two baking sheets with aluminum foil.

Place the foil-wrapped ribs, meat side up, on the baking sheets, and bake for 2 hours.

While the ribs are baking, make the sauce. In a medium pot, stir together the tomato sauce, ketchup, garlic, apple cider vinegar, lemon juice, Worcestershire sauce, molasses, brown sugar, black pepper, cumin, cayenne, and cloves. Bring to a boil, turn the heat down to low, and gently simmer for 30 minutes, occasionally stirring. (The sauce may splatter a bit.) After 30 minutes, stir in the smoked paprika and add salt to taste.

After 2 hours, remove the ribs from the oven, gently open the foil (a lot of steam will escape, so be careful), brush the meat side of the slabs with the sauce, and return to the oven. Bake for 30 minutes, uncovered, and then brush each slab with the sauce again. Bake for 30 more minutes.

Turn on the broiler and place a rack 6 inches away from the heating element. With tongs, remove the ribs from the foil packets, discarding the foil. (You can stir some of the rib juices into the sauce, if you like, or save it for another use.) Drain any remaining fat from the baking sheet and place the ribs back on the sheets. Brush each slab with sauce and broil for 1 to 3 minutes, or until dark spots appear. Sprinkle the ribs with the freshly cracked black pepper for garnish, and allow the ribs to rest for 10 minutes before serving.

NOTE: St. Louis–cut ribs are spare ribs from the belly side of the rib cage, which have had the tips removed.

PEPPERY BARBECUE SAUCE

1 cup canned tomato sauce

1 cup ketchup

2 cloves garlic, finely minced

2 tablespoons apple cider vinegar

2 tablespoons fresh lemon juice

1 tablespoon Worcestershire sauce

2 tablespoons molasses

2 tablespoons brown sugar

1 teaspoon black pepper

¼ teaspoon ground cumin

¼ teaspoon cayenne

Pinch of ground cloves

½ teaspoon smoked paprika

Salt

BALSAMIC-TARRAGON GLAZED HAM

✦

HAM HAS LONG BEEN a family favorite on Sundays and on big feast days, such as Thanksgiving and Christmas. My great-grandma, when she didn't have the time to prepare fried chicken for her guests, would have a ham waiting for them when they got home from church.

Many generations ago, my family would cold smoke their hams themselves after hog-butchering day. Today, the hams that we eat are from the store. That said, even if you didn't smoke it yourself, if you buy one with minimal processing that still has its bone, the ham will be moist and have a good flavor.

Any ham you buy from the store will be already-cooked (since cold smoking cooks the meat), so when you make one, you're simply reheating it in the oven. What you bring to the ham is the glaze that you add at the end. My favorite way to jazz up a ham is with a glaze made with the caramel notes of balsamic vinegar and the bitter-sweet bite of tarragon, delivered with a spread of lively mustard. Most ham glazes are cloying and too sweet, but this one has a good balance with the ham's rich, sweet flavor. SERVES 12

Preheat the oven to 275°F. Line a deep roasting pan with aluminum foil.

Place the ham in the pan and cover loosely with foil. Bake for 15 minutes per pound, or until a thermometer inserted in the thickest end reads 140°F.

Meanwhile, stir together the balsamic vinegar, mustard, garlic, tarragon, brown sugar, and pepper. Add salt to taste.

Once the ham reaches 140°F, remove it from the oven and turn up the oven temperature to 450°F. Brush the top and sides of the ham with the glaze, then return the ham to the oven. Bake, uncovered, for 15 minutes or until the glaze is browned. Allow the ham to rest for 20 minutes before slicing and serving.

1 (8- to 10-pound) semi-boneless cooked ham

¼ cup balsamic vinegar

¼ cup prepared yellow mustard

2 cloves garlic, finely minced

2 tablespoons dried tarragon

2 tablespoons brown sugar

1 teaspoon black pepper

Salt

MOLE CHORIZO

★

ON A VISIT TO SEE MY BROTHER'S FAMILY in Oregon, I stopped over in Seattle for a couple of days. While there, I had incredible salami that was goosed up with red chiles, cinnamon, and chocolate instead of more traditional Italian flavors, such as fennel and nutmeg. The shop called the salami *mole* salami, because mole (pronounced moe-lay) is a Mexican sauce made with chiles and spices. There are many different moles found in Mexico, but the one we most often see on menus in Texas is the mole poblano, with said red chiles, cinnamon, and chocolate.

While salami requires aging, Mexican chorizo can be made and eaten on the same day. Likewise, you don't have to worry about stuffing it into casing as it's always cooked loose. While in my first book I included two more traditional recipes, the Seattle salami inspired me to make a mole chorizo for this book.

At first it seemed odd to be combining the ground pork with chiles blended with sesame seeds, aromatics, raisins, spices, cocoa, and vinegar. After I fried up my first taste, however, I was amazed at the depth of flavor. When I shared it with friends, they all raved.

Texans love to eat chorizo, and this sausage makes a fine addition to breakfast tacos, on top of nachos, or in a molten cheese dish known as Choriqueso (page 62). Admittedly, the mole sauce portion of the recipe takes a little bit of time, but you can make big batches of this sausage, and it freezes well. MAKES ABOUT 1 POUND (2 CUPS)

2 ancho chiles, rehydrated, stemmed, and seeded (see page 9)

2 canned chipotle chile in adobo sauce

2 tablespoons raisins

1 tablespoon sesame seeds

½ yellow onion, chopped

4 cloves garlic, chopped

1 tablespoon cocoa powder

1 teaspoon ground cumin

1 teaspoon paprika

1 teaspoon dried oregano

½ teaspoon ground cinnamon

¼ teaspoon ground allspice

¼ teaspoon cayenne

Combine the ancho chiles, chipotle chiles, raisins, sesame seeds, onion, garlic, cocoa powder, cumin, paprika, oregano, cinnamon, allspice, cayenne, salt, apple cider vinegar, and water in a blender or food processor. Puree until a smooth, bright red paste forms, scraping down the sides as you blend. (You can add more water, a tablespoon at a time, if it's still too dry to blend.) It will look like a dark ketchup.

Add the chile puree to the ground pork and mix well. To test the flavors, heat up a skillet over medium heat, pinch off a small piece of the mole chorizo and fry it up in a skillet for a minute or so. Taste and add more spices, if needed.

Let the meat mixture sit refrigerated for at least 4 hours so the flavors can meld.

To prepare, fry as you would ground beef in a lightly greased skillet, stirring occasionally. Please note that the cooked chorizo is very similar in color to the raw chorizo, so cook for 7 to 10 minutes, or until a thermometer inserted into the meat reads 145°F. Once cooked, serve the mole chorizo with eggs and potatoes (page 25), melted cheese (page 62) or with tortillas for tacos.

The cooked sausage will keep in the refrigerator for a week. It can also be frozen uncooked for 3 months.

NOTE: If you don't grind your own meat (you can do this either with a grinder or in a food processor), make sure that the ground pork you buy has at least 20 percent fat; otherwise the sausage will be too dry.

Pinch of ground cloves

2 teaspoons kosher salt

2 tablespoons apple cider vinegar

2 tablespoons water, plus more as needed

1 pound ground pork (see note)

CHICKEN SPAGHETTI

★

BACK IN THE 1960S, my great-uncle Jamey was the president of Texas A&M University–Kingsville. On the day of the inauguration, the whole family made the trip to South Texas to celebrate and see Governor John Connolly swear in Jamey to his new post.

While I'm not sure how much socializing occurred between my family and the Connollys, in my great-grandma's recipe collection was Mrs. Connolly's chicken spaghetti. As my great-grandma was quite gregarious, I like to think that while chatting, they decided to swap recipes, as people who love good food are wont to do.

Chicken spaghetti is an old Texan favorite, a casserole where spaghetti, chicken, tomatoes, chiles, and cheese all come together to create a, satisfying dish. Many recipes, including the one in my great-grandmother's collection, call for canned soup but I've replaced it with a simple cheese sauce instead. I also blacken grape tomatoes, jalapeños, garlic, and onion under the broiler, for a lively, fire-roasted flavor. SERVES 8

Lightly grease a 9 by 13-inch baking dish. Line a baking sheet with foil.

Cook the spaghetti according to the package instructions in a large pot of boiling salted water. Drain, rinse, and transfer the spaghetti to the baking dish.

Meanwhile, turn on the broiler and place a rack 6 inches away from the heating element. Place the grape tomatoes and jalapeños on the prepared baking sheet, skin side up, along with the whole garlic cloves and onion. Broil, for 5 to 7 minutes, until the tomatoes, jalapeños, garlic, and onion are softened and have begun to blacken. Remove from the oven, and when cool enough to handle, dice the tomatoes, jalapeños, garlic, and onion.

Turn the oven temperature down to 350°F.

To make the sauce for the spaghetti, in a saucepan, melt the butter over medium-low heat. Whisk in the flour until well combined and slightly browned, about 30 seconds. Slowly pour in the milk and cook, stirring, until the sauce thickens just a bit, 3 to 5 minutes. (You want it to coat the back of your spoon, but not be too thick, like custard. If it gets too thick, you can slowly add more milk, about a teaspoon at a time.)

Once the sauce thickens, immediately turn off the heat and slowly stir in half of the cheeses, about ¼ cup at a time, until melted and incorporated into the sauce. Stir in the diced vegetables, along with the cumin, cayenne, cilantro, and lime juice. Taste and adjust the seasonings, adding salt and black pepper to taste. Pour the sauce into the cooked spaghetti and then stir in the shredded cooked chicken. Cover the spaghetti with the remaining cheeses.

Bake, uncovered, for 20 minutes, or until brown and bubbling. Garnish with cilantro before serving.

8 ounces spaghetti

2 cups grape tomatoes, halved lengthwise

2 jalapeños, stemmed, seeded, and halved lengthwise

4 cloves garlic, left whole

½ yellow onion

2 tablespoons (¼ stick) unsalted butter

2 tablespoons all-purpose flour

2 cups whole milk, plus more as needed

2 cups (8 ounces) shredded cheddar cheese

2 cups (8 ounces) shredded Monterey Jack cheese

½ teaspoon ground cumin

¼ teaspoon cayenne

½ cup chopped fresh cilantro, plus more for garnishing

2 teaspoons fresh lime juice

Salt and black pepper

4 cups shredded cooked chicken

JALAPEÑO FRIED CHICKEN

★

WE ARE FRIED-CHICKEN PEOPLE. Some Texans like to celebrate with barbecue, but my family has always turned to fried chicken instead.

When my grandparents were married, it was fried chicken that was served at their rehearsal dinner. And whenever my great-grandmother had friends over for a meal, it was fried chicken that was waiting for them when they arrived.

Fried chicken is a dish that you can order from a restaurant, but it's the sort of thing that tastes much better when it's fresh and homemade. My recipe is essentially the same one my family has made for generations, though since I live in a New York apartment, I've left out my great-grandmother's first step, which was to go out into the yard, pick the chickens, and then wring their necks. (If you are so inclined, however, please feel free to begin the recipe this way.)

The key to a moist, tender chicken is to brine it first, and to add a bit of flavor to mine I throw in some jalapeños, garlic, and cilantro. Traditionally, fried chicken is best fried in lard, though vegetable shortening is good, too. The most important thing, however, is to use a cast-iron skillet. Fried chicken is pan-fried, not deep-fried, as this yields a more tender bird.

Fried chicken can be served hot or cold, and it goes terrific with hot rolls, mashed potatoes, and ice cream for dessert. SERVES 4

JALAPEÑO BRINE

½ cup white vinegar

4 cloves garlic, smashed

4 jalapenos, halved lengthwise

1 bunch cilantro

¼ cup kosher salt

1 teaspoon black pepper

8 cups cold water

1 (3- to 4-pound) chicken, cut into parts, or 3 to 4 pounds bone-in, skin-on breasts, thighs, and/or drumsticks

To make the brine, in a large, nonreactive food-storage container, mix together the vinegar, garlic, jalapeños, cilantro, salt, and pepper. Stir in the water. Add the chicken parts and place in the refrigerator for 4 to 8 hours. This process will make the chicken more juicy and tender as it fries.

To make the breading, stir together the flour, cayenne, salt, pepper, paprika, oregano, and granulated garlic. Taste and adjust the seasonings, though I wouldn't recommend adding any more salt since the chicken will already be salty from the brine.

Remove the chicken from the brine, dredge each piece into the flour until well coated, and place the flour-coated chicken pieces on a baking sheet. (They can be close together, but should not overlap.) Allow the flour-coated chicken pieces to sit out for 1 hour. This step will help the coating adhere better when the chicken fries.

To fry the chicken, heat ½ inch of lard in a large heavy skillet, preferably cast iron, over medium-high heat to 350°F. If you don't have a candy thermometer, after 5 minutes of heating, stick a wooden spoon into the oil. If the oil bubbles around the spoon, it should be hot enough. Working in batches, place a single layer of chicken pieces in the oil, skin side down, turn down the heat to medium, cover the skillet, and cook for 10 minutes.

Take off the cover, gently turn over the chicken with tongs or a wooden spoon, and continue to cook, uncovered, for 10 more minutes. Stick an instant-read thermometer in the largest piece and check that it reads 165°F. If so, place the fried chicken on brown paper bags or a rack to drain. If not, continue to cook for a couple more minutes. Repeat for the remaining pieces, using the same oil. Allow to cool for 15 minutes then serve.

BREADING

2 cups all-purpose flour

¼ teaspoon cayenne

1 teaspoon kosher salt

1 teaspoon black pepper

½ teaspoon paprika

½ teaspoon dried oregano

½ teaspoon granulated garlic

Lard, vegetable shortening, or vegetable oil, for frying

TURKEY ENCHILADAS WITH SWEET POTATO–CHIPOTLE SAUCE

⭐

THE DAY AFTER THANKSGIVING, when you're staring at a refrigerator full of leftovers and you've already reached your annual quota of turkey sandwiches, perhaps it's time to try these enchiladas stuffed with turkey and cranberries and generously draped in a creamy sweet potato–chipotle sauce and melted cheese.

That said, these enchiladas should not be thought of as a second-tier meal. Matter of fact, my dad and my stepmother even declared that they preferred them over the main event enjoyed the previous day, which is high praise indeed. SERVES 4 TO 6

To make the sweet potato chipotle sauce, in a pot, heat the oil over medium-low heat. Add the onion and cook until translucent, 5 minutes. Add the garlic and cook for 30 seconds more.

Turn off the heat and transfer the onion and garlic into a blender or food processor. Add the sweet potato, chipotle chile, chicken broth, chili powder, cumin, allspice, cinnamon, and cayenne. Blend until smooth. Return the sweet potato sauce to the pot and add the cilantro. Bring to a boil, then turn the heat down to low, and gently simmer for 5 minutes, occasionally stirring. (Please note that the sauce will probably splatter.) Stir in the sour cream and lime juice, adjust the seasonings, and add salt to taste. Remove from the heat.

Preheat the oven to 350°F. Lightly grease a 9 by 13-inch baking dish.

Spread 1 cup of the sweet potato–chipotle sauce along the bottom of the baking dish. Stir ¼ cup of the sweet potato–chipotle sauce into the shredded cooked turkey.

In a medium skillet, heat the oil over medium-low heat. One at a time, heat up the tortillas in the oil, and then keep them wrapped in a cloth or tortilla warmer until all the tortillas are heated.

To assemble the enchiladas, take a heated tortilla, spread 1 tablespoon of the cranberry sauce on the tortilla, then place ¼ cup of the cooked turkey down the center. Roll the tortilla. Place the filled tortilla seam-side down in the baking dish and repeat. Pour the remaining sauce over the enchiladas and top with the cheese.

Bake for 15 minutes, or until cheese is lightly browned and bubbling.

Serve topped with sour cream and pecans.

SWEET POTATO–CHIPOTLE SAUCE

1 tablespoon vegetable oil

½ yellow onion, chopped

2 cloves garlic, chopped

1 cup mashed sweet potato

1 canned chipotle chile in adobo sauce

3 cups chicken broth or water

1 teaspoon chili powder

½ teaspoon ground cumin

¼ teaspoon ground allspice

¼ teaspoon ground cinnamon

Pinch of cayenne

¼ cup chopped fresh cilantro

½ cup sour cream

1 teaspoon fresh lime juice

Salt

ENCHILADAS

2½ cups shredded cooked turkey, white and/or dark meat

1 tablespoon vegetable oil

12 corn tortillas

¾ cup cranberry sauce

2 cups (8 ounces) shredded Monterey Jack cheese

Sour cream, for serving

Roasted pecans, for serving

CHICKEN FAJITAS

★

"AUSTIN MADE ME the best chicken fajitas," said my grandma. "I have never had chicken taste so good." Now, I have to admit, chicken fajitas are not something I've ever been inspired to make. Perhaps it's because they're made with boneless, skinless chicken breasts, which isn't the most flavorful cut.

And then there's the language purist inside of me, who knows that calling something "chicken fajitas" is simply wrong; the word *fajitas* originally referred to a cut of beef. Naming the dish chicken fajitas is like saying it's "steak-sliced chicken." Of course, this battle was lost long ago, and it's silly for me to not favor a dish because of its inaccurate name.

I also have to admit there's a thrill when the sizzling chicken arrives on a bed of sautéed peppers and onions, along with the required bowls of salsa, guacamole, and sour cream, and a stack of warm flour tortillas to make the meal complete. For me, fajitas are definitely more than the sum of their parts, so I decided to follow my uncle's lead.

The marinade started with a base of fresh lime juice and balsamic vinegar, along with some chiles, garlic, and cumin added for earthy heat. While I don't have a grill, which is how fajitas are traditionally made, cooking the chicken in a sizzling cast-iron skillet gave it a decent char. And when I tucked the chicken into flour tortillas and topped them with guacamole, sour cream, and sautéed peppers and onions, I had to admit, naming issues aside, chicken fajitas are pretty darn good. SERVES 4 TO 6

CHICKEN

¼ cup fresh lime juice

¼ cup extra-virgin olive oil

1 tablespoon balsamic vinegar

1 teaspoon Worcestershire sauce

6 cloves garlic

1 teaspoon ground cumin

4 dried chiles de árbol, stems removed

1 teaspoon kosher salt

½ teaspoon black pepper

2 pounds boneless, skinless chicken breasts or thighs

In a blender or food processor, mix together the lime juice, olive oil, balsamic vinegar, Worcestershire sauce, garlic, cumin, and chiles de árbol. Blend until smooth and add the salt and black pepper. Pour the marinade over the chicken and marinate, refrigerated, for 1 to 2 hours.

To make the fajitas, drain the chicken from the marinade. In a large, heavy skillet, heat up 1 tablespoon of oil on medium heat. Add the chicken and cook, covered, for about 5 minutes per side, or until the internal temperature is 160°F. Remove the chicken from the skillet, and allow to rest for 10 minutes.

Meanwhile, heat the remaining 1 tablespoon of oil in the skillet. Add the bell peppers and onion and cook until tender and soft, 7 to 10 minutes. Add salt to taste. While the peppers and onions are cooking, heat up the flour tortillas by either cooking each one over a burner or in a hot, dry skillet until they puff, about 15 seconds per side.

Slice the chicken and serve with the bell peppers and onions, warm flour tortillas, guacamole, salsa, and sour cream, so people can make their own fajita tacos.

FAJITAS

2 tablespoons vegetable oil

2 bell peppers, stemmed, seeded, and thinly sliced

1 yellow onion, thinly sliced

Salt

12 Buttermilk Bacon-Fat Tortillas (page 26) or other flour tortillas, warmed

Guacamole (page 66), for serving

Peach Salsa (page 245) or other salsa, for serving

Sour cream, for serving

POLLO ASADO

★

ALL OVER TEXAS, there are restaurants and food trucks that specialize in *pollo asado*, or grilled chicken. They take a whole marinated chicken, grill it, and then serve it with tortillas, beans, and a creamy green salsa. It makes for a great family dinner, and while it's quick to pick up a chicken at a restaurant, I think that it's even better when you make it at home.

I don't have a grill, but I've found that after a spell in a flavorful marinade made with ancho chile, vinegar, orange juice, and lime juice, the chicken takes on a great flavor no matter how it's prepared.

Because I'm oven-roasting my chicken, for more even cooking I spatchcock it, which is just a fancy term for cutting out the backbone and butterflying the bird. After it's roasted in the oven, I then slide it under the broiler for a few minutes so it gets some good char and smoke. And when I serve it on a platter with all of its typical accoutrements, everyone agrees that it tastes as good, if not better, than what they could have bought at the store. SERVES 4

To make the marinade, in a blender or food processor, combine the rehydrated ancho chile, oregano, cumin, cloves, cinnamon, garlic, onion, white vinegar, orange juice, lime juice, olive oil, and salt and blend until smooth.

With kitchen shears or a sharp knife, remove the spine from the back of the chicken and save for stock. Finish spatchcocking by opening the bird and gently pressing on the breast to flatten. Take the marinade and rub it all over the chicken, gently lifting the skin so you can spread some of it on the meat under the skin. Place the coated chicken in a plastic bag and refrigerate for at least 2 hours, and up to 8 hours.

Preheat the oven to 400°F. Line a baking sheet with aluminum foil.

Take the chicken out of the refrigerator and lay it flat, breast side up, on the baking sheet with the legs on the outside. Let it come to room temperature, about 20 minutes.

Roast for 45 minutes, or until a thermometer inserted in the thigh reads 160°F. Remove the chicken from the oven. Turn on the broiler and place a rack 6 inches from the heating element. Broil the chicken for 1 to 2 minutes, until the skin has dark spots. Remove from oven and let it rest for 10 minutes.

Serve with the creamy green salsa, hot sauce, and tortillas.

1 ancho chile, rehydrated, stemmed, and seeded (see page 9)

1 teaspoon dried oregano

1 teaspoon ground cumin

¼ teaspoon ground cloves

¼ teaspoon ground cinnamon

4 garlic cloves, minced

¼ yellow onion

¼ cup white vinegar

¼ cup fresh orange juice

¼ cup fresh lime juice

1 tablespoon olive oil

1 teaspoon kosher salt

1 (3-pound) chicken

Creamy Green Salsa (page 248), for serving

Old-Fashioned Texas Hot Sauce (page 241) or store-bought salsa, for serving

Corn or flour tortillas, warmed, for serving

CHICKEN TAMALES WITH TOMATILLO-GUAJILLO SALSA

⭐

WHEN I VISITED MY BROTHER, my dad, and their families in Oregon for Christmas one year, I suggested that we make tamales. "We've never done that before," they said, so I sent along detailed instructions on what we'd need.

Making tamales at the holidays is a long-standing Texan tradition. Well, really, it's a long-standing Mexican tradition that migrated to Texas. Though even if you don't spend the time making homemade tamales at Christmas, most Texans still serve them at the holiday table, which is what my family did when I was growing up.

It's true, tamales take a whole day to make, but when you have enough hands helping out, the process goes by fast. Plus, it's fun to have an activity that everyone— younger kids included—can join in and become a part of, as it makes the later eating of the tamales so much more meaningful.

When I went to Oregon, my plan had been to have my two-year-old nephew Austin Jack join us at the tamale-making table. He likes to cook with his parents, and the skills needed for making tamales are not too complex. But two-year-olds are famously unpredictable—so I shouldn't have been surprised that he said "no" when we asked him to join us and opted to play with his trucks instead. No matter, we still had a lot of fun rolling out the tamales. And hopefully next year he'll change his mind. SERVES 4 TO 6

CHICKEN

1 (4-pound) chicken

Water

2 cloves garlic

1 sprig cilantro

1 jalapeño, halved

1 bay leaf

1½ teaspoons kosher salt, plus more as needed

1 teaspoon black peppercorns

TOMATILLO-GUAJILLO SALSA

8 ounces tomatillos, husked and halved

¼ yellow onion

2 cloves garlic, left whole

2 cups water

Place the chicken in a large pot and cover with water by 1 inch. Add the garlic, cilantro, jalapeño, bay leaf, salt, and peppercorns. Bring to a boil, then turn the heat down to low. Simmer, uncovered, for 45 minutes.

Remove the chicken from the broth with tongs and place in a large bowl. When cool enough to handle, remove the skin and bones and shred the chicken. Meanwhile, strain the broth, discarding the vegetables, then remove the fat from the broth with a gravy separator. If you don't have a separator, you can take a quart-sized plastic storage bag and pour some broth into it. Snip a bottom corner of the bag and drain the broth, stopping when you get to the fat layer that is on top. (You will probably have to remove the fat in batches.) Add salt to taste. Reserve 1½ cups for the tamale dough, saving the rest for another use.

Toss the chicken with ¼ cup of the cooking broth. Taste and add salt if needed.

Meanwhile, to make the salsa, combine the tomatillos, onion, garlic, and water in a pot. Bring to a boil, turn the heat down, and simmer until the tomatillos are soft, about 10 minutes. Remove from the heat and allow to cool, about 10 minutes.

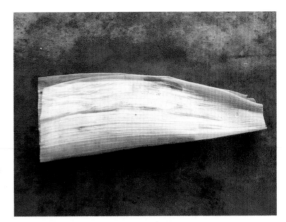
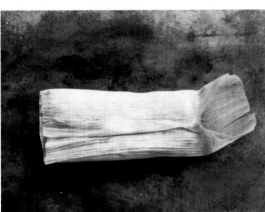

Combine the tomatillo mixture in a blender or food processor with the guajillo chiles, cumin, and allspice. Blend on high until smooth, 3 to 5 minutes; guajillo chiles have tough skins.

Using the same pot, heat the oil over medium-low heat. Pour in the salsa and cook, occasionally stirring, until the flavors have deepened, about 10 minutes. Taste and add salt—I usually start with ¼ teaspoon. Toss ½ cup of the salsa with the shredded chicken, reserving the rest for serving.

To make the tamales, submerge the cornhusks in a pan of warm water; they must be completely covered. Let soak until soft and pliable, 45 minutes.

To make the masa dough, in a stand mixer fitted with the paddle attachment on medium speed, beat the lard until fluffy and creamy. Add the masa harina, chicken broth, and cayenne and continue to beat until the dough comes together into a moist paste.

CONTINUED

4 guajillo chiles, rehydrated, stemmed, and seeded (see page 9)

½ teaspoon ground cumin

¼ teaspoon ground allspice

1 teaspoon vegetable oil

Salt

TAMALES

32 dried cornhusks

1 cup lard or unsalted butter (2 sticks), at room temperature

4 cups masa harina

1½ cups chicken broth, from the poached chicken, or store-bought, or vegetable broth

¼ teaspoon cayenne

To form the tamales, take a cornhusk, which you'll notice has four sides and is in sort of a cone shape. Place the cornhusk in front of you, with the pointed end at your right. On the top, wide part of the husk, spoon out ¼ cup of the masa and spread it out leaving a clean ¼-inch border around the masa on the sides and top. Place 2 tablespoons of the shredded chicken in the center of the masa.

To roll the tamales, fold the husk in half, joining together the two long sides (not the pointed end or wide top). Fold again, again folding the two long sides together. Now take the pointed end and fold it up about one-quarter way of the way up the tamale to secure it. Alternatively, you can rip strips from a cornhusk and after rolling, tie up each end like it's a package.

Place a steamer basket or a colander in a tall pot. Add water to the pot just to the base of the basket (don't let the water get into it). Place the tamales in the basket seam-side up, stacking them flat on top of each other, bring the water to a boil, and then cover the pot and turn the heat down to low. You can stack the tamales to the top of the basket or colander. If your basket or colander is not tall enough to contain all of them, however, you can steam the tamales in batches.

Check the water level occasionally to make sure there's enough in the pot (if it's getting too dry, take out the tamale basket and add more water), and steam the tamales for 2 hours. You'll know they're done when the masa pulls cleanly away from the husk.

Let them rest for a few minutes, and then serve warm with the tomatillo-guajillo salsa.

NOTE: If you like, you can fill these with pork, beef, chicken, or refried beans. You'll need 2 cups of whatever filling you choose to use.

BEER-BATTERED CATFISH TACOS

★

THERE WAS A PERIOD IN MY NEW YORK LIFE when just about every new person I met was from England. One Fourth of July, the Brits (as we called them) asked the Texans (as we called ourselves) if they could join us for a holiday lunch in the spirit of ironic good fun.

They asked what the usual Independence Day dish was, and I said fried chicken. They then suggested we try fried fish instead, perhaps in an effort to assert a little Anglophilia on the affairs. I agreed that sounded fun, but suggested we fry the very American (and Texan) catfish instead of the usual English whiting. It was our holiday after all. And instead of serving the fish with chips (the British term for French fries), we'd serve the fried fish with tortillas so people could make tacos.

The result was a hit. The fluffy yet crisp batter perfectly draped the tender catfish. We then stuffed the fried fish into tortillas and topped them with a cabbage slaw. On the side, salsas and a buttermilk dressing were offered for livening up the tacos, too.

Sure, it wasn't the usual way we celebrated the Fourth. That said, there is something about seafood that always reminds me of summer. So while the menu may have seemed odd at first, both the Brits and the Texans later agreed it was a fresh twist on both of our traditions. SERVES 4

To make the cabbage topping, toss the cabbage with the salt and allow to sit for 1 hour, refrigerated.

Rinse and drain the cabbage. Stir in the garlic, jalapeño, cilantro, cumin seeds, and vinegar. Taste and adjust the seasonings, and then keep refrigerated until you are serving.

To make the beer batter, whisk together the flour, cornmeal, baking powder, cumin, salt, pepper, and cayenne until well combined. Beat the egg with the beer and then pour into the flour mixture and stir until a smooth batter forms. Allow the batter to rest at room temperature for 1 hour. If it separates a bit during this time, simply whisk it again before using.

After the batter has rested, in a large, heavy skillet, heat 2 inches of oil over medium heat until it reaches 350°F. If you don't have a candy thermometer, after 5 minutes of heating, you can stick a wooden spoon into the oil to see if it's ready. If the oil bubbles around the spoon, it should be hot enough. Line a baking sheet with paper towels.

CONTINUED

CABBAGE TOPPING

2 cups shredded cabbage

1½ teaspoons kosher salt

2 cloves garlic, minced

1 jalapeño, stemmed, seeded, and finely minced

¼ cup chopped fresh cilantro

¼ teaspoon toasted cumin seeds

2 tablespoons white vinegar

BEER BATTER

¼ cup all-purpose flour

¼ cup cornmeal

1 teaspoon baking powder

½ teaspoon ground cumin

1 teaspoon kosher salt

¼ teaspoon black pepper

Pinch of cayenne

1 egg

1 cup dark Mexican beer

CATFISH

Oil, for frying

1 pound catfish fillets, cut into thin sticks or bite-sized nuggets

1 teaspoon kosher salt

½ teaspoon black pepper

1 tablespoon fresh lime juice

¼ cup all-purpose flour

Corn or flour tortillas, warmed, for serving

Lime wedges, for serving

Old-Fashioned Texas Hot Sauce (page 241), or store-bought salsa, for serving

Poblano Buttermilk Dressing (page 140), for serving (optional)

To fry the catfish, first season it evenly with the salt, pepper, and lime juice. Place the ¼ cup of flour on a plate, then, working in batches, lightly dredge the catfish in the flour. Holding it by one end, dip the catfish in the beer batter until well coated, and then gently lower into the oil. Fry for 2½ to 3 minutes, or until golden, turning once. Remove from the oil with a slotted spoon and drain the catfish on the paper towels. Repeat for the remaining fish.

Serve the fried fish with the warm tortillas, lime wedges, cabbage topping, salsa, and Poblano Buttermilk Dressing and let diners assemble their own tacos.

TORTILLA-CRUSTED TILAPIA

★

WHEN I WAS YOUNG, once a week my family would eat dinner at the local cafeteria restaurant. It was an interactive dining experience; you grabbed a tray and then slid it down the line, choosing your food as you went along.

Most cafeterias serve up traditional dishes such as roast beef, chicken-fried steak, and enchiladas. One of my favorite dishes at Luby's, the cafeteria that my family used to frequent, was the breaded and baked fish. This tortilla-crusted tilapia is an homage to that dish, with a Tex-Mex twist. SERVES 4

Preheat the oven to 400°F. Lightly grease a baking sheet or line with parchment paper.

Sprinkle the lime juice on both sides of the fish, then season both sides with the salt and pepper. Stir together the tortilla chips and cayenne on a plate. Beat the egg in a bowl. Dip each fillet in the egg, then roll in the tortilla chips. Place each coated fillet on the prepared baking sheet.

Bake for 15 to 17 minutes, or until the fish flakes.

While the fish is baking, make the tartar sauce. Mix together the mayonnaise, jalapeño chile, garlic, cilantro, and lime juice. Taste and add salt.

Serve the sauce with the cooked fish.

FISH

1 tablespoon fresh lime juice

4 (6-ounce) tilapia fillets

1 teaspoon kosher salt

½ teaspoon black pepper

1 cup finely crushed tortilla chips

¼ teaspoon cayenne

1 egg

JALAPEÑO TARTAR SAUCE

½ cup mayonnaise

1 jalapeño chile, stemmed, seeded, and finely diced

1 clove garlic, minced

1 teaspoon chopped fresh cilantro

1 teaspoon fresh lime juice

Salt

TUNA WITH AVOCADO AND RED PEPPER BAKED IN PARCHMENT

⭐

MY DAD'S BEEN LIVING in Oregon for about 10 years, and this baked fish has become his signature dinner-party dish. He says it's because it's a snap to make, but I think the real reason is that its flavors are a combination of both Texas and the Pacific Northwest—his old home and his new. He makes it with halibut because it's so fresh and plentiful in Oregon, but it's also terrific with yellowfin tuna from the Gulf. While it takes little effort to make, the final presentation and flavor are outstanding, making it suitable for both festive occasions and more quiet affairs. SERVES 4

4 (6- to 8-ounce) tuna or other thick fish fillets

4 teaspoons fresh lime juice

Salt and black pepper

¼ cup sour cream

1 small red bell pepper, stemmed, seeded, and sliced into 8 rounds

1 avocado, peeled, pitted, and cut into 12 slices

½ red onion, cut into 12 slivers

¼ cup chopped fresh cilantro

Preheat the oven to 375°F. From a roll of parchment paper, cut off four 18-inch pieces, fold each in half, and then cut each into a heart shape.

Season each fillet on both sides with lime juice, salt, and pepper. Place a fillet on one side of the parchment heart, in the center. Spread over the fillet 1 tablespoon of the sour cream. Layer on top of the fish 2 slices of bell pepper, 3 slices of avocado, and 3 red onion slivers. To seal the package, take the other side of the parchment and fold it over the fish, meeting the edges. Fold and crimp the edges until sealed, then place the package in a baking dish. Repeat the process for the remaining fillets.

Bake for 15 to 17 minutes. Open the pouches, sprinkle the fish with cilantro, and immediately serve.

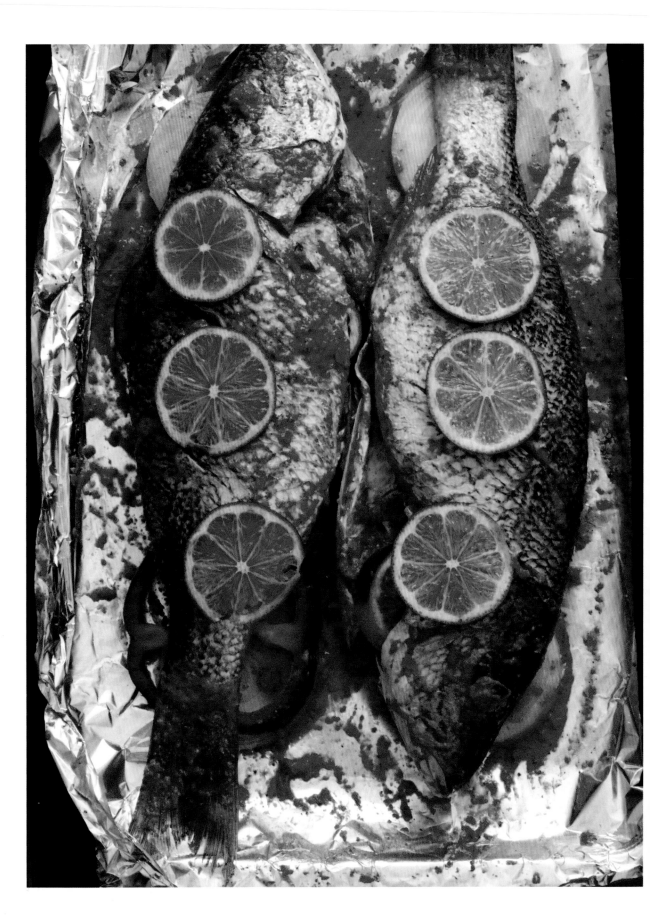

ROASTED WHOLE FISH

⭐

ALONG THE TEXAS GULF COAST, Mexican seafood restaurants specialize in cooking whole fish. The fish, which is usually snapper or redfish, is seasoned and then roasted or grilled. It's then presented with peppers, salsas, and tortillas, so people can take pieces of the fish and make tacos.

Recreating this at home is not difficult, especially if you have an able fishmonger who can scale and gut your fish for you. I first marinate my fish in a tangy, spicy marinade comprised of jalapeños, cilantro, garlic, and lime, then I roast it for about half an hour and serve it along with said accoutrements. It's a snap to make, and it always elicits a few oohs and ahs.

The only trick with eating a whole fish is that the bones are still there. I also leave on the head, as some folks find the fish cheeks the most delicate part. Though if your friends are squeamish, you can always discreetly cover the eyes with a slice of lime. As long as your fellow diners are hip to this, it should be fine. While some might think this sort of eating should only be reserved for weekend or special occasions, I'm convinced that it's just as welcome on the weeknight table, too. SERVES 4

Cut three vertical slashes from spine to belly on each side of each fish and place in a food-safe storage bag. To make the marinade, combine the jalapeños, garlic, cilantro, lime juice, ¼ cup of the olive oil, and cumin in a blender or food processor. Blend until smooth, then taste and add salt and black pepper. Pour the marinade over the fish. Lay the bag flat in the refrigerator for 2 to 4 hours, turning the bag once.

Allow the fish to come to room temperature, about 30 minutes. Preheat the oven to 450°F. Line a baking sheet with foil. Lightly toss the sliced bell pepper and onion with the remaining 1 tablespoon olive oil, then arrange on the sheet. Place the fish on top of the peppers and onions, and then top the fish with the lime slices.

Bake, uncovered, for 20 minutes, or until the fish flakes. Serve the fish with the onions and peppers, along with cilantro, guacamole, salsa, and tortillas on the side for passing around the table.

2 (1- to 1½-pound) whole red snappers, scales removed and gutted, leaving on the head and tail

2 jalapeños, stemmed, seeded, and chopped

4 cloves garlic, chopped

½ cup chopped fresh cilantro, plus more for serving

¼ cup fresh lime juice

5 tablespoons extra-virgin olive oil

¼ teaspoon ground cumin

Salt and black pepper

1 bell pepper, stemmed, seeded, and sliced into rings

1 yellow onion, sliced into rings

1 lime, thinly sliced

Chopped fresh cilantro, for serving

Guacamole, for serving (page 66)

Old-Fashioned Texas Hot Sauce (page 241) or store-bought salsa, for serving

Corn or flour tortillas, warmed, for serving

FRIED OYSTERS WITH CHIPOTLE-LIME DIPPING SAUCE

✪

I HAVE TO ADMIT that I'm not in love with raw oysters. Nope, if I'm going to eat an oyster, I prefer that it be fried.

This is not to say that I haven't had many memorable experiences with fresh oysters. For instance, there were freshly shucked oysters a friend's chef uncle shared with us the night before she got married. Then there were the numerous oysters enjoyed with friends outside of a café on a crisp October afternoon in Paris.

But still, I'd rather eat oysters battered and fried. I realize that preferring fried oysters over raw oysters may make me sound like a rube, but when it's done well, a freshly fried oyster is a thing to savor. The crunchy coating is a wonderful contrast to the soft, juicy oyster inside. Often, fried oysters can be so succulent that no sauce is even necessary, though I would never say no to a dollop or two of chipotle-lime dipping sauce. SERVES 4

1 pint shucked oysters

1 egg, beaten

¼ cup buttermilk

1 cup finely crushed saltines

½ cup yellow cornmeal

Salt and black pepper

Cayenne

Oil, for frying

Sliced limes, for serving

CHIPOTLE-LIME DIPPING SAUCE

1 canned chipotle chile in adobo sauce, finely chopped

½ teaspoon adobo sauce

½ cup mayonnaise

1 teaspoon chopped fresh cilantro

1 teaspoon fresh lime juice

¼ teaspoon ground cumin

1 teaspoon fresh lime juice

Salt

Drain the oysters, reserving ¼ cup of the liquid. Pat the oysters dry.

In a bowl, mix together the egg, buttermilk, and reserved oyster liquid. In another bowl or on a plate, stir together the crushed saltines and the cornmeal. Add a sprinkle of salt, black pepper, and cayenne to both the egg mixture and the breading mixture.

In batches, dip the oysters into the breading, then into the eggs, and then back into the breading. Place the breaded oysters on a large plate or baking sheet. Repeat until all the oysters are coated.

In a large, heavy skillet, heat ½ inch of oil over medium heat until it reaches 350°F. If you don't have a candy thermometer, after 5 minutes of heating, you can stick a wooden spoon into the oil to see if it's ready. If the oil bubbles around the spoon, it should be hot enough.

While the oil is heating, make the chipotle-lime dipping sauce by stirring together chipotle, adobo sauce, mayonnaise, cilantro, lime juice, and cumin. Taste, add salt, and adjust the seasonings. Refrigerate until you are ready to serve.

When the oil is ready, fry the oysters, turning once, until they are light brown, 2 to 3 minutes. Depending on the size of your skillet, you will probably have to do this in several batches. Drain on paper towels. Serve with chipotle-lime dipping sauce and sliced limes.

ANCHO CHILE SHRIMP QUESADILLA

⭐

WHILE ON MY WAY to Kingsville to visit the Texas A&M University library named after my great-uncle Jamey, my foot got a little heavy, and I suddenly found myself on the side of the road passing my driver's license to a police officer.

I explained to him that I had simply been lost in happy thoughts, recalling that the last time I had been to Kingsville was for my cousin's wedding. That happy occasion had occurred many years ago, and I was simply excited about finally going back. The police officer shook his head and told me it didn't matter *why* I was speeding, just the fact that I was. He then issued me a ticket for going too fast and being a menace on the road.

Once in Kingsville, I grabbed lunch at a local Tex-Mex restaurant. The shrimp quesadilla caught my eye and seemed to be a specialty of the house. When it arrived, it was even better than anticipated as the homemade flour tortillas were oozing with melted white cheese and tangy, spicy shrimp. It was an extremely satisfying dish that took away some of the sting of the earlier events and made Kingsville again feel warm and welcoming, just as it had all those years ago. SERVES 4

To make the marinade, combine the ancho chile, orange juice, lime juice, olive oil, ground cumin, ground allspice, cayenne, and garlic in a blender or food processor. Blend until smooth. Add salt to taste. Pour the marinade into a non-reactive container and add the shrimp. Toss to coat, then store in the refrigerator for 2 to 8 hours.

To cook the shrimp, melt the butter over medium-low heat in a large skillet and add the shrimp. Cook for a couple of minutes on each side, or until pink. (You may have to do this in batches.) Coarsely chop the cooked shrimp and toss with some of the pan sauce, if you like.

To make the quesadillas, in a clean skillet heated on medium, melt the butter. Add a tortilla and cook it on one side until it puffs (about 30 seconds). Flip the tortilla over and sprinkle over entire surface with ¼ cup of the Monterey Jack, ¼ cup of the Muenster, one-quarter of the chopped shrimp, one-quarter of the chopped jalapeños, one-quarter of the bacon, and 1 tablespoon of the chopped cilantro. Top with another tortilla, and after cheese has melted and the two tortillas stick together, flip the quesadilla and cook for a couple of minutes more.

Repeat with the remaining tortillas and filling. Cut into slices and serve warm with salsa.

SHRIMP

1 dried ancho chile, rehydrated, stemmed, and seeded (see page 9)

¼ cup fresh orange juice

1 tablespoons fresh lime juice

2 tablespoons extra-virgin olive oil

½ teaspoon ground cumin

¼ teaspoon ground allspice

Pinch of cayenne

2 cloves garlic, coarsely chopped

Salt

1 pound large uncooked shrimp, peeled and deveined

1 tablespoon unsalted butter

QUESADILLAS

1 tablespoon unsalted butter

8 Buttermilk Bacon-Fat Flour Tortillas (page 26) or other 6-inch flour tortillas

1 cup (4 ounces) shredded Monterey Jack cheese

1 cup (4 ounces) shredded Muenster cheese

2 jalapeño chiles, stemmed, seeded, and chopped

2 slices bacon, cooked and crumbled (optional)

¼ cup chopped fresh cilantro

Tomatillo-Chipotle Salsa (page 242) or store-bought salsa, for serving

SHRIMP BOIL

★

SHRIMP BOILS ARE COMMON at church suppers, veteran's groups, school fundraisers, and other large get-togethers in Texas. It's community dining, Gulf Coast style.

When you walk into the gathering place, you'll see long tables covered with newspaper, with bowls of melted butter and cocktail sauce placed every few feet. A team of cooks mans a huge pot, and the air will be thick with a delicious smelling steam. You take your seat at the table, and when the shrimp are done (it doesn't take long), they'll pour out the shrimp along with the other items in the pot, such as corn and potatoes onto a platter. You then peel, dip, and eat the shrimp, throwing the remains onto the newspaper-lined table. People keep track of how much they've eaten by the size of their peel pile, and much ribbing or bragging can ensue.

While it's fun to have a shrimp boil with hundreds of people, Texans like to do them on a smaller scale at home, too. The hardest part of the boil is ensuring you have a pot large enough to hold all the ingredients. The rest, such as finding people to enjoy the shrimp with you, is not difficult at all. SERVES 4

SHRIMP

¼ cup kosher salt

2 tablespoons black pepper

1 tablespoon celery seed

1 tablespoon mustard seeds

1 tablespoon whole allspice

2 teaspoons cayenne

2 limes, halved

1 yellow onion, peeled and quartered

4 cloves garlic, left whole

4 ears corn, shucked and halved

1 pound red potatoes

2 pounds medium shrimp

½ cup (1 stick) unsalted butter, melted

RED SAUCE

1 cup ketchup

1 clove garlic, finely minced

1 teaspoon prepared horseradish

1 canned chipotle chile in adobo sauce, minced (optional)

Fill a large pot two-thirds full with water and add the salt, black pepper, celery seeds, mustard seeds, allspice, cayenne, limes, onion, and garlic. Bring the pot to a boil. Place a steamer basket in the pot and add the potatoes. After 5 minutes, add the corn. Let the pot boil for 10 minutes.

Meanwhile, to make the red sauce, stir together the ketchup, garlic, horseradish, and chipotle chile.

After the pot has boiled for 15 minutes, lightly salt the shrimp and then add them to the steamer basket in the pot. Turn the heat down to low and continue to cook until the shrimp are pink, about 5 minutes.

Turn off the heat, lift out the steamer basket, and pour out the shrimp, potatoes, and corn onto a serving platter. Line a table with newspaper. Stir 1 tablespoon of the cooking liquid into the melted butter, discarding the rest. Serve the shrimp with the red sauce and melted butter on the side, for dipping.

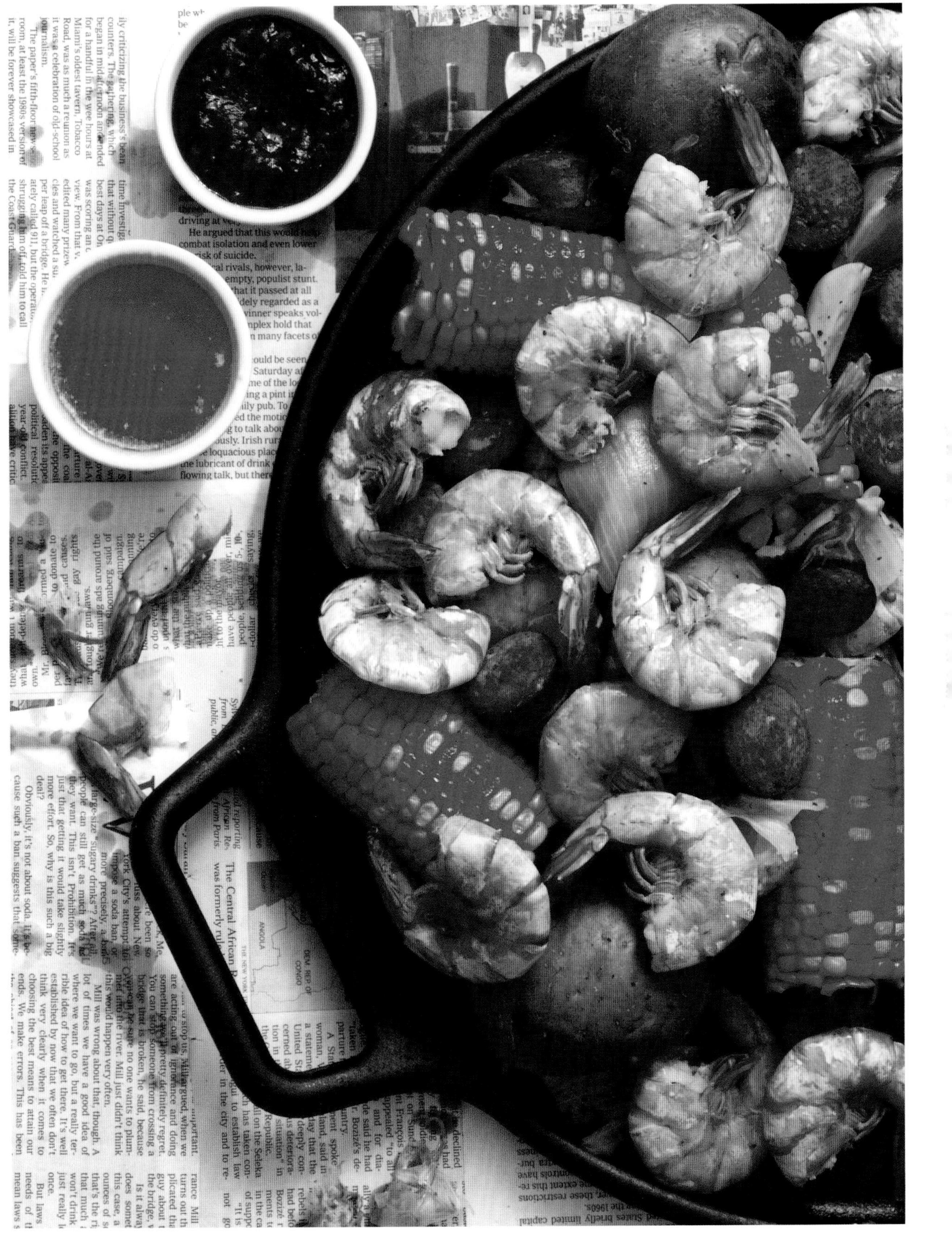

SAUSAGE AND SHRIMP JAMBALAYA

★

A FRIEND MENTIONED her husband was making jambalaya. This rice-based Cajun dish, chock-full of tomatoes, sausage, and shrimp was something I had grown up eating in Houston, yet my recent experiences with it had been limited to singing its praises along with Hank Williams. And while I love a good honky-tonk tune, I love a hearty meal even better. It was time to put this Southeast Texan standard back into my cooking rotation.

This is a simple one-skillet dish, which makes it work well during the week. Yet if you're having a get together or celebrating a special moment, jambalaya is certainly festive enough for those bigger nights, too. SERVES 4 TO 6

In a 4-quart pot or large, deep skillet, heat the oil over medium-low heat. Add the onion, jalapeños, and bell pepper, and cook, occasionally stirring, until the onions are translucent and the peppers are softened, 7 to 10 minutes. Stir in the garlic and sausage, and continue to cook, occasionally stirring, until the sausage begins to crisp, about 5 minutes more.

Add the tomatoes (do not drain the cans), parsley, thyme, oregano, cayenne, chicken broth, and rice. Stir until well combined, turn the heat up to high, and bring to a boil. Then turn the heat down to low, cover the pot, and cook until the rice is tender and has absorbed a lot of the liquid, 20 to 25 minutes.

Remove the lid and stir in the shrimp. Cook until the shrimp is pink, about 5 minutes. Stir in the smoked paprika and green onions, and then adjust the seasonings and add salt to taste. Serve immediately.

1 teaspoon vegetable oil or bacon grease

1 yellow onion, diced

2 jalapeños, stemmed, seeded, and diced

1 bell pepper, seeded, stemmed, and diced

4 cloves garlic, minced

4 pieces (12 to 14 ounces total) Andouille or other smoky sausage, sliced into rounds

2 (14.5-ounce) cans diced tomatoes

½ cup chopped fresh parsley

1 teaspoon dried thyme

1 teaspoon dried oregano

¼ teaspoon cayenne

2 cups chicken broth

1 cup rice

1 pound medium shrimp, peeled and deveined

1 teaspoon smoked paprika

4 green onions, green part only, chopped

Salt

STACKED JALAPEÑO-CHEESE ENCHILADAS

································ ★ ··

THESE ENCHILADAS ARE A FUSION of two dear favorites of mine. When I was growing up in Houston, there was a Mexican restaurant called Amalia's that served perhaps the finest enchiladas verdes I had every eaten. Every time I got off the plane to visit, we'd drive straight there, and I would dive into a plate of enchiladas made with a bright jalapeño salsa verde.

Then there are the enchiladas found in El Paso. While I have no family connection to El Paso, I've grown to love this West Texas border town for its natural beauty of desert landscapes, rocky hills, and canyons. The food there is also excellent, and when you're there, you'll eat enchiladas, though they will be stacked like pancakes instead of rolled.

Now, if you were in El Paso, chances are you'd make these stacked enchiladas with Hatch green chiles, which is a milder green chile that has its peak season in the late summer. You're certainly welcome to use them here, too. Though since the enchiladas verdes I grew up eating were made with the more piquant jalapeño, I've opted to use it instead, making these stacked enchiladas a marriage of two loves into one. SERVES 4

···

SALSA

1½ pounds tomatillos, husked and halved

½ yellow onion, cut into wedges

2 cloves garlic, left whole

2 jalapeño chiles, stemmed and halved

3 cups water

1 cup chopped fresh cilantro

Salt

To make the salsa, combine the tomatillos, onion, garlic, and jalapeño chiles in a large pot. Add the water and bring to a boil over high heat. Turn the heat down to low and simmer, uncovered, for 10 minutes, or until the tomatillos go from a bright green to a light, muted green.

Turn off the heat and let cool for 10 minutes. (If you don't let the vegetables cool, the steam will make the blender lid pop off, which makes a bit of a mess.) Transfer the pot contents including the liquid to a blender or food processor, add the cilantro, and blend until smooth. Add salt to taste. Return the salsa to the pot and keep warm over low heat.

Preheat the oven to 350°F. Spread ¼ cup of the salsa on each of four oven-proof plates. Place the plates on two large baking sheets.

To make the enchiladas, in a medium skillet, heat 1 tablespoon of the oil over medium-low heat. One at a time, heat the tortillas in the oil, and then keep them wrapped in a cloth or tortilla warmer until all the tortillas are heated.

Each enchilada stack will be made up of four tortillas. To assemble the enchiladas, take a tortilla and using tongs, dip it in the salsa until lightly coated. Place the tortilla on one of the oven-proof plates, and evenly top with ¼ cup shredded Monterey Jack, 1 teaspoon diced onion, and 1 tablespoon diced jalapeños. Dip another tortilla in salsa, lay it on top of the cheese and again, evenly top with ¼ cup of the shredded Monterey Jack, 1 teaspoon diced onion, and 1 tablespoon diced jalapeños. Repeat one more time. For the fourth tortilla in the stack, dip it in salsa, lay it on top of the previous layer, evenly spread over the tortilla 1 tablespoon of sour cream, then top with ¼ cup shredded Monterey Jack. Repeat the full procedure for the remaining enchilada stacks.

When done assembling, drizzle the remaining salsa over the stacks, slide the baking sheets into the oven, and bake for 10 to 15 minutes, until cheese is melted and beginning to bubble.

Meanwhile, heat the remaining 1 tablespoon oil over medium-high heat in a large skillet, and fry the eggs two at a time, to your preference.

Serve the enchiladas warm, each topped with a fried egg and chopped cilantro.

ENCHILADAS

2 tablespoons vegetable oil

16 corn tortillas

4 cups (1 pound) shredded Monterey Jack cheese

¼ yellow onion, diced

4 jalapeños, roasted (see page 9), stemmed, seeded, and diced

¼ cup sour cream

4 eggs

Chopped fresh cilantro, for serving

BLACK BEAN SOPES WITH CHIPOTLE CREMA

★

THE FIRST TIME I had sopes was not in Texas. No, I was in New York City enjoying a Mexican feast with new friends who were from the Southwest. Sopes, which are essentially a thick, chewy corn tortilla that's been shaped into a sort of cup, are a hearty vehicle for toppings such as beans.

While they are indeed more associated with Mexican cuisine than with Tex-Mex, you do see them in Texas, most often in San Antonio. There I had black bean sopes drizzled with a smoky, spicy chipotle crema. The presentation was gorgeous, and it was humble food made elegant.

To make this dish requires a bit of patience, as making sopes for the first time takes a little finesse. But once you get the hang of it, the process goes quickly. And while I still prefer mine with black beans, I find that the basic sopes can be a vehicle for just about anything. SERVES 4

SOPES

1¾ cups masa harina

¼ cup all-purpose flour

1 teaspoon baking powder

½ teaspoon kosher salt

1 tablespoon lard or vegetable shortening, at room temperature

1¼ cups water, plus more as needed

Oil, for frying

FILLING

½ cup sour cream

2 tablespoons whole milk

1 canned chipotle chile in adobo sauce

2 cups Refried Black Beans (page 109), or other refried beans

2 cups shredded iceberg lettuce

2 avocados, peeled, pitted, and cubed

½ cup (2 ounces) Cotija or feta cheese, crumbled

To make the sopes, whisk together the masa harina, flour, baking powder, and salt. Add the lard and water and stir until a soft, smooth ball is formed. If the dough is too dry, add more water, 1 teaspoon at a time.

Divide the dough into twelve balls. Roll or press out each one until it's about 3 inches wide and ¼ inch thick.

In a lightly oiled skillet over medium heat, cook each sope for 1 minute on one side. Remove from the heat and place on a plate, uncooked side up. While still warm, pinch the edges to form a ¼-inch raised edge.

Meanwhile, heat 2 inches of oil in a heavy skillet to 350°F. Line a baking sheet with paper towels. If you don't have a candy thermometer, after 5 minutes of heating, you can stick a wooden spoon into the oil to see if it's ready. If the oil bubbles around the spoon, it should be hot enough.

Working in batches, lower the sopes into the hot oil, flat side down, and fry until crisp, turning once, about 1 minute. Drain the sopes, flat side down, on the paper towels.

For the filling, first make a chipotle crema by combining the sour cream, milk, and chipotle chile in a blender or food processor and blend until smooth.

To assemble the sopes, top each sope in this order: refried beans, shredded lettuce, avocado, Cotija cheese, and chipotle crema. Serve immediately.

PECAN PIE, PAGE 224, AND LEMON PIE, PAGE 223

CHAPTER 6

SWEETS

After a fine Tex-Mex dinner in town, my grandma and I headed back to the farm. While the light had been harsh during the afternoon, it was now early evening and an excellent time to take photos of the bluebonnets blooming around her house. As we drove along, a line of heavy dark clouds appeared on the horizon.

We were talking about what we'd have for dessert. She mentioned there was cake at the house and some cookies, but no pie. I was going to say something about there not being pie, as she's quite famous for her pies, but before I could open my mouth the rain started pounding so hard, I couldn't see more than a few feet in front of the car. I slowed down and pulled over to let the storm pass. Then the rain stopped, as soon as it had begun.

"Welcome to springtime in Texas!" laughed my grandma.

As the large clouds faded away, there was a sharp diagonal line marking the border between clear sky and gray. It was stunning, so I asked her if she minded if I stopped the car to take a picture. She said she didn't mind at all.

After I took a few pictures, she mentioned she knew another spot where there would be a great view of this unusual sky. We drove along the country road and ended up at her neighbor's farm. He wasn't there, so his gate was closed, but I got out of the car, walked over to his fence, and started taking photos of his land and the sky.

Then I heard a honk. I turned around and my grandma was gesturing with her hands, pointing upward. I looked up and saw a rainbow. As I began taking pictures of the rainbow, I heard her honking

Butterscotch Brownies 203

Banana Pudding with Peanut Butter–Oatmeal Cookies 205

Mom's Raspberry Bars 207

Caballero Cookies 208

Spicy Snickerdoodles 211

Strawberry Shortcake 212

Apple Cake 215

Mexican Chocolate Cake 216

Gingerbread 219

Ruby Red Grapefruit and Pecan Sheet Cake 220

Lemon Pie 223

Pecan Pie 224

Sweet Potato Pie 226

My Family's Pie Dough 227

Plum Cobbler 229

Molasses and Spiced-Pecan Ice Cream 232

Peach Ice Cream 235

Divinity 236

again. I turned around and again she gestured, this time pointing off to the side. I looked over, and above where the first rainbow ended, I could see the arch of another.

A double rainbow! They spanned across the horizon, and while I wanted to take a photo of the two, I realized that my lens wasn't wide enough. I kept stepping back, and back, but it wasn't any use—I couldn't capture both of them in their full glory with my camera at the same time.

I returned to the car, and we sat in silence, admiring the sky. After a while, as the sun started to set, the rainbows began to fade. I considered driving around the countryside to see if I could find them again, but Grandma reminded me about the bluebonnets in her yard, adding that she was now ready for dessert.

"I'm sorry I didn't bake you a pie this trip," she said. I laughed and told her it was okay. Who was I to complain when all my life she's generously made the family countless pies, cookies, candies, and cakes. One night without homemade pie was going to be fine.

"Next time you come, I'm baking you a lemon pie. It was my mother's recipe and you're going to love it," she said. I told her it was a deal.

BUTTERSCOTCH BROWNIES (PAGE 203)

BUTTERSCOTCH BROWNIES

✪

MY GREAT-AUNT DORIS, whom I never had the pleasure of meeting, was famous in the family for making sweets. She had a debilitating heart condition, so she seldom left home and could do few activities that called for much exertion. But she had no problem stirring batters and doughs or slipping trays and pans of sweets in and out of the oven, so that's what she did.

While she was known to bake just about anything that my mom and uncles requested, it was these butterscotch brownies that made them smile the most. "She used a whole box of brown sugar!" said my uncle Austin with wonder, when recalling his memories of her baking them.

When I finally found her original recipe, it didn't call for a whole box of brown sugar, unless boxes were smaller back then. But it's still a terrific bar cookie, chock full of pecans. MAKES 20 BUTTERSCOTCH BROWNIES ★ PICTURED OPPOSITE

Preheat the oven to 350°F. Lightly grease a 9-inch square baking pan.

Melt the butter over low heat in a medium pan. Stir in the pecans and cook, occasionally stirring, until the pecans are slightly darker and fragrant, about 2 minutes. Remove from the heat and allow to cool, about 10 minutes. Stir in the brown sugar, eggs, and vanilla.

In a separate bowl, whisk together the flour, baking powder, and salt until well combined. Pour into the liquid ingredients and stir until a thick batter forms. Pour the batter into the prepared baking pan.

Bake, uncovered, for 20 to 25 minutes, until the edges are set. (Be sure to not overbake; the brownies will harden as they cool.) Allow to cool for 20 minutes before serving.

½ cup (1 stick) unsalted butter

2 cups coarsely chopped pecans

2 cups packed brown sugar

2 eggs, beaten

1 teaspoon vanilla extract

1½ cups all-purpose flour

2 teaspoons baking powder

½ teaspoon kosher salt

BANANA PUDDING WITH PEANUT BUTTER–OATMEAL COOKIES

BANANA PUDDING IS A CLASSIC Texan dessert found at most barbecues, outdoor gatherings, and potlucks. Texans have been serving it since the 1800s, but the dish has evolved from its beginnings as a sponge cake filled with custard and sliced bananas to a trifle layered with custard, bananas, and vanilla cookies, with everything, save for the bananas, usually coming from a box.

That kind of banana pudding is popular, but think about how much better it could be if you made the vanilla custard from scratch. And while I do enjoy the vanilla cookies in this dish, as I adore the combination of nuts and bananas, I usually make my pudding with peanut butter–oatmeal cookies instead.

Lest you think this version sounds like too much work, know that it's simple enough for a two-year-old to handle (with adult supervision, of course), as my nephew Austin Jack proved when he made it with his grandma. And if you're loyal to the usual vanilla cookies, that's okay; but if you love peanut butter, I do suggest giving these cookies a try. Just be warned that they're outrageously crisp, nutty, and good, and you might have a hard time saving enough for the banana pudding main event.

SERVES 6 TO 8

Preheat the oven to 350°F. Line two baking sheets with parchment paper. Place a metal mixing bowl in the freezer.

To make the cookies, cream together the brown sugar, granulated sugar, and butter. Add the peanut butter, egg, and vanilla, and mix until well combined. In a separate bowl, whisk together the oats, flour, baking soda, baking powder, cinnamon, and salt until well combined. Add this to the sugar mixture and stir until a soft cookie dough forms.

Working in batches, using a heaping teaspoon, form the dough into balls and place on the prepared baking sheets 2 inches apart. Bake, one sheet at a time, for 13 to 15 minutes, or until the edges are set. Cool on the sheet for 5 minutes then transfer to a wire rack to continue cooling (the cookies will harden as they cool). Repeat for the remaining cookie dough. You should have about 36 cookies.

CONTINUED

PEANUT BUTTER–OATMEAL COOKIES

½ cup packed brown sugar

½ cup granulated sugar

½ cup (1 stick) unsalted butter, at room temperature

½ cup chunky peanut butter

1 egg, beaten

1 teaspoon vanilla extract

1 cup rolled oats (not instant)

½ cup all-purpose flour

¼ teaspoon baking soda

¼ teaspoon baking powder

1 teaspoon ground cinnamon

¼ teaspoon kosher salt

PUDDING

2 cups whole milk

½ cup granulated sugar

¼ cup all-purpose flour

3 egg yolks

¼ teaspoon kosher salt

2 tablespoons (¼ stick) unsalted butter

1 teaspoon vanilla extract

4 bananas

2 tablespoons fresh lemon juice

WHIPPED CREAM TOPPING

1 cup heavy cream

2 tablespoons honey or powdered sugar

To make the pudding, whisk together the milk, granulated sugar, flour, egg yolks, and salt in a pot. Cook over medium-low heat, continuously stirring, until the mixture starts to bubble and then thicken, 4 to 6 minutes. Turn the heat down to low and stir in the butter and vanilla. Turn off the heat.

To make the whipped cream, take the bowl out of the freezer, add the cream and honey, and then beat until soft peaks form.

Peel and slice the bananas into ¼-inch rounds. Sprinkle the slices with the lemon juice to prevent them from turning brown.

To assemble, place a layer of cookies and bananas in the bottom of an 8-inch square baking dish. Layer on half of the pudding. Add another layer of cookies and bananas and then top with the remaining pudding. Spread on top the whipped cream, and then decorate with the remaining cookies and bananas. Chill for at least 4 hours before serving, though if you prefer, you can eat it warm.

Alternatively, you can serve the pudding in six ½-pint Mason jars or bowls. Evenly divide the cookies, sliced bananas, and pudding, and then proceed as above.

MOM'S RASPBERRY BARS

★

MOM HAS BEEN BAKING these for years, and they are addictive. She fills tin after tin with raspberry bars at the holidays, and if there are any left by Christmas Day, it's only because I've squirreled some away to take back to New York with me. She sends them to me in the mail from time to time, and it's always a happy day when she does, as even the most curmudgeonly grumps will soften after one bite. Or as one friend once said, "These are the most decadent things ever! Can I have another, please?"

They're not complex—just a mixture of raspberry jam, almonds, and white chocolate chips all nestled on a buttery, cake-y base. But it's the combination of flavors that make me (and everyone else) swoon. They're highly portable and make a great gift or dessert offering. MAKES ABOUT 48 BARS (DEPENDING ON HOW LARGE YOU CUT THEM)

Preheat oven to 325°F. Lightly grease a 9 by 13-inch baking dish.

In a small pot, melt the butter over medium heat. Remove from the heat and pour in 2 cups of the white chocolate chips. Do not stir.

Using a stand mixer fitted with the paddle attachment, beat the eggs on high speed until foamy. Add the sugar and continue to beat until lemon colored, about 2 minutes. Stir in the butter and white chocolate chip mixture, the flour, salt, and almond extract. Beat on low speed until well combined. Spread half the batter in the baking pan. Bake, uncovered, for 15 to 20 minutes, until golden brown.

Meanwhile, stir the remaining 2 cups white chocolate chips into the remaining batter. In a small pot over low heat, heat the raspberry preserves until melted.

Once the bottom layer is done, remove from the oven. Evenly spread the raspberry preserves over the baked layer. Gently spoon the remaining batter over the fruit and then sprinkle with almonds.

Bake, uncovered, for 30 to 35 minutes, until the almonds are lightly browned and an inserted knife comes out clean. Cool for 15 minutes before serving.

1 cup (2 sticks) unsalted butter

4 cups white chocolate chips

4 eggs

1 cup sugar

2 cups all-purpose flour

1 teaspoon kosher salt

2 teaspoons almond extract

1 cup raspberry jam

½ cup sliced almonds

CABALLERO COOKIES

★

COWBOY COOKIES ARE A TEXAN STAPLE. If you're not familiar with the cowboy cookie, it's an oatmeal cookie stuffed with nuts and chocolate chips. Despite the name, however, I'm pretty sure that these cookies were not served on the trail. That said, Texas does have a rich cowboy tradition, and along the border there's a long Mexican cowboy tradition, too.

One word for cowboy in Spanish is *caballero*. And since I've taken the basic cowboy cookie and given it a Tex-Mex flair with lots of cinnamon, vanilla, coffee, and cayenne, I thought calling these caballero cookies instead of cowboy cookies seemed like a good idea.

These cookies travel well, and I've shared them with colleagues and given boxes of them as birthday gifts, too. No matter when you serve them, they will go fast.

MAKES ABOUT 24 COOKIES

6 tablespoons (¾ stick) unsalted butter, at room temperature

¼ cup granulated sugar

½ cup packed brown sugar

1 egg, beaten

1 teaspoon vanilla extract

¾ cup all-purpose flour

¾ teaspoon baking powder

¾ teaspoon baking soda

1 teaspoon ground cinnamon

1 teaspoon finely ground coffee beans or espresso powder

¼ teaspoon kosher salt

Pinch of cayenne

½ cup rolled (not instant) oats

½ cup semisweet chocolate chips

½ cup white chocolate chips

½ cup chopped roasted pecans

Preheat the oven to 350°F. Lightly grease two baking sheets, or line them with parchment paper.

Cream together the butter, granulated sugar, and brown sugar until smooth. Add the egg and vanilla and beat until creamy.

Whisk together the flour, baking powder, baking soda, cinnamon, ground coffee, salt, and cayenne. Add the dry mixture to the liquid mixture. Stir until well combined. Stir in the oats, both types of chocolate chips, and the pecans.

Working in batches, form the dough into walnut-size balls (if the dough is too soft, you can place it in the refrigerator for 10 minutes), then place the dough balls 2 inches apart on the prepared baking sheets. Bake, one sheet at a time, for 11 to 14 minutes, or until flattened, lightly browned, and set. Cool on the sheet for 5 minutes then transfer to a wire rack to continue cooling. Repeat for the remaining cookie dough.

SPICY SNICKERDOODLES

★

THERE'S A PHOTO OF ME baking with my mom when I'm about two years old. We're making cookies, and while it's not exactly clear what kind of cookie we were baking, I'm guessing it was probably snickerdoodles.

Snickerdoodles are a classic cookie, and if for some sad reason you've never had one, it's a simple sugar cookie that has been rolled in cinnamon and sugar before baking, which lends a sweet and spicy crunch to each bite.

The cookie's origin is not Texan; its provenance is said to be Colonial Dutch (the "snicker" in the cookie's name may have come from the Dutch word *snekrad*, which means snail wheel). Some, however, speculate that its name comes from Germany, where there is a cinnamon sugar swirled pastry known as *Schnecke*, which is the German word for snail. The theory is that the German pastry was the inspiration for the American snickerdoodle, and its name stems from that German word.

No matter its etymology, it's still a fun word to say and the cookie is even more fun to eat. While the cinnamon-sugar combination is satisfying, I like to add some smoky heat in the form of chipotle chile powder to my snickerdoodles, as well. This gives it an added depth of flavor not found in the original, but certainly welcome to the bold Texan palate. MAKES 24 COOKIES

Preheat the oven to 350°F. Lightly grease two baking sheets or line them with parchment paper.

Cream together the granulated sugar, brown sugar, butter, and shortening. Stir in the eggs and vanilla. Whisk together the flour, cream of tartar, baking soda, cinnamon, chipotle powder, and salt. Add to the liquid ingredients, mixing until a soft dough comes together.

For the topping, stir together the granulated sugar, cinnamon, and chipotle powder.

Working in batches, form the dough into walnut-size balls, roll each ball in the sugar mixture, then place the balls 2 inches apart on the prepared baking sheets. Bake, one sheet at a time, for 10 to 12 minutes, or until the edges are set. When you remove the cookies from the oven, they will be puffy but will deflate and crackle as they cool. Cool on the sheet for 5 minutes then transfer to a wire rack to continue cooling. Repeat for the remaining cookie dough.

1 cup granulated sugar

½ cup packed brown sugar

½ cup (1 stick) unsalted butter, at room temperature

8 tablespoons vegetable shortening

2 eggs, beaten

1 teaspoon vanilla extract

2¾ cups all-purpose flour

2 teaspoons cream of tartar

1 teaspoon baking soda

½ teaspoon ground cinnamon

¼ teaspoon chipotle chile powder

¼ teaspoon kosher salt

TOPPING

¼ cup granulated sugar

1 teaspoon ground cinnamon

¼ teaspoon chipotle chile powder

STRAWBERRY SHORTCAKE

⭐

ALONG WITH WILDFLOWERS, nothing says spring to me more than freshly picked strawberries. To celebrate their arrival, my mom would always make strawberry shortcake—a simple yet satisfying way to enjoy this delicate fruit. While there's nothing finer than a freshly picked berry, after a light sprinkle of sugar and lemon zest, you'll need something to sop up all the juice. Fortunately, warm flaky biscuits and cold whipped cream can help with that. SERVES 8

1 quart strawberries, rinsed, hulled, and quartered

¼ cup sugar

1 teaspoon lemon zest

BISCUITS

2 cups all-purpose flour, plus more as needed

1 tablespoon baking powder

2 tablespoons sugar

¼ teaspoon ground cinnamon

½ teaspoon kosher salt

½ cup (1 stick) unsalted butter, cold

¾ cup half-and-half

WHIPPED CREAM TOPPING

1 cup heavy cream

1 teaspoon vanilla

2 tablespoons honey

Toss the strawberries with the sugar and lemon zest in a bowl, and leave out at room temperature for an hour, stirring occasionally.

Preheat the oven to 450°F. Lightly grease a baking sheet. Place a metal mixing bowl in the freezer.

To make the biscuits, mix together the flour, baking powder, sugar, cinnamon, and salt. Cut the stick of butter into pieces and work it into the flour mixture with your hands or a pastry blender until the mixture resembles pea-size crumbs. Pour in the half-and-half, mixing until the dough is a bit loose and sticky.

Pour the dough onto a floured surface and knead for a few minutes. The dough should be smooth and no longer wet. (You can sprinkle more flour on the surface if you find it's sticking.) Gather the dough into a ball and hit it with a rolling pin, turning and folding it in half every few whacks. Do this for a couple of minutes.

Roll out the dough until it's ¼ inch thick, and then fold it in half. Using a 3-inch biscuit cutter or a glass, cut out the biscuits from the folded dough. (You may have to gather the scraps and roll out again.) Place on the greased baking sheet 1 inch apart. Bake for 15 minutes, or until the tops are golden brown.

To make the whipped cream topping, take the metal mixing bowl out of the freezer. Pour in the cream and with an electric mixer, whisk, or eggbeater, beat the cream until it triples in size and makes soft peaks. Stir in the vanilla and honey.

To assemble the shortcakes, slice a biscuit in half. Place ¼ cup of the strawberries on one half of the biscuit and top with whipped cream and the other half of the biscuit. Serve immediately.

APPLE CAKE

★

THIS APPLE CAKE is what my grandma calls a "share cake." She'll bake up a pan, cut it into squares, and take it with her to share with friends at Bible study, afternoon teas, or potluck luncheons. It also makes a fine snack when her neighbors drop by to say howdy, and as they sit and chat she'll pass around a plate stacked high with square pieces of cake.

It's an old recipe, one that she got from Mary Lou Williams, an old dear friend of hers. It calls for apples, which is one reason my grandma likes it, because she has a tree and is always looking for ways to use up its fruit. It's also a hit with folks as it's full of sweet, crunchy pecans, the Texas state nut. But I think the main reason why everyone loves it is because it's the perfect cake for snacking—it's not too heavy and not too sweet, and the apples keep it moist, so it tastes good whether it's a day old or fresh from the oven. SERVES 12 TO 20

Preheat the oven to 350°F. Lightly grease a 9 by 13-inch pan. Sprinkle it with sugar.

In a large bowl, combine the oil, melted butter, eggs, sugar, and vanilla and mix with a spoon until smooth. Stir in the apples and pecans. Sift together the flour, salt, baking soda, and cinnamon and add to the egg mixture. Mix together well and then pour into the pan.

Bake for 40 to 45 minutes, or until an inserted knife comes out clean. Allow to cool for 10 minutes before serving. Stored covered at room temperature, this will keep for 3 days.

1 cup vegetable oil

¼ cup (½ stick) unsalted butter, melted

2 eggs, beaten

2 cups sugar

2 teaspoons vanilla extract

3 cups chopped peeled raw apple

1 cup chopped pecans

3 cups all-purpose flour

1 teaspoon kosher salt

1 teaspoon baking soda

1 teaspoon ground cinnamon

MEXICAN CHOCOLATE CAKE

★

THIS CAKE IS MY TWIST on the classic German chocolate cake, which isn't actually German. Nope, it's rumored to hail from East Texas and was known as such because of the brand of chocolate used, not the country of origin.

For my Mexican chocolate cake, I took my family's German chocolate cake recipe and then added lots of cinnamon and vanilla with a pinch of cayenne, too. The cake itself is tender and sweet, but it's the frosting that takes this cake over the top. The frosting is made with pecans, cream, and coconut, and as it cools, it becomes a little crisp and tastes like Mexican coconut candy. SERVES 16

CAKE

3 cups all-purpose flour

2 teaspoons ground cinnamon

1 teaspoon kosher salt

½ teaspoon baking soda

Pinch of cayenne (optional)

2 cups granulated sugar

1 cup (2 sticks) unsalted butter, at room temperature

1 cup buttermilk, at room temperature

4 eggs, at room temperature, beaten

2 teaspoons vanilla extract

4 ounces semisweet baking chocolate (not chocolate chips), chopped

COCONUT-PECAN FROSTING

½ cup unsweetened coconut flakes

½ cup chopped pecans

¼ cup (½ stick) unsalted butter

¼ cup whole milk or half-and-half

½ cup packed brown sugar

¾ cup confectioners' sugar

1 teaspoon vanilla extract

¼ teaspoon kosher salt

Preheat the oven to 300°F. Lightly grease and flour a 10-cup tube pan.

To make the cake, whisk together the flour, cinnamon, salt, baking soda, and cayenne. In a separate bowl, cream together the granulated sugar and butter. Stir in the buttermilk, eggs, and vanilla. Stir in the flour mixture until well combined.

Put the chocolate in the top of a double boiler and melt over simmering water while stirring, until the chocolate is melted and smooth. Remove from the heat and stir the melted chocolate into the batter until well combined. Pour the batter into the pan.

Bake, uncovered, for 1½ hours, or until an inserted knife comes out clean. Allow the cake to cool for 15 minutes, and then invert the pan onto a platter, sticking a knife between the cake and the edges of the pan to help remove it, if necessary. Continue to let it cool to room temperature before frosting, about 1 hour.

To make the frosting, in a dry skillet on low heat, toast the coconut, occasionally stirring, until lightly colored, about 2 minutes. Transfer the coconut to a bowl and add the pecans to the skillet. Toast until a little darker in color and fragrant, about 3 to 4 minutes. Transfer the pecans to the same bowl as the coconut.

In a saucepan, combine the butter, milk, brown sugar, and confectioners' sugar. Cook over low heat, occasionally stirring, until the butter is melted and the frosting has thickened, about 5 minutes. Remove from the heat, stir in the vanilla and salt, then stir in the coconut and pecans. While still warm, spread the frosting on top of the cooled cake.

GINGERBREAD

★

BOTH SIDES OF MY FAMILY make gingerbread at the holidays, and both use methods that have been with them for generations. This recipe is a combination of the two recipes, and it makes for a tender, spicy cake that isn't too sweet.

While it's good on its own, I like to sprinkle it with confectioners' sugar that's been enlivened with a bit of lemon zest. It goes well with a dollop of whipped cream, too.

From Thanksgiving to New Year's, you'll see gingerbread on our family table. And though it's most often served as a dessert, we've been known to enjoy slices of it for breakfast, too. SERVES 12

Preheat the oven to 350°F. Lightly grease and flour a 9-inch square baking dish.

Cream together the butter and granulated sugar. Stir in the egg and molasses until well combined. In a separate bowl, whisk the flour with the baking powder, cloves, ginger, cinnamon, nutmeg, and salt. Stir the dry ingredients into the butter-sugar mixture. Stir in the warm water until smooth. Pour the batter into the baking dish.

Bake, uncovered, for 25 to 30 minutes or until an inserted knife comes out clean. Be sure not to overcook it, because it will harden a bit as it cools.

While the cake is baking, whisk together the confectioners' sugar and lemon zest. Sprinkle over the baked gingerbread while it is still warm. Serve warm, or store, covered, at room temperature for up to 3 days.

½ cup (1 stick) unsalted butter, at room temperature

½ cup granulated sugar

1 egg, beaten

1 cup molasses

2½ cups all-purpose flour

2 teaspoons baking powder

1 teaspoon ground cloves

1 teaspoon ground ginger

1 teaspoon ground cinnamon

¼ teaspoon ground nutmeg

½ teaspoon kosher salt

½ cup warm water

TOPPING

2 tablespoons confectioners' sugar

1 teaspoon finely grated lemon zest

RUBY RED GRAPEFRUIT AND PECAN SHEET CAKE

✦

TEXAS INDEPENDENCE DAY is March 2. On this day, a group convened at Washington-on-the-Brazos (back then simply known as Washington) to craft a declaration of independence from Mexico. From that moment, the Republic of Texas was born.

While it's not a get-out-of-school holiday, it's still widely celebrated throughout the state. And because it's Texas's birthday, you clearly have to have cake! My preferred birthday cake is chocolate sheet cake. I wondered, however, what would happen if I changed it and made it more Texan. So instead of adding cocoa to my cake batter, I added our state fruit, the Ruby Red grapefruit, and our state nut, the pecan.

The result? A tangy and nutty cake made extra decadent because it's topped with cream cheese frosting loaded with chopped pecans and Ruby Red zest. This is a keeper, and I do believe a new tradition has been born. SERVES 16 TO 20

1 cup (2 sticks) unsalted butter

½ cup Ruby Red grapefruit juice

½ cup water

2 cups all-purpose flour, sifted

2 cups granulated sugar

1 teaspoon baking soda

½ teaspoon ground cinnamon

¼ teaspoon kosher salt

1 cup roasted pecans, coarsely chopped

2 tablespoons Ruby Red grapefruit zest

½ cup buttermilk

2 eggs, lightly beaten

1 teaspoon vanilla extract

FROSTING

8 ounces cream cheese, at room temperature

¼ cup (½ stick) unsalted butter, at room temperature

2 tablespoons Ruby Red grapefruit juice

2 teaspoons finely grated Ruby Red grapefruit zest

1 teaspoon vanilla extract

4 cups confectioners' sugar

Preheat the oven to 375°F. Grease and flour a 9 by 13-inch pan or a 15 by 10 by 1-inch jelly roll pan.

In a small pan on low heat, melt the butter with the Ruby Red grapefruit juice and water.

Mix together the flour, granulated sugar, baking soda, cinnamon, and salt. Stir in the pecans and grapefruit zest. Pour in the melted butter mixture, along with the buttermilk, eggs, and vanilla. Mix until a smooth batter forms. Pour the batter into the pan.

Bake for 25 to 30 minutes, checking it at 20 minutes, until the cake is lightly browned and an inserted knife or toothpick comes out clean. (If using a jelly roll pan, it should take about 20 minutes, so check it at 15 minutes.) Let the cake cool in the pan.

As the cake cools, prepare the frosting. Cream together the cream cheese, butter, grapefruit juice, grapefruit zest, and vanilla. Add the confectioners' sugar and stir until smooth.

Once the cake is cool to the touch (about an hour or so after baking), frost the cake. Serve immediately, or store, covered, at room temperature for up to 3 days.

LEMON PIE

★

WHEN YOU HAVE A COLD, you begin to crave large doses of citrus in order to knock out that bug. At least I do. Though if it's Christmas, you might want something a little more festive than a cup of lemon tea, which is where this pie comes into play.

This tart and tangy lemon pie, a recipe that my grandma got from her mother, isn't one that we normally eat, as we're more inclined to eat pecan or sweet potato pies. But when I was feeling under the weather and had a mad craving for lemons, my grandma offered to make this as a form of medicine for me. The pie was incredible, and while it didn't cure me immediately, I'm certain that its infusion of vitamin C helped get me back on the road to recovery.

Even better, however, was my family's rediscovery of this classic pie. Its bright sunshiny flavor has become one of my favorites, and I'm so pleased that it's back on our family table, where it belongs. SERVES 8

Preheat the oven to 350°F.

Poke holes in the unbaked pie crust with a fork and bake it for about 20 minutes or until it's lightly browned. (Some people prefer to weigh it down with pie weights or beans as it may bubble a bit.)

Meanwhile, make the filling. In a pot, stir together the sugar, flour, and hot water. While stirring, cook over medium heat until the sugar dissolves, a couple of minutes. Beat the egg yolks with the cold water and add to the pot, then stir in the lemon juice, butter, and salt. Stir and cook until thick, about 3 minutes. Remove from the heat.

To make the meringue, beat the egg whites with the sugar and salt until they are smooth, light, and fluffy and form soft peaks like whipped cream. This should take anywhere from 5 to 10 minutes. (If you don't have a stand mixer, a strong arm with a whisk or an eggbeater can accomplish this task, too. Please note that by hand it will take much longer than 10 minutes.)

Pour the lemon custard into the baked pie shell and top with the meringue. Bake until the peaks on the meringue are lightly browned, about 10 minutes. Cool for 10 minutes, then serve. Covered, this will keep in the refrigerator for up to 3 days.

1 unbaked 9-inch pie shell (page 227)

FILLING

1 cup sugar

⅓ cup all-purpose flour

1 cup hot water

3 egg yolks

¼ cup cold water

⅓ cup fresh lemon juice

1 tablespoon unsalted butter

Pinch of kosher salt

MERINGUE

3 egg whites

⅓ cup granulated sugar

Pinch of kosher salt

PECAN PIE

★

THE PECAN IS THE STATE NUT of Texas and, like many Texans, my grandma has a few pecan trees on her farm. While sometimes the critters get to the nuts before we do, when we are able to harvest its sweet pecans, they're the best that I've ever had.

Pecans are in season in the fall. For this reason, pecan pie is a traditional addition to the Thanksgiving table. That said, pecans store well so people do serve this pie year-round, and my grandma has even been known to mail me a frozen pecan pie for my birthday in June.

As the pecan is our state nut, it makes sense that pecan pie has been declared the state pie of Texas, too. The recipe that my grandma uses is one she learned from her mother, and it's a classic rendition that yields a nutty, dense, and rich pie. While it's best warm from the oven, perhaps topped with whipped cream, it also makes for a fine breakfast when cold, too. SERVES 8

¾ cup sugar

¾ cup light corn syrup

3 eggs, beaten

1 teaspoon vanilla extract

2 tablespoons whole milk

2 tablespoons all-purpose flour

¼ cup (½ stick) unsalted butter, melted

1 cup pecans

1 unbaked 9-inch pie shell (page 227)

Preheat the oven to 350°F.

Mix together the sugar, the corn syrup, eggs, and the vanilla. Stir in the milk, flour, melted butter, and pecans. Pour the filling into the pie shell. Bake for 45 to 50 minutes, or edges are set and an inserted knife comes out clean. Allow to cool for 10 minutes, then serve. Stored covered and at room temperature, this will keep for up to 3 days.

SWEET POTATO PIE

★

SWEET POTATO PIE is always on our Thanksgiving table—my family prefers it to pumpkin pie, though the two are similar in texture and taste. But sweet potatoes give the custard a bit more heft and are, as the name implies, more naturally sweet than pumpkins.

I asked my grandma for the family recipe, but she pointed me in the direction of my uncle Richard. "Richard makes the best sweet potato pie," she said. And after years of eating it, I have to agree that indeed he does.

Richard loves his pies, and when my brother got married, my uncle helped co-ordinate a marathon pie-baking party on that side of the family. See, my brother had decided that instead of a groom's cake, he wanted a table filled with pies. And so my family's repertoire was on full display—chocolate, chess, apple, peanut butter, and, of course, Uncle Richard's sweet potato.

When you make a sweet potato pie, the most important thing is the spice. Richard uses the usual suspects, such as cinnamon and nutmeg. But he also adds ginger and cloves, which I think add a bit of heat and zing. MAKES 2 PIES; SERVES 16

1½ cups mashed cooked sweet potatoes or 1 (15-ounce) can mashed sweet potatoes

3 eggs, beaten

¾ cup packed brown sugar

1 teaspoon ground cinnamon

½ teaspoon ground ginger

½ teaspoon ground cloves

¼ teaspoon ground nutmeg

¾ teaspoon kosher salt

1 (12-ounce) can evaporated milk

2 unbaked 9-inch pie shells (page 227)

WHIPPED CREAM TOPPING

1 cup heavy cream

2 tablespoons honey

1 teaspoon ground ginger

Preheat the oven to 375°F. Place a metal mixing bowl in the freezer.

Combine the sweet potatoes, eggs, brown sugar, cinnamon, ginger, cloves, nutmeg, salt, and evaporated milk in a blender or food processor and blend until smooth. Pour the sweet potato mixture into the unbaked pie shells, dividing it equally.

Bake, uncovered, for 55 minutes or until set and an inserted knife comes out clean. Allow the pies to cool for 1 hour.

Once the pies have cooled, make the whipped cream topping: Take the mixing bowl out of the freezer, and pour in the cream, honey, and ground ginger. Either by using the beater attachment on your mixer or an eggbeater, beat until soft peaks form.

Serve each slice topped with the whipped cream.

MY FAMILY'S PIE DOUGH

★

IF YOU DON'T ALREADY have a favorite pie crust, here is the one my family uses. It's unusual in that it calls for vegetable oil and milk, instead of the usual butter or lard, but it's easy to make and has a salty flavor that's a good contrast to sweet fillings. Please note that it's important to use whole milk; you'll need the fat to make a tender crust. MAKES 2 SINGLE-LAYER 9-INCH PIE SHELLS OR 1 DOUBLE-LAYER PIE CRUST

In a bowl, mix together the flour and salt. Add the oil and milk and stir until well combined. (If the dough is too crumbly and dry, you can add a bit more milk, about a teaspoon at a time.)

Halve the dough into two balls. If you only need one crust, you can freeze the other dough ball for up to 3 months.

To line a pie pan, take one ball of dough, place it between two sheets of waxed paper, and roll out into about an 11-inch circle. Lift the top sheet of waxed paper off the rolled-out dough and flip the dough into the pie pan, lifting off the other piece of waxed paper. Press until smooth and trim the edges. Use a fork or your fingers to crimp for decoration. Use with your preferred pie recipe.

2 cups all-purpose flour

1 teaspoon kosher salt

½ cup vegetable oil

¼ cup whole milk, plus more as needed

PLUM COBBLER

★

DURING THE SUMMER, when my grandma's plum trees yield abundantly, she typically makes jam with all of the excess fruit. I thought, however, it would be fun to come up with another way to use up this sweet and tart stone fruit.

Cobblers have long been a popular dessert in Texas, though we are more inclined to make them with peaches and dewberries, which are a wild Texas blackberry. Plums, however, also make for a fine cobbler. There are different ways to approach a cobbler, and this one goes with a biscuit-like topping; the softer, fluffier dough is all the better for sopping up the plum's juices. SERVES 6 TO 8

Preheat the oven to 350°F.

In a large cast-iron skillet or a 9-inch square baking dish, toss the plums with the sugar, flour, cinnamon, nutmeg, and lemon zest.

To make the topping, in a small pot, melt the butter over low heat. In a separate bowl, whisk together the flour, sugar, baking powder, and salt. Pour the melted butter and the buttermilk into the dry ingredients, and then stir until a sticky, wet dough forms.

Using a spoon, drop spoonfuls of the dough evenly over the plums, though it's okay if some of the plums are exposed. Bake, uncovered, for 40 minutes, or until the crust is light brown and the plums are bubbling. Allow to cool for 10 minutes before serving. Stored covered in the refrigerator, this will keep for up to 3 days.

3 pounds plums, pitted and sliced

¾ cup sugar

¼ cup all-purpose flour

1 teaspoon ground cinnamon

¼ teaspoon ground nutmeg

1 teaspoon finely grated lemon zest

TOPPING

¼ cup (½ stick) unsalted butter

1 cup all-purpose flour

½ cup sugar

2 teaspoons baking powder

½ teaspoon kosher salt

½ cup buttermilk

MOLASSES AND SPICED-PECAN ICE CREAM

⭐

DURING THE FALL IN TEXAS, on Friday nights you'll find most folks at the local high school football game. This tradition crosses all borders, and it's almost liturgical in its strict adherence to ritual. While there are many dishes associated with Friday night games, such as Frito pie, nachos, and pickles, ice cream is usually on hand, too. It's not only offered in the concession stands, but also found at drive-in restaurants where people congregate after the game to talk about what happened while enjoying a scoop or two.

Now, I have to admit that I've never seen a molasses-pecan ice cream at any high school game. That said, the dark, bittersweet notes of the molasses gives this ice cream an autumnal air, a theme that is continued with the buttery crunch of pecans, a nut that comes into season in late October.

This ice cream is a perfect after-game dish, as a way to toast a big win or soothe a tragic loss. It also goes well scooped onto warm slices of pecan or sweet potato pie, especially after a holiday meal. That said, this ice cream isn't limited to the cooler months. I've been known also to enjoy bowls in the summer, because its flavor is both bracing and restorative, much like a cup of strong coffee. MAKES 1 QUART

1 cup heavy cream

2 cups half-and-half

¼ cup molasses

¼ cup packed brown sugar

1 teaspoon ground cinnamon

¼ teaspoon ground ginger

¼ teaspoon kosher salt

Pinch of ground nutmeg

4 egg yolks, beaten

1 teaspoon vanilla extract

SPICED PECANS

1 tablespoon unsalted butter

1 cup pecans, chopped

2 tablespoons brown sugar

¼ teaspoon ground cinnamon

¼ teaspoon kosher salt

In a large saucepan, stir together the cream, half-and-half, molasses, brown sugar, cinnamon, ginger, salt, and nutmeg. Place over medium-low heat and cook just until the mixture is warm—do not let it boil.

When the cream is warm, scoop out ¼ cup of the mixture and stir it into the beaten egg yolks until well combined. Slowly pour the cream and egg yolks back into the pot, whisking constantly. Continue to cook until the mixture is thickened and coats the back of a spoon, 2 to 4 minutes. Again, do not let it boil. Remove the cream mixture from heat, stir in the vanilla, and then cool in the refrigerator for at least 4 hours.

Meanwhile, to make the pecans, melt the butter in a skillet over medium-low heat. Add the pecans and cook, occasionally stirring, until the pecans are slightly darker in color and fragrant, 3 to 5 minutes. (Be observant; they can quickly burn!) Remove the pecans from the heat and stir in the brown sugar, cinnamon, and salt. Taste and adjust the seasonings.

After the cream mixture has cooled, freeze in an ice-cream machine according to the manufacturer's instructions. Just before it's done, add the pecans and allow it to churn until they are well incorporated. Chill in the freezer for 4 hours for a firmer ice cream or serve immediately for a softer ice cream.

PEACH ICE CREAM

★

BEFORE THE ADVENT of air-conditioning, on summer afternoons Texans would sit on the porch to keep cool. They would sip tall, cool glasses of iced tea or lemonade, and if they were feeling especially industrious, they would crank up a batch of ice cream, too.

While Texans love many different flavors of ice cream, peach ice cream may be the flavor most connected with Texan summers, as this delicate, sweet fruit can be grown in a large portion of the state. While today most folks have electric ice cream makers and tend to stay inside on the hottest days, there is something to be said for sitting on the porch and eating ice cream with your family and friends, and saying howdy to the neighbors as they stroll by. MAKES 1 QUART

Toss the peaches with ¾ cup of the granulated sugar, the lemon juice, and cinnamon. Cover, refrigerate, and let macerate for 2 to 8 hours, until softened.

Divide the peach mixture in half. Pour half the mixture, both peaches and liquid, into the blender or food processor and puree until smooth. Gently mash the other half, and then refrigerate.

To make the ice cream base, pour the peach puree into a saucepan and add the cream, half-and-half, remaining ¼ cup granulated sugar, and brown sugar. Cook over medium-low heat until warm but not boiling, 3 to 5 minutes. Meanwhile, beat the egg yolks with the vanilla. Take the cream mixture off the heat, mix ½ cup of the cream mixture into the beaten egg yolks, and then add the egg yolk mixture back into the pot with the rest of the cream mixture. While stirring, continue to cook until the mixture is slightly thickened and coats the back of a spoon, about 2 minutes. Refrigerate the ice cream base until cool, 2 to 4 hours.

Freeze in an ice-cream machine according to the manufacturer's instructions. Halfway through the freezing process, pour in the reserved mashed peaches and their syrup.

Serve immediately, if you want a softer ice cream, or chill in the freezer for 2 hours for a firmer ice cream.

2 cups sliced peeled peaches

1 cup granulated sugar

2 tablespoons fresh lemon juice

½ teaspoon ground cinnamon

1 cup heavy cream

2 cups half-and-half

¼ cup packed brown sugar

4 egg yolks

1 teaspoon vanilla extract

DIVINITY

★

"SAY, WHAT DO YOU THINK about divinity candy?" asked my uncle Richard. I replied that to be honest I hadn't thought about it very much. To my mind, it was a traditional Texan treat that my family used to serve at holidays. He said this was true, but that perhaps I should ponder it a bit more.

Had I ever even eaten divinity? I couldn't recall, though in my great-grandmother's letters she often reports making it for people. Perhaps when I was young she had offered it to me, but as with many old-fangled things, it had gone out of style.

I went looking for a recipe and did indeed find one in my family's collection. Like most candies, it called for sugar, but I was surprised that there were egg whites, too. I made the recipe, using a candy thermometer for accuracy and on a cool, dry day, so the candy would set properly, and while there was a little effort involved, it wasn't too difficult.

As I dropped spoonfuls of the white candy onto a sheet to harden, I thought about the name. I had asked my mom why it was called divinity, and she replied that it was because of the way it tasted. This is true, but with its fluffy peaks and soft shape, the candy reminded me of clouds, which may also be why its name connotes the heavens.

This sweet candy has a crisp outer texture that gives way to a creamy center. I like to flavor mine with pecans and orange zest, though people have been known to add peanuts, chocolate, and candied fruit to their divinity instead. It stores well in an airtight container and makes for a fine holiday gift. And if my uncle were to ask me now what I thought about divinity, I'd reply that I think it's divine. MAKES ABOUT 30 PIECES

3 cups sugar

1 cup water

½ cup light corn syrup

2 egg whites, at room temperature

1½ teaspoons vanilla extract

¼ teaspoon kosher salt

1 cup chopped pecans

2 teaspoons finely grated orange zest

Line two baking sheets with parchment paper and lightly grease two dessert spoons.

In a tall pot, stir together the sugar, water, and corn syrup. Insert a candy thermometer into the pot and cook over high heat, while stirring, to bring the syrup to a boil. Turn the heat down to medium-low and continue to cook until it reaches the hardball stage, 250°F, or when a small amount of the syrup turns into a hard ball when dropped into a glass of cold water.

Meanwhile, with a stand mixer fitted with the whisk attachment, beat the egg whites on medium speed until soft peaks form, 3 to 5 minutes.

When the syrup reaches 250°F, remove from the heat. With the stand mixer on medium speed, slowly pour the syrup over the beaten egg whites. The egg white mixture will just be a dark thick liquid at first, but continue to beat until it begins to thicken and turn white, 3 to 5 minutes. At this point, add the vanilla, salt,

pecans, and orange zest. Continue to beat until the mixture is thick and no longer glossy. From the moment you pour in the syrup to this point, it can take anywhere from 5 to 10 minutes.

Once the divinity candy is no longer glossy, turn off the mixer. Scoop out about a tablespoon-size portion of the candy with one of the greased spoons and use the other spoon to slide it onto the parchment paper. It should not be shiny and should easily form into a cloud-shaped mound. Work quickly, because the candy will begin to harden in the mixer as it cools. Don't worry if it does get too hard, you can add a little bit of warm water and beat it for a few seconds to make it soft again.

Let the divinity rest until no longer sticky, about 1 hour. It will keep in an airtight container for 1 week.

NOTE: When you stir in the egg whites, you can also add dried fruit and/or shredded coconut.

CHAPTER 7

ACCOMPANIMENTS

They say there is power in names. Take my nephew, for example.

His name is Austin (like his father and great-grandfather before him), and we call him Austin Jack. Austin Jack does not live in Austin—no, he doesn't even live in Texas. Austin Jack was born and raised in Oregon, but his father is a native Texan, and he is named after a long line of Texans, so I do believe he has an inherent link to the state.

For instance, there was Austin Jack's first Thanksgiving visit to Texas when he was a one-year-old. After dinner the family was watching the annual Dallas Cowboys holiday game, while Austin Jack took a nap. When he woke up, he toddled over to the set, pointed at it, and yelled, "Fooooball!" Just like a Texan.

The next day, the family rode into McKinney to have lunch at San Miguel's, our family's favorite Tex-Mex restaurant. His mother ordered the chicken fajitas for him. After his mother cut the chicken into bite-size pieces and drizzled them with mild salsa, Austin Jack ate his plate of fajitas with great joy. Just like a Texan.

A few months later, I visited my family in Oregon. Upon my arrival, my brother took us to a Mexican restaurant. The waiter brought out a basket of chips and a bowl of salsa and Austin Jack smiled and clapped his hands. Then, while sitting in his mother's lap, I watched him grab a chip from the basket, dip it into the fiery sauce, and take a bite. Just like a Texan.

"Isn't that too hot for him?" I asked. My brother shook his head and said that it was not. In fact, Austin Jack loved chips and salsa, and they fed it to him all the time at home. (Apparently, he's also a huge fan of guacamole, and when the waiter

Old-Fashioned Texas Hot Sauce 241

Tomatillo-Chipotle Salsa 242

Peach Salsa 245

Red Chile Salsa Picante 246

Creamy Green Salsa 248

Corn–Black Bean Salsa 249

Cranberry–Green Chile Salsa 252

Asparagus Pickles 253

Dilly Green Beans 254

Chipotle Pickled Carrots 255

Pickled Red Onions 256

Pickled Whole Peppers 258

Sorghum Mustard Pickles 259

Fresh Watermelon Rind Pickles 261

Corn Relish 262

Plum Jam 265

Blueberry-Pecan Jam 266

brought out a bowl, the adults had to figure out a way to outsmart this determined toddler, so we could at least get one bite.)

My nephew's love of salsa clearly shows that my brother and sister-in-law are raising him right. Though I wonder just how much of this love is genetic, as I've never met a Texan who didn't instinctively know that chips and salsa are good.

See, Texans love a good salsa. We enjoy it as both a dip and a topping, and most Texans eat it at least once a day. You could say the same about our sauces, pickles, and salad dressings, too. It is the odd Texan meal that doesn't have some sort of delectable condiment on the side—often homemade, in a jar on the table for folks to apply as needed. This is just how it's done.

While there are plenty of commercial versions of our favorite condiments on offer, I think you'll find that when you make a fresh batch of hot sauce, peach salsa, or corn relish, it will taste far better than anything that you could buy in a bottle or a jar. They may not seem like the stars of the meal—but they're as important to a Texan as the ribs, tacos, or salad they're meant to accompany. So I say, eat these flavorful condiments often and with gusto. Just like a Texan.

OLD-FASHIONED TEXAS HOT SAUCE

⭐

ON OUR FAMILY'S TABLE, you will usually find a small bowl of salsa that is used as both a condiment and a dipping sauce to crisp, salty tortilla chips. If you're of a certain age, you probably grew up calling this concoction *hot sauce* instead of salsa, as it's now more commonly known. And while in the past few years Texans have started serving a variety of salsas, this old-fashioned hot sauce remains a favorite of mine.

While it's made with only three ingredients—tomatoes, jalapeños, and garlic, along with dashes of black pepper and salt—it still has a depth of flavor that belies its simplicity. Even now, when we have access to a host of other chile peppers and spices, this traditional hot sauce is still in style. MAKES ABOUT 2 CUPS

In a large pot, combine the plum tomatoes, jalapeños, garlic, and water. Bring to a boil, turn the heat down to low, and gently simmer for 10 minutes, or until the tomatoes are soft.

Turn off the heat and allow to cool for 10 minutes. Pour the contents of the pot into a blender or food processor and blend until well combined. Add salt and black pepper to taste. Serve immediately, or store in the refrigerator for up to 1 week.

NOTE: While this salsa is good on its own, if you're so inclined, feel free to add a squirt of lime juice or a handful of chopped cilantro.

1 pound plum tomatoes, stemmed and halved lengthwise

1 or 2 jalapeños (depending on how hot you want the salsa), stemmed, seeded, and halved

4 cloves garlic, peeled

1 cup water

Salt and black pepper

TOMATILLO-CHIPOTLE SALSA

★

WHEN ASKED TO PROVIDE SALSA for a backyard barbecue, I knew exactly what I'd make—tomatillo-chipotle salsa. Now, you might think bringing salsa to a barbecue might seem out of place. But Texans are just as prone to put salsa on smoked meat, as some are inclined to apply barbecue sauce, or, as it's done in Central Texas, some are inclined to apply no sauce at all.

This tangy salsa has hints of smoke from the chipotle chiles, which go very well with smoked meats. But you certainly don't need to fire up the smoker to enjoy this salsa; it also makes a fine accompaniment to tortilla chips, tacos, and eggs.

MAKES ABOUT 3 CUPS

1 pound tomatillos, husked and halved

¼ yellow onion

4 cloves garlic

2 cups water

1 canned chipotle chile in adobo sauce

Salt

In a pot, combine the tomatillos, onion, garlic, and water and bring to a boil. Turn the heat down and simmer for 10 minutes, or until the tomatillos are soft. Remove from the heat and allow to cool, about 10 minutes. Drain the vegetables, reserving the liquid. Pour the vegetables into a blender or food processor and add the chipotle chile. Puree until smooth; if the sauce is too thick, add the reserved cooking liquid as needed. Add salt to taste. Serve immediately, or store in the refrigerator for up to 1 week.

PEACH SALSA

★

IN THE SUMMER, you'll find peaches growing all over Texas. While folks love to argue over which region produces the best (with the fruit from either Fredericksburg or Fairfield receiving the most support), I've yet to find a bad peach in Texas. Please permit me to brag a little, but I do believe that Texas peaches are indeed the best.

There are many ways to enjoy Texas peaches. One of my favorites is with this fresh salsa, chock-full of other summertime favorites. such as fresh tomatoes, jalapeños, and cilantro. Unlike more traditional Texas salsas, this one is both a little spicy and a little sweet, which makes it a perfect for those long, languid days. While it's terrific with just a basket of tortilla chips, it also goes well on chicken, fish, and tacos, too. MAKES ABOUT 2 CUPS

Combine the peaches, tomatoes, jalapeño, bell pepper, garlic, red onion, and water in a pot. Bring to a boil, then turn the heat down and simmer until the tomatoes are soft, about 10 minutes. Remove from the heat and allow to cool, about 10 minutes.

Pour the contents of the pot into a blender or food processor along with the lime juice and pulse on low until chunky. Stir in the chopped cilantro and add salt to taste. Serve immediately, or store in the refrigerator for up to 1 week.

NOTE: To peel the peaches, fill a large pot with water and bring to a boil. Cut a small "X" on the top and bottom of each peach. Add them to boiling water and let them cook for 30 seconds. Using tongs or a long spoon, remove the peaches, rinse with cold water and then peel off the skin by gently rubbing the peach. Halve and then pit the peeled peaches.

1 pound peaches, peeled (see note below) and quartered

1 pound plum tomatoes, halved

1 jalapeño, stemmed, seeded, and halved

½ bell pepper, stemmed and seeded

3 cloves garlic

¼ red onion

1 cup water

2 teaspoons fresh lime juice

½ cup chopped fresh cilantro

Salt

RED CHILE SALSA PICANTE

★

BOTTLES OF CHILE PEPPER SALSAS are as ubiquitous on the Texan table as bowls of tomato salsa. We like to add a few dashes of this piquant condiment to almost everything—from scrambled eggs to fried chicken. People usually fall into two camps with these more potent salsas—either you prefer the thin, vinegary ones that hail from our neighboring state of Louisiana, or you're a fan of the thicker, spicier salsas that come from our southern neighbor, Mexico.

As I fall into the latter camp, my homemade red chile salsa is a take on that style, with its blend of fiery chiles de árbol and fruity guajillo chiles, with a bit of garlic, cumin, oregano, and allspice thrown in to give the blend depth. For tang, I stir in some vinegar, then cook the salsa for a few minutes to soften the flavors.

You are welcome to begin eating this immediately, though the salsa will taste even better if you allow it to deepen and mellow for a few days in the refrigerator. While this salsa makes a fine topping for dishes such as tacos or eggs, my favorite way to use it is slathered on a batch of Fired-Up Wings (page 58). MAKES ABOUT 2 CUPS

10 chiles de árbol, rehydrated, stemmed, and seeded (see page 9)

6 guajillo chiles, rehydrated, stemmed, and seeded (see page 9)

2 cloves garlic

1 teaspoon ground cumin

1 teaspoon dried oregano

¼ teaspoon ground allspice

¾ cup water, plus more as needed

1 teaspoon vegetable oil

½ cup white vinegar, plus more as needed

Salt

Combine the chiles de árbol and guajillo chiles in a blender or food processor. Add the garlic, cumin, oregano, allspice, and water. Blend for 5 minutes until smooth. (You blend the chiles this long because they have very tough skins and this ensures the salsa is smooth without having strain it and lose some of the flavor.)

In a skillet, heat the oil on low and pour in the salsa. Cook for 5 minutes, stirring occasionally. (Please note that the salsa will probably splatter.) Remove from the heat, stir in the vinegar, and add salt to taste. You can add more vinegar or water if you desire a thinner sauce. Serve immediately, or store in the refrigerator for up to 1 week.

CREAMY GREEN SALSA

⭐

THE FIRST TIME I had this salsa I was at a Tex-Mex joint in Bryan with my family. "Get the green salsa," said one cousin. "It's addictive."

The waiter brought out a large bowl filled with a smooth, army-green substance. It was thick and luscious, and I could have sworn there were avocados or perhaps even dairy involved, it was so creamy and good.

My family and I kept dipping our chips into the salsa, trying to figure out its secrets. The waiter was not forthcoming, so it took some research and testing on my behalf to crack the code. After much trial and error, however, I discovered this beguiling salsa is simply an emulsion of jalapeño chiles, serrano chiles, garlic, and oil.

This extra-fiery salsa makes a fine addition to any taco, and it goes especially well with chicken dishes such as Pollo Asado (page 175), evidenced by how it's commonly found at the Mexican grilled chicken restaurants that are popular throughout the state. It can also be used as a dipping sauce for chips or crunchy vegetables, too.

MAKES ABOUT ¾ CUP

8 jalapeño chiles, roasted (see page 9), stemmed, and seeded

4 serrano chiles, roasted (see page 9), stemmed, and seeded

2 cloves garlic

½ cup vegetable oil

Salt

Combine the jalapeño chiles, serrano chiles, garlic, and vegetable oil in a blender or food processor and blend until smooth. Add salt to taste. Serve immediately, or store in the refrigerator for up to 1 week.

CORN–BLACK BEAN SALSA

✪

THERE ARE SEVERAL corn salsa recipes in my repertoire, but this one is notable for the fact that you don't have to turn on your oven, stove, or grill. You simply take uncooked freshly shucked corn and cooked black beans, and toss them with some fresh jalapeños, bell peppers, cilantro, lime juice, and olive oil.

This corn and black bean salsa is terrific with tortilla chips and makes a good side dish, too. It's also a fine topper on shrimp, scallops, fish, and chicken. But no matter how you eat it, know that it will keep you cool. SERVES 4 TO 6

Mix together the corn, black beans, red onion, garlic, jalapeño, red bell pepper, cilantro, and cumin. Stir in the olive oil and lime juice. Add salt and cayenne to taste, and adjust the seasonings. Allow to chill for at least 30 minutes before serving. Stored in the refrigerator, this will keep for up to 1 week.

2 cups freshly shucked corn (from about 4 ears) or 2 cups frozen

1½ cups cooked black beans, drained or 1 (15-ounce) can black beans, drained

¼ small red onion, diced

2 cloves garlic, minced

2 jalapeños, stemmed, seeded, and diced

½ small red bell pepper, stemmed, seeded, and diced

¼ cup chopped fresh cilantro

½ teaspoon ground cumin

¼ cup extra-virgin olive oil

1 tablespoon fresh lime juice

Salt and cayenne

CRANBERRY–GREEN CHILE SALSA

★

FOR MANY PEOPLE, "cranberry sauce" evokes the image of a tubular, red, gelatinous substance that slithers out of a can. You'd think with so many people interested in fresh, local foods, it would be a relic from the past. But it's still a popular holiday item, and at Thanksgiving you'll see stacks of this canned product on prominent display at grocery stores, which always makes me sad.

Making homemade cranberry salsa is simple and tastes miles beyond its canned cousins. While basic cranberry sauce is tart and good, I like to liven mine up with roasted chiles, pecans, cilantro, and orange zest. We've been serving it at my family's Thanksgiving for years, and once you try it, I believe that it will become a new Thanksgiving tradition for your family, too. MAKES 2½ CUPS

12 ounces fresh cranberries or frozen cranberries, thawed

¾ cup sugar

½ cup fresh orange juice

¼ teaspoon ground cinnamon

2 poblano chiles, roasted (see page 9), peeled, stemmed, seeded, and diced

2 jalapeño chiles, roasted (see page 9), stemmed, seeded, and diced

¼ cup chopped toasted pecans

2 tablespoons finely grated orange zest

½ cup chopped fresh cilantro

¼ teaspoon ground cumin

Pinch of ground ginger

Pinch of cayenne

Salt

In a pot, stir together the cranberries, sugar, orange juice, and cinnamon. Cook over medium heat until the sugar is dissolved and the cranberries are soft, about 10 minutes. Remove from the heat.

Stir in the poblano and jalapeño chiles, pecans, orange zest, cilantro, cumin, ginger, and cayenne. Add salt to taste. Refrigerate for 2 hours before serving. Stored in the refrigerator, this will keep for up to 1 week.

ASPARAGUS PICKLES

★

WHEN MY GRANDMA WAS YOUNG, she used to keep her own patch of asparagus at her family's farm, as she was the only one in her family who enjoyed eating it. I can understand her family's aversion, as it took me quite a while to decide that I like asparagus, too.

Asparagus has a strong flavor that is mellowed by cooking, so sometimes you sacrifice some of its crisp texture for that milder flavor. When you pickle asparagus, however, it has both a terrific flavor and a satisfying crunch.

Asparagus is one of the first signs of spring, both in Texas and in many other parts of the world. Matter of fact, in Germany they make a huge deal out of the arrival of asparagus, with festivals and much fanfare. Because parts of Texas were settled by Germans and still retain a strong German flavor, I think you'll find these pickles are a fine addition to the Texan table.

While these pickles are excellent on their own, their brightness also adds life to a pickle platter, in salads, or alongside rich meats, such as ham or sausage.

MAKES 2 QUARTS

Sterilize two quart canning jars with lids and bands (see page 267).

Trim the asparagus to fit into the jars by cutting away from the bottom of each stalk. The asparagus should fit in the jar with a ½ inch headspace at the top. Divide the garlic, tarragon, salt, peppercorns, and mustard seeds between the two jars. Pack half of the asparagus into each jar, with the pointy tips pointing upward.

Combine the water and vinegar in a pot and bring to a boil. Evenly pour the boiling liquid into each jar, filling any remaining space with additional warm water, leaving ½ inch of headspace. Put the lids on the jars and give them a good shake. Place the jars in the refrigerator, and the asparagus will be ready in 24 hours, though their flavor will improve after a couple more days.

The asparagus will last refrigerated for 1 month. Alternatively, you can process the jars for 15 minutes in a boiling water bath (see page 267) for long-term storage.

2 pounds asparagus

4 cloves garlic, minced

2 sprigs fresh tarragon

¼ cup kosher salt

1 teaspoon black peppercorns

1 teaspoon mustard seeds

1 cup water, plus more warm water as needed

2 cups white vinegar

DILLY GREEN BEANS

★

IF YOU'VE NEVER had dilly green beans, which are pickled green beans made lively and bright from lots of fresh dill and garlic, don't be like me. See, back when I lived in Austin, my mom was going through a pickled green bean phase. Every time she came to visit, she'd bring me a jar, but because I was leery of them, I'd pass them off to friends instead.

One day, however, a friend insisted I try them, and I discovered that the snappy beans weren't strange at all—nope, they were refreshing, bright, and good. I predict that once you take a bite, you'll be a convert like me.

They're good eating on their own, straight from the jar, but I also enjoy throwing them into my German Potato and Green Bean Salad (page 86), because their tanginess pairs well with the heavier potatoes. MAKES 2 QUARTS

1 pound green beans

4 cloves garlic

4 large sprigs dill

2 jalapeños, seeded and halved

¼ cup kosher salt

2 teaspoons black peppercorns

2 teaspoons mustard seeds

1 teaspoon cumin seeds

1 cup water, plus more warm water as needed

1½ cups white vinegar

Sterilize two quart canning jars with lids and bands (see page 267).

Trim the ends from the green beans. Divide the garlic, dill, jalapeños, salt, peppercorns, mustard seeds, and cumin seeds between the two jars. Pack the green beans into the jars.

In a medium saucepan, combine the water and vinegar and bring to a boil. Evenly pour the boiling liquid into each jar, filling any remaining space with warm water, leaving ½ inch of headspace. Put the lids on the jars and give them a good shake. Place the jars in the refrigerator. The green beans will be ready in 24 hours, though their flavor will improve after a couple more days.

The green beans will last refrigerated for 1 month. Alternatively, you can process the jars for 15 minutes in a boiling water bath (see page 267) for long-term storage.

CHIPOTLE PICKLED CARROTS

⭐

PICKLED CARROTS have long been a feature at Tex-Mex restaurants. Their tangy, spicy crunch is a terrific contrast to rich, cheese-heavy dishes, such as enchiladas. I like to also put out a bowl of these before a meal and offer them as a refreshing starter. They are also wonderful in tacos and on burgers, and if you're feeling a little unorthodox, you can even dip them into a bowl of Choriqueso (page 62), too. MAKES 2 PINTS

Sterilize two pint canning jars with lids and bands (see page 267).

Divide the garlic, chipotle chiles, cilantro sprigs, salt, and cumin seeds between the two jars.

In a medium saucepan, combine the water, vinegar, and carrots and bring to a boil. Evenly pour the boiling liquid and carrots into each jar, filling any remaining space with warm water, leaving ½ inch of headspace. Put the lids on the jars and give them a good shake. Place the jars in the refrigerator, and the carrots will be ready in 24 hours, though their flavor will improve after a couple more days.

The carrots will last refrigerated for 1 month. Alternatively, you can process the jars for 15 minutes in a boiling water bath (see page 267) for long-term storage.

4 cloves garlic, chopped

2 canned chipotle chiles in adobo sauce, chopped

2 sprigs cilantro

2 tablespoons kosher salt

1 teaspoon cumin seeds

1 cup water, plus more warm water as needed

1 cup white vinegar

1 pound carrots, peeled and cut into rounds

PICKLED RED ONIONS

★

PICKLED RED ONIONS may be one of the prettiest pickles with their pastel pink tones. Typically in Texas, you find these pickles alongside the salsas, pickled jalapeños, and cilantro at taquerias. They're so simple to make that most people I know like to keep a jar at home, too.

Their tangy flavor adds brightness to rich meat dishes like Cochinita Pibil (page 157), though you can also enjoy them with eggs, seafood, and barbecue. MAKES 1 PINT

1 teaspoon kosher salt

1 teaspoon black peppercorns

¼ teaspoon cumin seeds

1 jalapeño, halved

1 cilantro sprig

1 red onion (6 to 8 ounces), peeled and cut into thin rings

½ cup water, plus more warm water as needed

½ cup white vinegar

Sterilize a pint canning jar with lid and band (see page 267).

Put the salt, peppercorns, and cumin seeds in the jar. Add the jalapeño, cilantro, and the onion. The jar should be full, with about ½ inch of headspace at the top.

In a small saucepan, combine the water and the vinegar and bring to a boil. Evenly pour the boiling liquid into each jar, filling any remaining space with warm water, leaving ½ inch of headspace. Place the lid on the jar and give it a good shake. Put the jar in the refrigerator, and the onions will be ready in 24 hours, though their flavor will improve after a couple more days.

The onions will last refrigerated for 1 month. Alternatively, you can process the jars for 10 minutes in a boiling water bath (see page 267) for long-term storage.

PICKLED WHOLE PEPPERS

★

IT'S A RARE TEXAN who doesn't have a jar of pickled whole peppers on hand, and they often make appearances at the table. While you might think these only go well with Tex-Mex, pickled whole peppers can be served with just about anything, from barbecue to fried chicken.

Traditionally, Texans pickle only jalapeño chiles. Because I enjoy a splash of red in my pickle jar, I've also started adding red Fresno chiles, since red jalapeños are more difficult to find. If you're not familiar with the Fresno, it's hot like a jalapeño, but has a slight sweetness to it, as well. This is why I not only enjoy plopping these red and green pickles on my plate, but I also find they make a far superior pimento cheese than the jarred red peppers you'll find at the store.

While these quick pickles will be ready in just a day, they only get better with time. If you're a fan of pickled whole peppers, you might want to make a double batch, as you'll find yourself eating these soon and often. MAKES 2 PINTS

4 cloves garlic, chopped

2 tablespoons kosher salt

1 teaspoon black peppercorns

1 teaspoon mustard seeds

1 teaspoon cumin seeds

2 sprigs cilantro

4 ounces jalapeño chiles (about 8)

4 ounces red jalapeño chiles or red Fresno chiles (about 8)

1 cup water, plus more warm water as needed

1 cup white vinegar

Sterilize two pint canning jars with lids and bands (see page 267).

Divide the garlic, salt, peppercorns, mustard seeds, cumin seeds, and cilantro between the jars. With a sharp knife, cut four ¼-inch slits lengthwise into each chile, two near the top and two near bottom, on each side. Pack the chiles into each jar.

In a small saucepan, combine the water and vinegar and bring to a boil. Evenly pour the boiling liquid into each jar, filling any remaining space with warm water, leaving ½-inch of headspace. Place the lids on the jars and give them a good shake. Place the jars in the refrigerator, and the peppers will be ready in 24 hours, though their flavor will improve after a couple more days.

The peppers will last refrigerated for 1 month. Alternatively, you can process the jars for 10 minutes in a boiling water bath (see page 267) for long-term storage.

SORGHUM MUSTARD PICKLES

★

SWEET PICKLES, known as bread-and-butter pickles, are popular across Texas. Both sides of my family have been making them for generations, and they are still many family members' absolute favorite pickle. My grandpa's family used to harvest cane for sorghum syrup, and while there is no proof that my great-grandma ever used it for her sweet pickles, I like to think that perhaps she did.

If you're not familiar with sorghum syrup, it has a buttery, slightly burnt flavor that reminds me of caramel. On the sweetness spectrum, it falls between honey and molasses. While I'm not a huge fan of overly sweet pickles, the sorghum gives these a nice hint of sweetness, with still enough tang to keep these pickles refreshing.

MAKES 2 QUARTS

Sterilize two quart canning jars with lids and bands (see page 267).

Divide the garlic, salt, peppercorns, mustard seeds, red pepper flakes, allspice berries, turmeric, and cloves between the jars. Divide the cucumbers and then pack into each jar.

In a small saucepan, combine the water, vinegar, sorghum syrup, and sugar and bring to a boil. Evenly pour the boiling liquid into each jar, filling any remaining space with warm water, leaving ½-inch of headspace. Place the lids on the jars and give them a good shake. Place the jars in the refrigerator, and the pickles will be ready in 24 hours, though their flavor will improve after a couple more days.

The pickles will last refrigerated for 1 month. Alternatively, you can process the jars for 10 minutes in a boiling water bath (see page 267) for long-term storage.

NOTE: You can substitute Persian or English cucumbers if you can't find Kirbys. You can also substitute honey for the sorghum syrup.

4 cloves garlic, minced

¼ cup kosher salt

1 tablespoon black peppercorns

1 tablespoon mustard seeds

2 teaspoons red pepper flakes

1 teaspoon allspice berries

¼ teaspoon ground turmeric

4 whole cloves

2 pounds Kirby or other small pickling cucumbers, sliced into ¼-inch rounds

2 cups water, plus more warm water as needed

2 cups apple cider vinegar

2 tablespoons sorghum syrup

¼ cup sugar

FRESH WATERMELON
RIND PICKLES

⭐

MY GRANDMA ADMITTED to me recently that she wasn't a big fan of watermelon rind pickles. Like most Texans of a certain era, her mother used to make them in the summer, as they're a wonderful way to use up your watermelon rinds. Traditionally, watermelon rind pickles are boiled until translucent with sugar, vinegar, and spices, such as cloves, allspice, and cinnamon. While these spices go with many things, I find that these warm flavors clash with the rind, which in its raw state is crisp and cool, much like a cucumber, to which the melon is related.

Yes, I have to admit that I'm also not a fan of the classic rind pickles, but I do admire my great-grandma's desire not to waste any of the fruit. What I like to do with my rind instead is make a fresh pickle with just salt, garlic, vinegar, and jalapeño. It's crisp, salty, and slightly sour, and they make a fine topping on a burger, can be tossed with cubed fresh watermelon, or eaten straight out of the jar. So while these may not be your great-grandmother's watermelon rind pickles, these still honor the fruit and are a refreshing addition to any warm-weather meal. MAKES 1 PINT

Place the rind in a food-storage container and toss with the salt. Pour over the salted rind enough water to cover by 1 inch, and then refrigerate the rind for 1 day.

Sterilize a pint canning jar (see page 267).

Once the rind has soaked in the salt solution, drain the rind and rinse. Put the jalapeños, garlic, and cilantro in the jar, then add the rinsed rind. Pour in the vinegar and add enough water to fill.

Refrigerate for 1 day before serving. The pickles will last refrigerated for 2 weeks.

2 cups peeled and cubed watermelon rind

1 tablespoon kosher salt

1 jalapeño, halved

1 clove garlic

2 sprigs cilantro

½ cup white vinegar

Water

CORN RELISH

★

WHEN YOU LOOK THROUGH old family recipes, you'll find that most Texans have at least one for corn relish in their recipe box. Except this Texan right here. That's right. When I was looking through my stacks of notes and cards, I couldn't find one recipe for this Texan summertime standard. This made no sense to me, as my family even grew corn! No matter, I started asking folks how they made their corn relish and then came up with my own.

You want to make this when corn is at its peak, as that's when it will be the most sweet and juicy. To eat it, simply spoon it onto hotdogs, into tacos, or on top of fish.

MAKES 1 PINT

2 cups fresh corn kernels from 4 ears of corn

1 red bell pepper, stemmed, seeded, and finely diced

2 jalapeños, stemmed, seeded, and finely diced

2 cloves garlic

½ cup chopped fresh cilantro

½ yellow onion, diced

¾ cup apple cider vinegar

1 tablespoon sugar

½ teaspoon kosher salt

¼ teaspoon ground turmeric

¼ teaspoon powdered mustard

Sterilize two half-pint canning jars or 1 pint-sized jar with lids and bands (see page 267).

Combine all the ingredients in a large pot and bring to a boil. Turn the heat down to low and simmer for 15 minutes, or until the vegetables are tender. Pour the relish into the jars, leaving ½ inch of headspace. Place the lids on the jars, allow to cool and then refrigerate. The relish can last 2 weeks in the refrigerator.

Alternatively, you can process the jars for 15 minutes in a boiling water bath (see page 267) for long-term storage.

PLUM JAM

✪

ONE OF THE LAST THINGS that my grandfather planted on the farm before he passed was a plum tree. He did it as an anniversary gift for my grandma, as plums were in season when they got married one July day many years ago. And every summer, when it starts to bear fruit, my grandma makes the family plum jam. While the jam is tart, sweet, and delicious, what makes this gift from her even more special is knowing that my now-gone grandfather played a small role in making those plum preserves, too.

Her recipe calls for Sure-Jell, a boxed pectin that for some strange reason I couldn't find in New York City. So I've slightly adapted her method and used lots of lemon juice to help the jam come together instead. While my plum jam is not nearly as good as hers, I believe it's not the lack of boxed pectin but because her plums come from a tree planted with love. That tree's fruit, which is a gift that keeps giving, is what makes her plum preserves taste so good. MAKES 2 PINTS

Sterilize 2 pint canning jars with lids and bands (see page 267). Place a plate in the freezer.

Combine the plums, sugar, lemon juice, and cinnamon in a pot. Allow the plums to macerate for 20 minutes, or until juicy. Bring the pot to a boil, then turn the heat down to low, and cook, stirring occasionally, for 40 minutes. (Don't worry if there's foam on top of the jam. While some advise to skim it, I leave it and find it doesn't affect the jam.)

Take the plate out of the freezer and place a spoonful of the jam on it. After a minute, tilt the plate. If the jam doesn't run, it's ready. If it does run, continue to cook it, occasionally stirring, for 5 more minutes; then check again. Continue to cook and test until the jam doesn't run.

Pour the jam into the jars, leaving ½ inch of headspace. Cover with the lids and rings. Allow to cool and then refrigerate. Alternatively, you can process the jars for 5 minutes in a boiling water bath (see page 267) for long-term storage.

2½ pounds plums, pitted

2 cups sugar

¼ cup fresh lemon juice

½ teaspoon ground cinnamon

BLUEBERRY-PECAN JAM

★

TEXANS LOVE BLUEBERRIES, as evidenced by the festivals and celebrations that mark their early summer arrival (not to mention my nephew Austin Jack's blueberry-stained face whenever a bowl is placed within his reach). Texans also love pecans, which is our state nut. And finally, Texans love jam, so combining the beloved blueberry with the iconic pecan seemed like an obvious thing to do.

The sweet berries go well with the nutty crunch of pecans, and you'll soon find yourself spreading this on a whole host of breads, rolls, and biscuits. MAKES 2 PINTS

2 cups blueberries

2 cups sugar

¼ cup fresh lemon juice

½ cup chopped roasted pecans

Sterilize 2 pint canning jars with lids and bands (see page 267). Place a plate in the freezer.

Combine the blueberries, sugar, and lemon juice in a pot. Allow the blueberries to macerate for 20 minutes, or until juicy. Bring the pot to a boil, turn the heat down to low, and cook, stirring occasionally, for 40 minutes. (Don't worry if there's foam on top of the jam. While some advise skimming it, I leave it and find it doesn't affect the jam.)

Take the plate out of the freezer and place a spoonful of the jam on it. After a minute, tilt the plate. If the jam doesn't run, it's ready. If it does run, continue to cook, occasionally stirring, for 5 more minutes; then check again. Continue to cook and test until the jam doesn't run.

Stir the pecans into the jam, then pour the jam into the jars, leaving ½ inch of headspace. Cover with the lid and rings. Allow to cool and then refrigerate. Alternatively, you can process the jars for 5 minutes in a boiling water bath (see page 267) for long-term storage.

CANNING

How to sterilize jars and lids

To sterilize jars and lids, you can either boil them in a large pot of water for 10 minutes or run them through the sterilizing cycle of your dishwasher. Afterward, remove the jars and lids with tongs and place them on a clean surface.

How to can by using a boiling water bath

While I prefer to keep my pickles and jams in the fridge and use them immediately, I realize there are times you'll want to preserve them to give as gifts or keep on your pantry shelves. The easiest way to do this is the water-bath method.

To can using a water bath, place a rack in the bottom of a canner or a tall stockpot. Fill the pot halfway with water and bring to a boil. (I also use this pot to sterilize my jars and lids.) Once you've filled your jars, wipe the rim with a damp cloth, top with the lid and then screw on the band. Lower the jars into the pot, making sure that 1 inch of water covers the top of the lids. If not, add more water. When the water returns to a boil, cover the pot, and then begin timing according to the recipe.

The times listed in this book are for an altitude of sea level to 1,000 feet. For an altitude 1,000 feet to 5,000 feet above sea level, add 5 minutes. For an altitude 5,000 feet and above, add 10 minutes.

Once done, remove the jars with a jar lifter or tongs, place on a kitchen towel, and allow to cool. If the jars have sealed properly, you will hear a slight popping sound a few minutes after removing from the bath. Though if you walk away and don't hear the pop, another way to test the seal, according to the National Center for Home Preservation, is by pressing on the lid after the jars have cooled for 12 hours. If the lid feels solid and doesn't move up and down, it's sealed. But if it feels loose, it hasn't. Another test is to hold the jar at eye level and look at the lid. If it's concave in the center, it's sealed. If you are processing this way, make sure that the lids have never been used before, as they will only seal once. These jars will not require refrigeration until after opening. If the seal didn't take, then refrigerate the jars and use within a month.

For more information, visit the National Center for Home Food Preservation at nchfp.uga.edu, or refer to one of the many fine books on home canning available.

RESOURCE GUIDE

★

Many of the ingredients in this book can be found at your local grocery store. A few of the sauces, spices, and chile peppers can be found at a Mexican grocer. If, however, you have a hard time sourcing certain items (such as dried chiles or masa harina), here are places where you can place mail orders for these ingredients.

AMAZON
www.amazon.com (US)
www.amazon.co.uk (Europe)

A great source for just about any equipment or pantry item you need, including cast-iron cookware, tortilla presses, chili powder, dried chiles, masa harina, canned jalapeños, and pecans.

CADDO VALLEY PECANS
www.caddovalleypecans.com

Native Texas organic pecans.

CAJUN GROCER
www.cajungrocer.com

A good online source for filé powder, a necessary ingredient for gumbo.

LODGE
www.lodgemfg.com

Affordable, dependable cast-iron cookware.

MEXGROCER
www.mexgrocer.com (US)
www.mexgrocer.co.uk (Europe)

Beans; canned chipotle, jalapeño, poblano, and serrano chiles; cornhusks; dried chiles; masa harina; Mexican chocolate; posole (hominy); spices; tortilla presses; and tortillas.

PENDEREY'S
www.penderys.com
800-533-1870

Chili powder, cornhusks, dried chiles, spices, and vanilla extract.

SOUTHTEX ORGANICS
www.stxorganics.com

Texas citrus.

ACKNOWLEDGMENTS

★

You're reading this book due to the hard work, kindness, and generosity of quite a few people. I am so grateful to have them all in my life.

First, a big thank you to my agent and fellow homesick Texan, Brettne Bloom. She works tirelessly to support her authors, and I'm thankful every day that she's on my side.

The fine folks at Ten Speed Press took my words and photos and created a beautiful book, beyond what I ever could have imagined. My editor Emily Timberlake has been a joy to work with and I'm grateful she challenged me to produce the best book possible. I'd also like to thank Aaron Wehner for starting the conversation, Katy Brown for her gorgeous, impeccable design, Kristin Casemore for spreading the word, copyeditor Andrea Chesman for making the manuscript sparkle, and the marketing folks—Hannah Rahill, Michele Crim, Ali Slagle, and Ashley Matuszak—for all their hard work. Brad Thomas Parsons also deserves thanks for initially introducing me to Ten Speed.

It's important to hear other people's opinions when you create recipes, and I am grateful for the sage advice and feedback from my team of terrific testers: Mike Bierschenk, Erin Bryan, Steff Childs, Kristine Laudadio Devine, Rachel Dubose, Travis Dubose, Sharon Dunn, Linda Ford, Bill Gunter, Ginny Heckel, Celeste Lipp, Kathi Malin, Mijke Rhemtulla, Cheryl Rode, Carolyn Woolley, Sarah Whetsell, and Kelly Yandell.

As I was traveling around Texas to research and take photos, I was much obliged to the generous people who fed me, housed me, and let me photograph their property, including Wendy Adams, Monica Crowley, Mark Dominguez, Eric Grossman, Jerita Howard, Laura Kopchick, Hillary Netardus, and Tim Richardson.

A hearty shout-out to all the bloggers and booksellers who said nice things about my first book to their readers and customers, with a special thanks going to Faye Bowles and her team at my neighborhood shop, Posman Books. Your hard work is much appreciated.

I am so grateful to have such a supportive family, including my grandmother who baked countless pies, my mom and dad who helped test recipes, my brother, sister-in-law, and step-mother who provided feedback on said recipes, and the two newest members of the family, Austin and Jonas, who bring much happiness into our lives.

Last but not least, I want to thank all of my readers. Without your encouragement and support, this couldn't be possible. Thank you.

MEASUREMENT
CONVERSION CHARTS

VOLUME

US	IMPERIAL	METRIC
1 tablespoon	½ fl oz	15 ml
2 tablespoons	1 fl oz	30 ml
¼ cup	2 fl oz	60 ml
⅓ cup	3 fl oz	90 ml
½ cup	4 fl oz	120 ml
⅔ cup	5 fl oz (¼ pint)	150 ml
¾ cup	6 fl oz	180 ml
1 cup	8 fl oz (⅓ pint)	240 ml
1¼ cups	10 fl oz (½ pint)	300 ml
2 cups (1 pint)	16 fl oz (⅔ pint)	480 ml
2½ cups	20 fl oz (1 pint)	600 ml
1 quart	32 fl oz (1⅔ pints)	1 l

TEMPERATURE

FAHRENHEIT	CELSIUS/GAS MARK
250°F	120°C/gas mark ½
275°F	135°C/gas mark 1
300°F	150°C/gas mark 2
325°F	160°C/gas mark 3
350°F	180 or 175°C/gas mark 4
375°F	190°C/gas mark 5
400°F	200°C/gas mark 6
425°F	220°C/gas mark 7
450°F	230°C/gas mark 8
475°F	245°C/gas mark 9
500°F	260°C

LENGTH

INCH	METRIC
¼ inch	6 mm
½ inch	1.25 cm
¾ inch	2 cm
1 inch	2.5 cm
6 inches (½ foot)	15 cm
12 inches (1 foot)	30 cm

WEIGHT

US/IMPERIAL	METRIC
½ oz	15 g
1 oz	30 g
2 oz	60 g
¼ lb	115 g
⅓ lb	150 g
½ lb	225 g
¾ lb	350 g
1 lb	450 g

INDEX

★

A

Achiote Marinade, 157–58
Almonds
    Blueberry Granola, 34
    Mom's Raspberry Bars, 207
Ambrosia Salad, 95
Ancho chiles, 8
    Ancho Chile Applesauce, 96
    Ancho Chile Shrimp
        Quesadilla, 189
    Mole Chorizo, 164–65
    Pollo Asado, 175
    Ranch-Style Beans, 108
    Shredded Beef Enchiladas
        with Three-Chile Sauce,
        142–43
    Venison Chili, 118–19
Angel Biscuits, 39
Apples
    Ancho Chile Applesauce, 96
    Apple Cake, 215
    Apple-Jalapeño Dutch Baby
        Pancake, 29
    Apple-Walnut Salad, 78
Apricot Bread, 31
Artichoke, Spinach, and Bacon
    Dip, 53
Asparagus Pickles, 253
Avocados
    Guacamole, 66
    Guacamole Salad, 77
    Tuna with Avocado and
        Red Pepper Baked in
        Parchment, 184

B

Bacon
    Bacon and Chipotle Corn
        Pudding, 101
    Bacon-Cheddar-Chipotle
        Biscuits, 40
    Bacon-Jalapeño Cheese
        Ball, 57
    Bacon-Molasses Breakfast
        Sausage, 16
    Breakfast Enchiladas,
        22–23
    Buttermilk Bacon-Fat Flour
        Tortillas, 26
    Buttermilk Potato Soup with
        Bacon and Jalapeño,
        122–23
    Chipotle–Blue Cheese
        Wedge Salad, 82
    Chipotle-Cheddar
        Scalloped Potatoes, 99
    Creamy Macaroni and
        Cheese, 104
    German Potato and Green
        Bean Salad, 86
    grease, 26
    Oyster Casserole, 100
    Spinach, Bacon, and
        Artichoke Dip, 53
    Venison Chili, 118–19
Balsamic-Tarragon Glazed
    Ham, 163
Banana Pudding with Peanut
    Butter–Oatmeal Cookies,
    205–6
Barbecue Sauce, Peppery, 160
Bars, Mom's Raspberry, 207

Beans
    Black-Eyed Pea and
        Mexican Chorizo
        Soup, 117
    Cowboy Beans, 107
    Crazy Nachos, 65–66
    Frito Salad, 85
    Ranch-Style Beans, 108
    See also Black beans;
        Green beans
Beef
    Brisket Tacos, Dallas Style,
        148–49
    Chipotle Taco Meat, 65
    Cowboy Beans, 107
    Crazy Nachos, 65–66
    Crispy Tacos, 151
    Michelada Flank Steak
        Tortas with Poblano-
        Buttermilk Dressing,
        139–40
    Shredded Beef Enchiladas
        with Three-Chile Sauce,
        142–43
    Steak Fingers with Jalapeño
        Cream Gravy, 146–47
    Sunday Brisket, 145
Beer
    Beer-Battered Catfish Tacos,
        179–80
    Michelada Flank Steak
        Tortas with Poblano-
        Buttermilk Dressing,
        139–40
    Venison Chili, 118–19
Bell peppers
    Chicken Fajitas, 172–73

Bell peppers, *continued*
 Tuna with Avocado and Red Pepper
  Baked in Parchment, 184
Biscuits
 Angel Biscuits, 39
 Bacon-Cheddar-Chipotle
  Biscuits, 40
Black beans
 Black Bean Sopes with Chipotle
  Crema, 196
 Chilaquiles in Black Bean Salsa, 21
 Corn–Black Bean Salsa, 249
 Refried Black Beans, 109
Black-Eyed Pea and Mexican Chorizo
 Soup, 117
Blueberries
 Blueberry Granola, 34
 Blueberry-Pecan Jam, 266
Bread
 Apricot Bread, 31
 Cranberry-Gruyère Scones, 37
 Great-Grandma Blanche's
  Chocolate Muffins, 30
 Jalapeño Corn Sticks, 47
 Michelada Flank Steak Tortas with
  Poblano-Buttermilk Dressing,
  139–40
 Oatmeal Bread, 44
 Pecan-Lime French Toast
  Casserole, 33
 Sausage and Pepper Breakfast
  Casserole, 19
 See also Biscuits; Rolls; Tortillas
Breakfast Enchiladas, 22–23
Brine, Jalapeño, 168
Brisket
 Brisket Tacos, Dallas Style, 148–49
 Sunday Brisket, 145
Brownies, Butterscotch, 203
Buttermilk
 Angel Biscuits, 39
 Buttermilk Bacon-Fat Flour
  Tortillas, 26
 Buttermilk Dinner Rolls, 38
 Buttermilk Potato Soup with Bacon
  and Jalapeño, 122–23
 Poblano-Buttermilk Dressing, 140
Butterscotch Brownies, 203

C
Caballero Cookies, 208
Cabbage
 Beer-Battered Catfish Tacos,
  179–80
 Macaroni Salad, 90
 Mustard Coleslaw, 94
Cakes
 Apple Cake, 215
 Gingerbread, 219
 Mexican Chocolate Cake, 216
 Ruby Red Grapefruit and Pecan
  Sheet Cake, 220
Candy
 Divinity, 236–37
 thermometers, 4
Canning, 4, 267
Carrots
 Chipotle Pickled Carrots, 255
 Macaroni Salad, 90
Cast-iron skillets, 4
Catfish Tacos, Beer-Battered, 179–80
Cheese
 Ancho Chile Shrimp
  Quesadilla, 189
 Apple-Walnut Salad, 78
 Bacon and Chipotle Corn
  Pudding, 101
 Bacon-Cheddar-Chipotle
  Biscuits, 40
 Bacon-Jalapeño Cheese Ball, 57
 Black-Eyed Pea and Mexican
  Chorizo Soup, 117
 Breakfast Enchiladas, 22–23
 Brisket Tacos, Dallas Style, 148–49
 Chicken Spaghetti, 167
 Chipotle–Blue Cheese Dressing, 82
 Chipotle–Blue Cheese Wedge
  Salad, 82
 Chipotle-Cheddar Scalloped
  Potatoes, 99
 Choriqueso, 62
 Cranberry-Gruyère Scones, 37
 Crazy Nachos, 65–66
 Cream Cheese Frosting, 220
 Creamy Macaroni and
  Cheese, 104
 Crispy Tacos, 151
 Frito Salad, 85
 Green Chile Baked Eggs, 20
 Green Chile Hominy
  Casserole, 103

 Jalapeño Pimento Cheese, 56
 Klobasnek (Sausage Kolaches),
  42–43
 Michelada Flank Steak Tortas with
  Poblano-Buttermilk Dressing,
  139–40
 Pigs in Jalapeño-Cheddar
  Blankets with Jalapeño Dipping
  Sauce, 61
 Sausage and Pepper Breakfast
  Casserole, 19
 Shredded Beef Enchiladas with
  Three-Chile Sauce, 142–43
 Spicy Pea Salad, 89
 Spinach, Bacon, and Artichoke
  Dip, 53
 Stacked Jalapeño-Cheese
  Enchiladas, 194
 Turkey Enchiladas with Sweet
  Potato–Chipotle Sauce, 171
Chicken
 Chicken Fajitas, 172–73
 Chicken Soup, 125–26
 Chicken Spaghetti, 167
 Chicken Tamales with Tomatillo-
  Guajillo Salsa, 176–78
 Chipotle Chicken and Dumplings,
  125–26
 Fired-Up Wings, 58
 Jalapeño Fried Chicken, 168–69
 Pollo Asado, 175
 Sopa de Lima (Mexican Lime
  Soup), 127
Chilaquiles in Black Bean Salsa, 21
Chile powder, 8, 9
Chiles, dried
 buying, 7
 rehydrating and roasting, 9
 storing, 7
 varieties of, 8
 See also individual varieties
Chiles, fresh
 buying, 6
 roasting, 9
 storing, 6
 varieties of, 6–7
 working with, 6
 See also individual varieties
Chiles, ground, 8
Chiles de árbol, 8
 Chicken Fajitas, 172–73
 Red Chile Salsa Picante, 246

Chili
    Pork Chili Verde, 121
    Venison Chili, 118–19
Chili powder, 8, 9
Chipotle chiles, 8
    Achiote Marinade, 157–58
    Bacon and Chipotle Corn
        Pudding, 101
    Bacon-Cheddar-Chipotle
        Biscuits, 40
    Chipotle–Blue Cheese Dressing, 82
    Chipotle–Blue Cheese Wedge
        Salad, 82
    Chipotle-Cheddar Scalloped
        Potatoes, 99
    Chipotle Chicken and Dumplings,
        125–26
    Chipotle-Lime Dipping Sauce, 188
    Chipotle Pickled Carrots, 255
    Chipotle Ranch–Spiced Oyster
        Crackers, 71
    Chipotle Taco Meat, 65

Coffee-Chipotle Pork Chops, 152
    Shredded Beef Enchiladas with
        Three-Chile Sauce, 142–43
    Sweet Potato and Chipotle
        Tortillas, 28
    Sweet Potato–Chipotle Sauce, 171
    Tomatillo-Chipotle Salsa, 242
    Venison Chili, 118–19
Chocolate
    Caballero Cookies, 208
    Great-Grandma Blanche's
        Chocolate Muffins, 30
    Mexican Chocolate Cake, 216
Chorizo
    Black-Eyed Pea and Mexican
        Chorizo Soup, 117
    Choriqueso, 62
    Green Chile Hominy
        Casserole, 103
    Potato-Chorizo Breakfast Tacos, 25
Cobbler, Plum, 229
Cochinita Pibil, 157–58

Coconut
    Ambrosia Salad, 95
    Blueberry Granola, 34
    Coconut-Pecan Frosting, 216
Coffee-Chipotle Pork Chops, 152
Coleslaw, Mustard, 94
Collard Greens, Smoky, 102
Cookies
    Caballero Cookies, 208
    Peanut Butter–Oatmeal Cookies,
        205
    Spicy Snickerdoodles, 211
Corn
    Corn–Black Bean Salsa, 249
    Corn Relish, 262
    Green Chile Hominy
        Casserole, 103
    Shrimp Boil, 190
    Zucchini-Corn Salsa, 131
    See also Cornmeal

Cornmeal
  Bacon and Chipotle Corn
    Pudding, 101
  Fried Oysters with Chipotle-Lime
    Dipping Sauce, 188
  Jalapeño Corn Sticks, 47
Cowboy Beans, 107
Crab
  Southeast Texas Gumbo, 132
Crackers
  Chipotle Ranch–Spiced Oyster
    Crackers, 71
  Oyster Casserole, 100
Cranberries
  Cranberry–Green Chile Salsa, 252
  Cranberry-Gruyère Scones, 37
Crazy Nachos, 65–66
Creamy Green Salsa, 248
Creamy Macaroni and Cheese, 104
Crispy Tacos, 151
Cucumbers
  Sorghum Mustard Pickles, 259
  Tomato, Cucumber, and Peach
    Salad, 81

D
Desserts
  Apple Cake, 215
  Banana Pudding with Peanut
    Butter–Oatmeal Cookies, 205–6
  Butterscotch Brownies, 203
  Caballero Cookies, 208
  Divinity, 236–37
  Gingerbread, 219
  Lemon Pie, 223
  Mexican Chocolate Cake, 216
  Molasses and Spiced-Pecan Ice
    Cream, 232
  Mom's Raspberry Bars, 207
  Peach Ice Cream, 235
  Pecan Pie, 224
  Plum Cobbler, 229
  Ruby Red Grapefruit and Pecan
    Sheet Cake, 220
  Spicy Snickerdoodles, 211
  Strawberry Shortcake, 212
  Sweet Potato Pie, 226
Dilly Green Beans, 254
Dips
  Guacamole, 66
  Spinach, Bacon, and Artichoke
    Dip, 53

Divinity, 236–37
Dumplings, Chipotle Chicken and,
  125–26
Dutch Baby Pancake, Apple-
  Jalapeño, 29

E
Eggs
  Green Chile Baked Eggs, 20
  Macaroni Salad, 90
  Pico de Gallo Deviled Eggs, 54
  Potato-Chorizo Breakfast Tacos, 25
  Sausage and Pepper Breakfast
    Casserole, 19
Enchiladas
  Breakfast Enchiladas, 22–23
  Enchilada Sauce, 22
  Shredded Beef Enchiladas with
    Three-Chile Sauce, 142–43
  Stacked Jalapeño-Cheese
    Enchiladas, 194
  Turkey Enchiladas with Sweet
    Potato–Chipotle Sauce, 171
Equipment, 3–4

F
Fajitas, Chicken, 172–73
Fired-Up Wings, 58
Fish
  Beer-Battered Catfish Tacos,
    179–80
  Roasted Whole Fish, 187
  Tortilla-Crusted Tilapia, 183
  Tuna with Avocado and Red Pepper
    Baked in Parchment, 184
French Toast Casserole,
  Pecan-Lime, 33
Fresh Watermelon Rind Pickles, 261
Fresno chiles, 6
  Jalapeño Pimento Cheese, 56
  Pickled Whole Peppers, 258
Fried Oysters with Chipotle-Lime
  Dipping Sauce, 188
Frito Salad, 85
Frostings
  Coconut-Pecan Frosting, 216
  Cream Cheese Frosting, 220
Fruits
  peeling, 4
  See also individual fruits

G
German Potato and Green Bean
  Salad, 86
Gingerbread, 219
Granola, Blueberry, 34
Grapefruit, Ruby Red, and Pecan
  Sheet Cake, 220
Gravy, Jalapeño Cream, 146
Great-Grandma Blanche's Chocolate
  Muffins, 30
Green beans
  Dilly Green Beans, 254
  German Potato and Green Bean
    Salad, 86
Green Chile Baked Eggs, 20
Green Chile Hominy Casserole, 103
Greens, Smoky Collard, 102
Guacamole, 66
  Guacamole Salad, 77
Guajillo chiles, 8
  Achiote Marinade, 157–58
  Breakfast Enchiladas, 22–23
  Enchilada Sauce, 22
  Red Chile Salsa Picante, 246
  Tomatillo-Guajillo Salsa, 176–77
Gumbo, Southeast Texas, 132

H
Ham, Balsamic-Tarragon Glazed, 163
Hatch chiles, 6
  Green Chile Baked Eggs, 20
  Hominy Casserole, Green Chile, 103
Horseradish Cream Sauce, 145
Hot Sauce, Old-Fashioned Texas, 241

I
Ice cream
  Molasses and Spiced-Pecan Ice
    Cream, 232
  Peach Ice Cream, 235

J
Jalapeño chiles, 6
  Apple-Jalapeño Dutch Baby
    Pancake, 29
  Bacon-Jalapeño Cheese Ball, 57
  Buttermilk Potato Soup with Bacon
    and Jalapeño, 122–23
  Cranberry–Green Chile Salsa, 252
  Crazy Nachos, 65–66
  Creamy Green Salsa, 248
  Frito Salad, 85

Green Chile Hominy
Casserole, 103
Jalapeño Brine, 168
Jalapeño Corn Sticks, 47
Jalapeño Fried Chicken, 168–69
Jalapeño Pesto–Stuffed Pork Roast,
155–56
Jalapeño Pimento Cheese, 56
Jalapeño Tartar Sauce, 183
Klobasnek (Sausage Kolaches),
42–43
Michelada Flank Steak Tortas with
Poblano-Buttermilk Dressing,
139–40
Old-Fashioned Texas Hot
Sauce, 241
Pickled Whole Peppers, 258
Pico de Gallo Deviled Eggs, 54
Pigs in Jalapeño-Cheddar
Blankets with Jalapeño Dipping
Sauce, 61
Pork Chili Verde, 121
Stacked Jalapeño-Cheese
Enchiladas, 194
Steak Fingers with Jalapeño Cream
Gravy, 146–47
Jambalaya, Sausage and Shrimp, 193
Jams
Blueberry-Pecan Jam, 266
canning instructions for, 267
Plum Jam, 265

K
Klobasnek (Sausage Kolaches),
42–43

L
Lemon Pie, 223
Limes
Achiote Marinade, 157–58
Chipotle-Lime Dipping Sauce, 188
Lime Curd, 33
Pecan-Lime French Toast
Casserole, 33
Sopa de Lima (Mexican Lime
Soup), 127

M
Macaroni
Creamy Macaroni and Cheese, 104
Macaroni Salad, 90
Marinade, Achiote, 157–58

Masa harina
Black Bean Sopes with Chipotle
Crema, 196
Chicken Tamales with Tomatillo-
Guajillo Salsa, 176–78
Mexican Chocolate Cake, 216
Mexican Lime Soup (Sopa de
Lima), 127
Michelada Flank Steak Tortas with
Poblano-Buttermilk Dressing,
139–40
Molasses and Spiced-Pecan Ice
Cream, 232
Mole Chorizo, 164–65
Mom's Raspberry Bars, 207
Muffins, Great-Grandma Blanche's
Chocolate, 30
Mustard Coleslaw, 94
My Family's Pie Dough, 227

N
Nachos, Crazy, 65–66

O
Oats
Blueberry Granola, 34
Caballero Cookies, 208
Oatmeal Bread, 44
Peanut Butter–Oatmeal
Cookies, 205
Okra
Southeast Texas Gumbo, 132
Old-Fashioned Texas Hot Sauce, 241
Onions
peeling, 4
Pickled Red Onions, 256
Oranges
Achiote Marinade, 157–58
Ambrosia Salad, 95
Orange-Cinnamon Candied
Pecans, 68
Oyster Casserole, 100
Oyster Crackers, Chipotle Ranch–
Spiced, 71
Oysters
Fried Oysters with Chipotle-Lime
Dipping Sauce, 188
Oyster Casserole, 100

P
Palote, 4
Pancake, Apple-Jalapeño Dutch
Baby, 29
Paprika, smoked, 8
Pasilla chiles, 8
Pumpkin Pasilla Soup, 128
Shredded Beef Enchiladas with
Three-Chile Sauce, 142–43
Venison Chili, 118–19
Pasta
Chicken Spaghetti, 167
Creamy Macaroni and Cheese,
104
Macaroni Salad, 90
Peaches
Peach Ice Cream, 235
Peach Salsa, 245
Tomato, Cucumber, and Peach
Salad, 81
Peanut Butter–Oatmeal Cookies, 205
Pea Salad, Spicy, 89
Pecans
Ambrosia Salad, 95
Apple Cake, 215
Apricot Bread, 31
Bacon-Jalapeño Cheese Ball, 57
Blueberry Granola, 34
Blueberry-Pecan Jam, 266
Butterscotch Brownies, 203
Caballero Cookies, 208
Coconut-Pecan Frosting, 216
Cranberry–Green Chile Salsa, 252
Cranberry-Gruyère Scones, 37
Divinity, 236–37
Jalapeño Pesto–Stuffed Pork Roast,
155–56
Molasses and Spiced-Pecan Ice
Cream, 232
Orange-Cinnamon Candied
Pecans, 68
Pecan-Lime French Toast
Casserole, 33
Pecan Pie, 224
Ruby Red Grapefruit and Pecan
Sheet Cake, 220
Peppery Barbecue Sauce, 160
Peppery Ribs, 160–61
Pickles
Asparagus Pickles, 253
canning instructions for, 267
Chipotle Pickled Carrots, 255

Pickles, *continued*
Dilly Green Beans, 254
Fresh Watermelon Rind Pickles, 261
Pickled Red Onions, 256
Pickled Whole Peppers, 258
Sorghum Mustard Pickles, 259
Pico de Gallo Deviled Eggs, 54
Pies
Lemon Pie, 223
My Family's Pie Dough, 227
Pecan Pie, 224
Sweet Potato Pie, 226
Pigs in Jalapeño-Cheddar
Blankets with Jalapeño Dipping
Sauce, 61
Pineapple
Ambrosia Salad, 95
Plums
Plum Cobbler, 229
Plum Jam, 265
Poblano chiles, 6–7
Brisket Tacos, Dallas Style, 148–49
Cranberry–Green Chile Salsa, 252
Green Chile Baked Eggs, 20
Green Chile Hominy
Casserole, 103
Poblano-Buttermilk Dressing, 140
Pork Chili Verde, 121
Squash Blossom Soup with
Zucchini-Corn Salsa, 131
Pollo Asado, 175
Pork
Balsamic-Tarragon Glazed
Ham, 163
Cochinita Pibil, 157–58
Coffee-Chipotle Pork Chops, 152
Jalapeño Pesto–Stuffed Pork Roast,
155–56
Peppery Ribs, 160–61
Pork Chili Verde, 121
Venison Chili, 118–19
See also Bacon; Chorizo; Sausage
Potatoes
Buttermilk Potato Soup with Bacon
and Jalapeño, 122–23
Chipotle-Cheddar Scalloped
Potatoes, 99
German Potato and Green Bean
Salad, 86
Potato-Chorizo Breakfast Tacos, 25
Shrimp Boil, 190

Puddings
Bacon and Chipotle Corn
Pudding, 101
Banana Pudding with Peanut
Butter–Oatmeal Cookies, 205–6
Pumpkin
Pumpkin Pasilla Soup, 128
Roasted Pumpkin Seeds, 67

Q
Quesadilla, Ancho Chile Shrimp, 189

R
Ranch-Style Beans, 108
Raspberry Bars, Mom's, 207
Red Chile Salsa Picante, 246
Red Sauce, 190
Refried Black Beans, 109
Relish, Corn, 262
Ribs, Peppery, 160–61
Rice
Sausage and Shrimp
Jambalaya, 193
Spanish Rice, 110
Roasted Pumpkin Seeds, 67
Roasted Whole Fish, 187
Rolls
Buttermilk Dinner Rolls, 38
Klobasnek (Sausage Kolaches),
42–43
Ruby Red Grapefruit and Pecan Sheet
Cake, 220

S
Salad dressings
Chipotle–Blue Cheese Dressing, 82
Poblano-Buttermilk Dressing, 140
Salads
Ambrosia Salad, 95
Apple-Walnut Salad, 78
Chipotle–Blue Cheese Wedge
Salad, 82
Frito Salad, 85
German Potato and Green Bean
Salad, 86
Guacamole Salad, 77
Macaroni Salad, 90
Mustard Coleslaw, 94
Sauerkraut Salad, 93
Spicy Pea Salad, 89
Tomato, Cucumber, and Peach
Salad, 81

Salsas and sauces
Ancho Chile Applesauce, 96
Black Bean Salsa, 21
Chipotle-Lime Dipping Sauce, 188
Corn–Black Bean Salsa, 249
Cranberry–Green Chile Salsa, 252
Creamy Green Salsa, 248
Enchilada Sauce, 22
Horseradish Cream Sauce, 145
Jalapeño Dipping Sauce, 61
Jalapeño Tartar Sauce, 183
Old-Fashioned Texas Hot
Sauce, 241
Peach Salsa, 245
Peppery Barbecue Sauce, 160
Red Chile Salsa Picante, 246
Red Sauce, 190
Sweet Potato–Chipotle Sauce, 171
Tomatillo-Chipotle Salsa, 242
Tomatillo-Guajillo Salsa, 176–77
Zucchini-Corn Salsa, 131
Sauerkraut Salad, 93
Sausage
Bacon-Molasses Breakfast
Sausage, 16
Klobasnek (Sausage Kolaches),
42–43
Pigs in Jalapeño-Cheddar
Blankets with Jalapeño Dipping
Sauce, 61
Sauerkraut Salad, 93
Sausage and Pepper Breakfast
Casserole, 19
Sausage and Shrimp
Jambalaya, 193
Southeast Texas Gumbo, 132
See also Chorizo
Scones, Cranberry-Gruyère, 37
Serrano chiles, 7
Creamy Green Salsa, 248
Squash Blossom Soup with
Zucchini-Corn Salsa, 131
Shortcake, Strawberry, 212
Shredded Beef Enchiladas with Three-
Chile Sauce, 142–43
Shrimp
Ancho Chile Shrimp
Quesadilla, 189
Sausage and Shrimp
Jambalaya, 193
Shrimp Boil, 190
Southeast Texas Gumbo, 132

Smoky Collard Greens, 102
Snapper
    Roasted Whole Fish, 187
Snickerdoodles, Spicy, 211
Sopa de Lima (Mexican Lime
    Soup), 127
Sopes, Black Bean, with Chipotle
    Crema, 196
Sorghum Mustard Pickles, 259
Soups
    Black-Eyed Pea and Mexican
        Chorizo Soup, 117
    Buttermilk Potato Soup with Bacon
        and Jalapeño, 122–23
    Chicken Soup, 125–26
    Chipotle Chicken and Dumplings,
        125–26
    Pumpkin Pasilla Soup, 128
    Sopa de Lima (Mexican Lime
        Soup), 127
    Squash Blossom Soup with
        Zucchini-Corn Salsa, 131
Southeast Texas Gumbo, 132
Spanish Rice, 110
Spicy Pea Salad, 89
Spicy Snickerdoodles, 211
Spinach, Bacon, and Artichoke
    Dip, 53
Squash Blossom Soup with Zucchini-
    Corn Salsa, 131
Stacked Jalapeño-Cheese
    Enchiladas, 194
Steak Fingers with Jalapeño Cream
    Gravy, 146–47
Strawberry Shortcake, 212
Sunday Brisket, 145
Sweet potatoes
    Sweet Potato and Chipotle
        Tortillas, 28
    Sweet Potato Pie, 226
    Turkey Enchiladas with Sweet
        Potato–Chipotle Sauce, 171

T
Tacos
    Beer-Battered Catfish Tacos,
        179–80
    Brisket Tacos, Dallas Style, 148–49
    Chipotle Taco Meat, 65
    Crispy Tacos, 151
    Potato-Chorizo Breakfast Tacos, 25
Tamales, Chicken, with Tomatillo-
    Guajillo Salsa, 176–78
Tartar Sauce, Jalapeño, 183
Tilapia, Tortilla-Crusted, 183
Tomatillos
    Pork Chili Verde, 121
    Stacked Jalapeño-Cheese
        Enchiladas, 194
    Tomatillo-Chipotle Salsa, 242
    Tomatillo-Guajillo Salsa, 176–77
Tomatoes
    Black-Eyed Pea and Mexican
        Chorizo Soup, 117
    Chicken Spaghetti, 167
    Chipotle–Blue Cheese Wedge
        Salad, 82
    Enchilada Sauce, 22
    Frito Salad, 85
    Old-Fashioned Texas Hot
        Sauce, 241
    Peach Salsa, 245
    Peppery Barbecue Sauce, 160
    Pico de Gallo Deviled Eggs, 54
    Ranch-Style Beans, 108
    Sausage and Shrimp
        Jambalaya, 193
    Smoky Collard Greens, 102
    Tomato, Cucumber, and Peach
        Salad, 81
Tortas, Michelada Flank Steak, with
    Poblano-Buttermilk Dressing,
    139–40
Tortilla chips
    Black-Eyed Pea and Mexican
        Chorizo Soup, 117
    Frito Salad, 85
    Tortilla-Crusted Tilapia, 183

Tortillas
    Ancho Chile Shrimp
        Quesadilla, 189
    Beer-Battered Catfish Tacos,
        179–80
    Breakfast Enchiladas, 22–23
    Brisket Tacos, Dallas Style, 148–49
    Buttermilk Bacon-Fat Flour
        Tortillas, 26
    Chicken Fajitas, 172–73
    Chilaquiles in Black Bean
        Salsa, 21
    Crazy Nachos, 65–66
    Crispy Tacos, 151
    Shredded Beef Enchiladas with
        Three-Chile Sauce, 142–43
    Sopa de Lima (Mexican Lime
        Soup), 127
    Stacked Jalapeño-Cheese
        Enchiladas, 194
    Sweet Potato and Chipotle
        Tortillas, 28
    Turkey Enchiladas with Sweet
        Potato–Chipotle Sauce, 171
Tuna with Avocado and Red Pepper
    Baked in Parchment, 184
Turkey Enchiladas with Sweet Potato–
    Chipotle Sauce, 171

V
Vegetables
    peeling, 4
    See also individual vegetables
Venison Chili, 118–19

W
Walnut Salad, Apple-, 78
Watermelon Rind Pickles, Fresh, 261
White chocolate
    Caballero Cookies, 208
    Mom's Raspberry Bars, 207

Z
Zucchini-Corn Salsa, 131